THE BIRTH OF RHETORIC

ISSUES IN ANCIENT PHILOSOPHY
General editor: Malcolm Schofield

GOD IN GREEK PHILOSOPHY
Studies in the early history of natural theology
L. P. Gerson

ANCIENT CONCEPTS OF PHILOSOPHY
William Jordan

LANGUAGE, THOUGHT AND FALSEHOOD
IN ANCIENT GREEK PHILOSOPHY
Nicholas Denyer

MENTAL CONFLICT
Anthony Price

Heavenly Father, Thank You for caring about
every area of my life. Thank You for Your protection
over the lives of my children. Allow me to rest in the
knowledge of Your care. Amen.

KIM BOYCE

....

....

....

....

....

....

....

....

*I*n peace I will both lie down and sleep, for You alone,
O Lord, make me to dwell in safety.

PSALM 4:8 NASB

I love these little people; and it is not a slight thing when they, who are so fresh from God, love us.

CHARLES DICKENS

....

....

....

....

....

....

....

....

....

....

....

....

....

THE BIRTH OF
RHETORIC

Gorgias, Plato and their successors

Robert Wardy

London and New York

First published 1996
by Routledge
11 New Fetter Lane, London EC4P 4EE

Simultaneously published in the USA and Canada
by Routledge
29 West 35th Street, New York, NY 10001

First published in paperback 1998

© 1996 Robert Wardy

Transferred to Digital Printing 2003

Typeset in Garamond by Florencetype Ltd
Stoodleigh, Devon
Printed and bound in Great Britain by
Selwood Printing Ltd, West Sussex

British Library Cataloguing in Publication Data
A catalogue record for this book is available from
the British Library

Library of Congress Cataloguing in Publication Data
Wardy, Robert.
The birth of rhetoric: Gorgias, Plato, and their successors/
Robert Wardy.
p. cm. – (Issues in ancient philsophy)
Includes bibliographical rerferences (p.) and index.
1. Plato. Gorgias. 2. Rhetoric, Ancient. 3. Gorgias, of Leontini.
I. Title. II. Series.

PA4279.G7W37   1996
170–dc20   95–48938
ISBN 0-415-14643-7 (pbk)

Uxori carissimae eloquentissimaeque
maritus loquax uxoriusque

CONTENTS

CONTENTS

INTRODUCTION

What is rhetoric? There are too many answers, too much at variance with each other. Rhetoric, let us say, is the capacity to persuade others; or a practical realisation of this ability; or, at least, an attempt at persuasion, successful or not. Furthermore, this capacity might, to one degree or another, be either natural or acquired. Again, rhetorical exercises might or might not be confined to language: if visual or architectural 'rhetoric' is a metaphorical extension of 'rhetoric', what does this metaphor preserve, and what does it discard, of the core meaning, rhetorical language? Again, rhetoric is 'mere' rhetoric: it is the capacity to get others to do what its possessor wants, regardless of what they want, except to the extent that their desires limit what rhetoric might achieve: this, of course, is the rhetoric of ideological manipulation and political seduction. And finally, rhetoric is for some a distinctive mode of communication, whether admirable or deplorable; for others, as soon as one person addresses another, rhetoric is present.

This book is devoted to helping the reader understand what rhetoric is. It does not pretend that only one conception of rhetoric is possible, let alone desirable; nor is the account it develops either complete or conclusive. That is as it should be: any study of rhetoric with pretensions to completeness or conclusiveness inevitably betrays a dogmatism which fails to do justice to the suggestiveness – at once bewildering and exciting – largely responsible for rhetoric's perennial attractions. This book will try to help readers indirectly, by showing them how it might come about that there are so many answers to the fundamental question with which we began. Any such approach must be rooted in Classical antiquity. Only Westerners ignorant of their own past traditions, and so, necessarily, ignorant of rival foreign institutions, would imagine that rhetoric is some sort

1

of cultural universal. Granted, it is a trivial enough truth that human societies are not to be found in which people do not engage in what we would call the activity of persuasion; indeed, one might reasonably contend that engagement in persuasive negotiation, very broadly conceived, is precisely what makes a collection of individuals into a community. But such an undeniable truth does not entail that multiple, profound differences do not exist between what we mean by 'persuasion', and whatever term we suppose approximates to it in the language of another society. So in some drastically etiolated sense, persuasion might well be a human universal; but what we in this culture mean by 'persuasion' cannot possibly be, because our concept is the product of a complicated historical process starting with the ancient Greek idea of rhetoric.

In the West, self-conscious reflection on the theory and practice of persuasion is a Greek achievement, initiated in the fifth century BCE and culminating in the fourth. But – and this is why Greek rhetoric continues to speak to us in a voice we cannot afford to ignore – such reflection was anything but a calm collective meditation issuing in a ruling consensus. Greek rhetoric was born in bitter controversy; and its most important legacy to us is a highly ramified debate, not a body of doctrine. This book will not, however, aim for anything like a comprehensive study of Greek rhetoric: it contains no study of the orators, for example, and no analysis of the elaborate technical handbook tradition, fascinating as these both are in their own right. That would be to attempt at once too much and too little: too much, obviously, because the field is so vast; not quite so obviously, too little, because wide-ranging surveys of rhetoric tend to represent it as a history from which the essential debate has been disastrously leached.

So this book is about Gorgias. The first answer to our question, that rhetoric is a persuasive ability, although a commonplace, derives from Plato's dialogue, the *Gorgias*, which also has something to say about the source of this capacity. The message of Gorgias' *Encomium of Helen* invokes the persuasive power of vision as well as of language. More than any other text, the *Encomium* invites us to confront the terrifying, exhilarating possibility that persuasion is just power, and that no human contact is innocent of its manipulative presence. Thus focusing sharply on Gorgias will eventually enable us to understand why our question calls forth a plurality of conflicting responses: the Greek debate over the nature and value of rhetoric, from which all the answers ultimately come, centres on his figure. This is a genetic thesis, but the justification for concentrating on Gorgias is not restricted to historical considerations; my hope is that this book will convince the reader that Gorgias not only inaugurated the great rhetoric debate, he also gave unequalled expression to some of its most vital components. To learn about Gorgias is to learn about what continues to matter in rhetoric.

There are additional limitations. Gorgias is significant for other reasons too, ones irrelevant to our concerns. This book does not delve into aspects of Gorgianic studies unconnected with Gorgias the rhetor or with the formative reactions to him. Even within these terms, there is no pretence that my coverage of the voluminous scholarship is anything like complete. My intention is that, since I am writing for readers keenly interested in the cardinal question of rhetoric, and such readers come from widely different backgrounds, they should not be put off by the rebarbativeness of a learned apparatus concealing the chief lines of the argument. Scholarly citations are accordingly of work the reader may find helpful in following those lines (whether the works referred to are insightful or misleading) and are in the form of end- rather than footnotes, to signal that involvement in the secondary literature is optional. For similar reasons the main text does not assume any knowledge of Greek or Latin; a few notes will be of interest only to the philologically inclined specialist. Nevertheless, because the composition of the texts considered is often careful and subtle in the extreme, I do not avoid the occasional transliteration, rather than translation, of certain key terms. Of course the point is to alert the reader without Greek or Latin to potentially misleading connotations, and so such transliteration will always be accompanied by an explanation of the distinctive semantics of the original term. At the same time, this is no 'introductory' text. The ambition of *The Birth of Rhetoric* is to be at once accessible, and intellectually challenging.

The first chapter is devoted to Gorgias' *On What Is Not*. A further answer to 'what is rhetoric?' is: 'not philosophy'. This need not be as resoundingly uninformative as it appears; indeed, as we shall discover, there is much to say for the thesis that the impact of *On What Is Not* on our conception of rhetoric is a function of the deliberately provocative stance which Gorgias adopted towards the Greek philosophical project. So an initial foray into Greek philosophy is unavoidable. Previous acquaintance with it is not assumed, although general interest in philosophy certainly is; but then, anyone who claims to be interested in rhetoric rather than philosophy is sadly deluded. By the same token, Gorgias will teach us that philosophers ignore the challenge of rhetoric only at their own peril. Chapter 2 concerns Gorgias' *Encomium of Helen*: it examines how Gorgias constructs a psychology which complements the arresting implications of *On What Is Not* and completes his radical alternative to the philosophical view of the use and abuse of language.

Chapter 3 turns to the *Gorgias*, Plato's massively influential counterblast on behalf of the philosophers. Once more, respecting the Gorgianic theme means that the chapter does not extend beyond this dialogue to grapple with Plato's other celebrated contribution to the debate about rhetoric, the *Phaedrus*; and our study of the *Gorgias* will centre on the first section of the dialogue, in which Gorgias himself is depicted as Socrates' interlocutor. This means that much of the dialogue with which philosophers have been preoccupied will be ignored. But since we shall find that the first section has typically been slighted as a consequence of the neglect, or misconstrual, of Gorgias' true importance, the reading adopted in this chapter, by redressing the balance, will reveal features of the dialogue otherwise overlooked.

Chapter 4 tries to substantiate the contention of the previous three chapters that Plato and Gorgias between them largely set the terms of the debate constituting rhetoric. In the nature of the case, such a thesis does not admit of anything like demonstrative proof. Our programme will be that establishing contact with related episodes in the history of rhetoric (again, not exhaustive, but selected for their exceptional importance) will demonstrate how very far the foundation laid by Gorgias extends beneath the structure of that history, and how recognition of his influence can reshape our interpretations of these episodes. Thus the second and third parts of this chapter investigate both Isocrates' devious compromise with Gorgias, and Cicero's historically decisive endorsement of Isocrates' anti-philosophical manœuvre. The fourth part analyses the *To Plato: In Defence of Rhetoric* of Aelius Aristides, which responds to the critique of the *Gorgias* at greater length and with greater intensity than does any other ancient work. The fifth chapter seeks to show that the other momentous reaction to Plato's reaction to Gorgias, that of Aristotle, strives after a far more difficult, and correspondingly provocative, compromise. The Epilogue looks further, albeit more tentatively, than the rest of the book. Gorgias' decision to exemplify the overwhelming control exercised by rhetoric over a passive, victimised auditor with the submission to seduction of the most famous (and most infamous) Greek woman, Helen of Troy, was far from casual, while Plato's (paradoxically belligerent) advocacy of impersonal dialectic emphatically rejects any suggestion that personal characteristics in general, never mind gender in particular, can or should impinge on the progress of a philosophical investigation. The issue of gender is thus inextricably bound up with the quarrel between rhetoric and philosophy from the outset; and since that issue (rightly) now dominates much of the best current thought in the least tractable areas of the quarrel, we finish with an effort to describe the connections between Gorgias' representation of persuasive power and some of our own, deepest, continuing anxieties.

The Birth of Rhetoric is a descendant of my teaching in the interdisciplinary course on rhetoric which I directed with Simon Goldhill at Cambridge. My first thoughts on Gorgias benefited considerably from his acute criticisms, and also from the brilliant originality of another teacher on the course, John Henderson. But my largest debt remains to those students whose questions and objections consistently punctured (some of) my complacency and encouraged me to think again; just who was teaching whom remains unclear to me. Real improvements in the first chapter are due to Jacques Brunschwig and throughout, as always, to Catherine Atherton and Myles Burnyeat. Malcolm Schofield enhanced the whole by rearranging the parts. Wardy 1996a incorporates some of the material now found in Chapters 1, 2 and 3, and I am grateful to Flammarion for permission to republish it. A version of Chapter 5 appears in Wardy 1996b; I am grateful for the permission of the trustees of the University of California Press to reprint.

1

MUCH ADO ABOUT NOTHING
Gorgias' *On What Is Not*

I am sitting with a philosopher in the garden; he says again and again
'I know that that's a tree', pointing to a tree that is near us. Someone
else arrives and hears this, and I tell him: 'This fellow isn't insane.
We are only doing philosophy.'

(Wittgenstein, *On Certainty* 467)

WHO WAS GORGIAS?

Who was Gorgias? Philostratus, a second- (or third-)rate writer of
later antiquity, reports that Gorgias is the man 'to whom we believe
the craft of the sophists is to be traced back as it were to its father'
(Buchheim test. 1).[1] Philostratus' mediocrity is precisely what renders
his opinion valuable: it reveals how Gorgias eventually appeared to
the ancient world. But why did it seem appropriate to make him
the father of sophistry? First, because of rhetorical innovations at a
basic technical level which Gorgias is supposed to have ushered in,
involving both structure and ornamentation (for example, poetic
diction and periodicity); second, and of considerably more interest,
because he introduced *paradoxologia*, which embraces both paradoxical thought and paradoxical expression. On the occasion of his
famous embassy to Athens seeking military aid for his home-city,
Leontini, in Sicily, his skill in speaking extempore reputedly brought
nearly all the leading politicians and intellectuals under his influence
(test. 1). Of the three most striking claims preserved in the largely
anecdotal biographical reports, one is that he pioneered impro-
visation, so that 'on entering the Athenian theatre, he cried out
"Give me a theme!" . . . in order to demonstrate that he knew everything' (test. 1a; again, this comes from Philostratus; but the claim
is already to be found in Plato, *Meno* 70B, test. 19); the second,

6

that his fancied pupil Isocrates declares in an apparently neutral tone that Gorgias accumulated relatively great wealth by travelling about unwed and childless, thus avoiding the civic and educational expenses of the paternal citizen (*Antidosis* 15.156, test. 18); the third, that 'among the Thessalians "to orate" acquired the name "to gorgiasise"' (test. 35).

Clichéd as they now are, these fragmentary portraits raise all the important questions about Gorgias. Why is Gorgias a 'sophist', and not only that, but the great original? And is there really such a thing as 'the craft of the sophists'? Whatever 'sophistry' might be, is it necessarily akin to 'rhetoric'? A 'paradox' is literally 'what opposes opinion': if Gorgias in some manner affronts people's beliefs, how can he successfully persuade them? Isocrates' denial of familial and civic identity to Gorgias does not sit easily with Gorgias' rôle in obtaining Athenian aid for his fellow-citizens: how, then, does rhetoric connect with political activity? An ability to improvise fluently gives the skilled speaker an obvious advantage; but need a sophist/rhetor really claim omniscience about the themes on which he can readily extemporise? What does the performative aspect of rhetoric (Gorgias impressing his public in the theatre) reveal about its nature?

Finally, to compound the confusion – reminiscent of the plurality of answers to our first question, 'what is rhetoric?' – many scholars lengthen the list of Gorgias' accomplishments with the title 'philosopher', albeit usually only for the early stages of his career.[2] The ancient sources claim a linkage with Empedocles: 'Empedocles was a doctor and supreme rhetor. Indeed, Gorgias of Leontini, a man excelling in rhetoric, became his pupil' (Diogenes Laertius 8.58–9, test. 3). Ancient doxographers' fondness for tutelary relationships as a standard organisational principle means that such statements must always be treated with extreme reserve. In this instance, however, whatever the historical fact of the matter might have been, one feature of the characterisation of Empedocles has the effect of harmonising the suggestion that he taught Gorgias with the other evidence. We might standardly think of Empedocles as a philosopher, with medicine and magic as more or less reputable sidelines, but Diogenes adds rhetoric. Furthermore, Sextus Empiricus reports that Aristotle in a lost work actually identified him as the founder of rhetoric: 'Aristotle says in the *Sophist* that Empedocles first set rhetoric in motion' (*Against the Mathematicians* 7.6, test. 3). Just as sophistry is traced back to Gorgias, so rhetoric is attributed to his teacher; just as the sources are unwilling or unable to keep Gorgias within a single pigeonhole, so too Empedocles is portrayed as crossing the boundary, usually so very strict, between rhetoric and philosophy. A reading of *On What Is Not* and *The Encomium of Helen* will reveal that this difficulty in classifying Gorgias, so far from being a mere taxonomic side-issue, goes to the heart of his unparalleled contribution to the history of rhetoric.

Other sources suggest that Gorgias' pioneering enthusiasm spilled over into naïvely exaggerated effects, and this reflects a somewhat embarrassed uncertainty about how it was that he made such a remarkable impression. One authority tells us that 'he was the first to use figures of speech rather unusual and remarkable for ingenuity . . . but what then commanded approbation on account of the novelty of the construction now seems laboured and often appears ridiculous and excessively contrived' (Diodorus, *Bibliotheca historica* 12.53.2, test. 4). Evidently later writers were hard put, on the basis of works in their possession ascribed to Gorgias, to understand what all the fuss was about. At least to some extent, what survives under Gorgias' name bears out Diodorus' negative judgement: it is true that Gorgias' prose is very highly wrought, in that it freely employs a large variety of aural effects, daring figurative language and formal patterns very far beyond the pale marked out by the (relatively) restrained stylistic taste of later Greeks. One way ancient scholars tried to make sense of history was in terms of a category of 'the first discoverer': they attempted to impose order on their past, real or imaginary, by setting up genealogical trees for each significant cultural domain, with an august 'first discoverer' at the root. This practice could clearly function in part as a way of smoothing over the awkwardness of Gorgias' perceived stylistic strain and bad taste – what more does one reasonably expect from a pioneer?

I am not concerned either to support or to reject this condemnation of Gorgias' style; such evaluation is notoriously a matter of fixed expectations verging on prejudice, for ancient and modern alike. What I am at pains to emphasise is that the puzzlement over Gorgias' merit might betray a much deeper insensitivity towards what he was really about. However these later thinkers might react to Gorgias' works, they take it for granted that the proper criteria to be brought to bear in evaluating them are those deriving from the elaborated rules of 'rhetorical' aesthetics, where 'rhetorical' is to be understood with reference to the technical handbook tradition. It was inevitable that Gorgias would not appear to best advantage in this light. In part his 'impropriety' is just the unsurprising consequence of his failing to adhere to conventions not as yet formulated, rather as if one were to impugn Monteverdi's musical credentials on the grounds that his operas do not conform to eighteenth-century standards. But, much more importantly, Gorgias was bound to disappoint because his greatest originality lay in deliberately subverting generic expectations: not only in confusing one type of rhetorical discourse with another, but also in eroding the distinction between rhetoric and philosophy itself.

It might be objected immediately that this suggestion cannot possibly be right, because such expectations only came into existence in the aftermath of self-conscious Greek recognition of distinctive literary or rhetorical genres and intellectual tasks; but (so the objection runs) Gorgias' context antedates any such recognition. The situation then, in the fifth century BCE, was intellectually fluid, compared with later rigidity. At this early juncture 'sophist' simply means 'wise man', primarily a poet, in contrast to the Platonic designation of a (sub-)philosophical type; and at this date there was no such thing as 'philosophy' as opposed to 'rhetoric', only very different would-be 'wise men' who came to be generically isolated long after the fact. The objection does not hold water. True, it would be rash to maintain that those thinkers we now call 'philosophers' used that very term to mark their special identity;[3] but it does not follow that they therefore also lacked the unique self-conception that by the fourth century was called 'philosophical'. And a far stronger, positive defence is available: Gorgias unmistakably challenges us to respond to *On What Is Not* against one quite specific and revolutionary philosophical backdrop, that of Parmenides' great argument. Accordingly our next move must be to extract some vital information from the figure depicted by Plato in the *Parmenides* as the father of philosophy, to match Gorgias as the father of sophistical rhetoric.

THE CHALLENGE OF PARMENIDES

Parmenides' spokeswoman, the goddess Justice, announces to him early in his philosophical poem: 'you must hear everything, both the unmoved heart of persuasive *alētheiē* and the opinions of mortals, wherein there is no *alēthēs* conviction', (Coxon fr. 1).[4] '*Alētheiē*' is conventionally rendered either 'truth' or 'reality', and often the context clearly favours one over the other. The problem here is that Parmenides seems not only to fuse the real with the true, but also

9

to suggest that truth/reality, unlike mere opinions, is *objectively persuasive*.[5] Persuasion in this special sense recurs significantly throughout the deduction: thus 'this road of inquiry, that it is and cannot not be, is the path of persuasion, for it follows truth/reality' (fr. 3).

Elsewhere the goddess warns Parmenides against any reliance on sense perception (and, perhaps, conventional language), since what we perceive (and, perhaps, say) invariably and fundamentally misrepresents the way things really are: 'do not permit greatly experienced habit to force you down this way of using an aimless eye and a ringing ear and tongue' (fr. 7). At this point, 'force' is attributed to pernicious, habitual delusion. It has long been recognised that one of the pre-eminent defining features of Greek culture is its concept of persuasion. In the first instance, this is a polar concept: persuasion is thought of as systematically opposed to force or compulsion. (This conceptual structure is most vividly portrayed at the conclusion of Aeschylus' *Eumenides*, when Athena uses persuasion on the Furies so as to break the horrific cycle of compelled violence which propels the action of the *Oresteia*.) So, since we have already been told that 'the path of persuasion' 'follows truth/reality', it would be reasonable to infer that Parmenides intends us to associate positive persuasion with what is, the only possible route of enquiry into any subject whatsoever, negative compulsion with what is not, what is impossible even to conceive or speak of.[6] And that is not surprising, since in the persuasion/force polarity, persuasion is usually, if not invariably, the positive member.

Later in the poem, however, the associations apparently shift: speaking of the 'one being', the goddess asks:

> how and whence could it have grown? I shall not permit you either to assert or to think 'from what is not' . . . And what necessity would have forced it to begin growing from nothing later rather than earlier? . . . Never will the strength of conviction permit something additional to come to be from what is not; that is why justice has released neither generation nor destruction by loosening their bonds, but holds them fast.
>
> (fr. 8)

These later declarations add the paradoxical dimension that persuasion, despite the standard opposition to force, actually shares in necessity; likewise, judicial imagery recurs in the famous claim that 'powerful necessity holds what is in the bonds of a limit' (fr. 8). Not only that, but rational conviction also seems to act on, or at least with, what is – so that, for example, 'generation and destruction have wandered very far away, pushed back by *alēthēs* conviction' (fr. 8) – as the goddess associates reality with reason ever more intimately; just as the goddess does not permit Parmenides certain thoughts, so the sole object of thought, what is, is itself constrained by what it must be.

Insofar as rational conviction acts in concert with what is and derives its persuasiveness from reality itself, the philosopher empowered to instil it would appear to possess complete control over our intellects. Yet when she passes from truth to human delusion, the goddess implicitly acknowledges that reality is unfortunately not alone in swaying minds,[7] although at the same time she emphatically divorces falsity from conviction: 'now I put an end to persuasive *logos* and thought about reality/truth, and from this point do you learn mortal opinions by listening to the deceptive *kosmos* of my words' (fr. 8). Two words in this programmatic statement have been merely transliterated because neither can be rendered straightforwardly into English. *Logos* resists translation even more than *alētheiē*. First, it often means 'verbal account'; but here it approximates to 'argument' or 'reasoning', and thus stands in polar opposition to the (mere) 'words', highlighting the exclusively logical, rational character of truth. Second, and crucially, we shall see that the debate between philosophy and rhetoric can be effectively formulated as a conflict over the very meaning of this word '*logos*', so that we must take care not to beg any questions about its semantics. What is a '*kosmos*'? Anything ordered or harmonious, but also, by an obvious extension, anything adorned by virtue of arrangement – hence our 'cosmetics'. Just as a painted face deceives the onlooker, so the goddess' phrase suggests the disturbing possibility that a *kosmos* of words – a *logos*, perhaps, albeit not hers – might mislead precisely in that these words wear an attractive appearance of superficial order masking essential incoherence.[8] Indeed, the *kosmos* the goddess goes on to describe (or construct), a *kosmos* akin to those constructed by Parmenides' more orthodox contemporaries and predecessors, the 'cosmologists', turns out to be a stunningly complex and complete fabrication, merely a *kosmos* of words – as any account of the world but the goddess' own monistic *logos* must be.

Why, then, utter such deceitful falsehoods at all? 'So that never shall any mortal outstrip you in judgement' (fr. 8). Thus the master-persuader Parmenides can be seen from our perspective as at once philosopher and rhetorician: philosopher, insofar as he has access to a *logos* whose inescapable logic persuades all those wise enough to follow the argument; rhetorician, insofar as his deception will – Parmenides assumes – persuade all those foolish enough not to grasp the repercussions of the *logos* – and will do so more effectively, in fact, than any other 'cosmology'.[9] But, in line with the qualifications expressed at the end of the previous section, it is essential that we do not import this possible conception of Parmenides' (claimed) status into his own self-conception. Explicit, contrastive definitions of philosophy and rhetoric first emerge in Parmenides' wake – in fact, emerge by way of various attempted resolutions of the tension created for his successors by his combination within a single work of genius of what was to become (be conceived as) philosophy with what was to become (be conceived as) rhetoric.

These features of Parmenides' discourse together make an essential context for the appraisal of Gorgias; together they constitute extremely problematic conditions on what can count as *logos* in the sense of 'argument' – conditions which he will deftly exploit. In the first place, even if the goddess insists that it is the force of the *logos* to which her auditor, Parmenides, must yield, the fact remains that in the manner of earlier Greek poets, he puts his deduction into the mouth of a divine, and thus supremely authoritative, figure. Both Gorgias and Plato will prove themselves very sensitive to the issue of whether genuine authority is impersonal, vested in the *logos* itself, or personal, depending on who says what to whom as much as on what is said. Again, Parmenides fuses reality with persuasive truth by way of rational compulsion, despite the traditional Greek opposition between force and persuasion to which I have alluded – making necessity and conviction strange bed-fellows indeed. Perhaps no one can simply will to believe (rationally): one must be *made* to believe, ideally by valid argument: hence Descartes' 'I move the more freely towards an object in proportion to the number of reasons which compel me' (letter to Mersenne).[10] Of course, rational constraint is not necessarily identical with compulsion: but both Gorgias and Plato will return to the obscure relation between them. Most bluntly, why should we accept Parmenides' assurance that truth/reality is in and of itself persuasive? After all, the goddess herself alerts us to the danger that a 'deceptive *kosmos*' is in the offing; and 'deceptive' *means* 'likely to deceive'. These mere 'words' presumably take in fools, not someone who has grasped the import of the goddess' legitimate reasoning; but that admission will not help, since the most conspicuous feature of Parmenidean persuasion is that it is ostensibly correlated with an objective factor, *alētheiē*, rather than being relative to a subjective or variable factor: it is not, say, 'persuasive for Peter' (but not for Paul), or 'persuasive today' (but not tomorrow). Next, when Parmenides contrasts *logos* with (mere) words, he must mean to convey the idea that the only vehicle of real conviction is rational argument: Gorgias will systematically undermine the claims of philosophical *logos* to this monopoly. The ambiguous attractions of *kosmos* will also make themselves felt in the *Encomium of Helen*.

Finally, the goddess' exhortation to 'judge by *logos* the contentious test [*elenchos*, the word later used to describe Socrates' dialectical method] I have expressed' (fr. 7) invites a trial-by-*logos*. Her 'test' for what genuinely is has itself to be judged, and in this trial there can be only one judge, reason or *logos*. The very fact that a judgement is needed is a result of the contentiousness of the test; it is itself an object of strife and controversy. But, as this controversy concerns what is to be or will be believed (the distinction between these is precisely one of the problems later thinkers had to wrestle with), surely one measure of success must be the extent to which an audience yields to what it is told – perhaps *the* measure, if Parmenides' linking of truth with persuasive power is as reliable as he assumes. Victory here may be victory, not over some rival, but over an audience, which is won over, overcome, vanquished by the account or whoever wields it. Do successful persuaders then inevitably victimise their audiences? We shall find that the equation of the power of persuasion with victimisation of the persuaded looms large both in Gorgias' own writing, and in Plato's writing about him.

Furthermore, the goddess' exhortation helps justify my insistence that if Gorgias does react to Parmenides, then he is indeed reacting to something which was at that time perceived as distinctively philosophical, even if Parmenides never defined himself explicitly as a 'philosopher'. The reason for this is simple: even if Parmenides fails to say anything like 'I am a philosopher, not a poet or rhetorician or . . .', he does insist that *logos* as exemplified by the first part of his poem is not just words. Admittedly, he does not proceed to explain what *logos* is for him; he must expect us to infer what a *logos* must be (like) from the example he provides in his deductive argument. Therefore we are entitled to conclude that Parmenides' readers would gather that he was presenting them with a new model of persuasion, according to which reputable conviction can only issue from proper reasoning (whatever precisely that is supposed to be).

I do not pretend that nothing else in what we call Greek philosophy could have prompted Gorgias' reaction. Heraclitus proclaims that 'listening not to me but to the *logos* it is wise to agree [*homologein* = share the same *logos*] that all things are one' (fr. 50). Heraclitus is, quite simply, the philosopher of the *logos*, and what could be less ambiguous than this assertion that authority rests impersonally with the *logos*, rather than with Heraclitus himself (cf. 'although the *logos* is common, the many live as if they had private wisdom' (fr. 2))? But of course ambiguity riddles Heraclitus' delphic pronouncements; even his choice of the common *logos* over personal enlightenment is counterbalanced by the assertion that 'I searched out myself' (fr. 101). This need not indicate that Heraclitus, unlike Parmenides, does not espouse a characteristically philosophical doctrine of *logos* as transcending human attachments, and free from the need for personal legitimation. Rather, it shows that on both conceptions, Parmenides' and Heraclitus' alike, the independence claimed for *logos* is intensely (and probably designedly) problematic. A more serious, if not insuperable, obstacle to the thesis that Heraclitus too might have contributed some material to Gorgias' philosophical target is that while Parmenides supplies a paradigm of deductive *logos*, and one which manifestly influenced Gorgias, the nature of Heraclitus' *logos* – cosmic principle, (concealed) argument, mathematical proportion, or all at once[11] – is notoriously unclear. That Heraclitus might have had a part to play in the formation of Gorgias' rejoinder to philosophy cannot, therefore, be established with anything like the degree of certainty that Parmenides did so.

THE IMPOSSIBILITY OF COMMUNICATION

Gorgias' *On What Is Not* has come down to us in two versions. One is preserved by the sceptical philosopher Sextus Empiricus (*Against the Mathematicians* (hereafter *M*) 7.65 ff.), the other in the Peripatetic *mélange About Melissus, Xenophanes and Gorgias* (hereafter *MXG*). Many scholars have long been exercised by the comparative merits of the versions, which differ considerably in both argumentation and expression. Their guiding principle – which cannot stand inspection – is that one candidate must be genuine, the other, spurious, so that comparing and evaluating the versions correctly will deliver *real* Gorgias to us.[12] There are indeed weighty reasons for dissatisfaction with the version recorded by Sextus Empiricus. We know on

14

independent grounds that the sceptics were interested in so-called 'sophistical' writings (the anonymous work entitled *Dissoi* [=*Double*] *Logoi* is contained in the MSS of Sextus, for example), and the portion of *M* 7 dealing with Gorgias bears many signs of heavy editorial intervention, such as the manufactured link with Protagoras (65). Most important, because this text incorporates the full technical vocabulary of Hellenistic epistemology, its author must be systematically reformulating and commenting on his material.[13] I shall therefore use *MXG* (references are to the text printed in Buchheim), but it too has the regimented format of a doxographical report, and it neither can preserve anything like Gorgias' own words, nor even necessarily keeps intact the sequence of his reasoning.[14] Although we should not believe that we have access to the Gorgianic original, we can nevertheless maintain, with due caution, that what we read is a reasonable extrapolation from the *On What Is Not* itself – and much less of an extrapolation than the version in *M*.[15] Our purpose is not to investigate *On What Is Not* in its entirety, but rather to home in on its illustration of *paradoxologia*, its discussion of communication and its problematic relation to philosophical thought.

In the very title we confront our first paradox: it actually bears a disjunctive name, *On What Is Not or On Nature* (*M* 7.65; Olympiodorus provides just the title *On Nature* (Buchheim fr. 2)). Unfortunately the alternatives might both be later impositions, but they could preserve a significant Gorgianic joke. For an ancient philosopher or scientist, 'nature' is what really is, so that *On Nature* became the standard designation eventually awarded to Presocratic writings. The recorded title of the work of Melissus, who was a follower of Parmenides, is also disjunctive: *On Nature or On What Is* (Kirk, Raven and Schofield 521 and 522); thus it is tempting to read Gorgias as setting out to shock philosophical expectations by inverting Melissus.[16] If the alternative titles are original with Gorgias, then he is blithely equating nature – what really *is* – with nothing; taken together, the titles constitute a self-negating claim, a saying which unsays itself. This phenomenon of arrested or self-destructive communication, introducing semantic convention only to flout it, will emerge as the hallmark of the entire work. On the other hand, even if the doubled label is not original, it remains of interest, since it would then so clearly betray the difficulty later readers experienced in attempting to classify Gorgias' text alongside less unorthodox Presocratic works.

The text begins disconcertingly enough: 'he says there is nothing; even if there is something, it is unknowable; even if it both is and is knowable, nevertheless it cannot be revealed to others' (*MXG* 979^{a}12–13). We shall not pause over the details of Gorgias' 'proof' of nihilism and unknowability, beyond remarking that it deliberately overturns Parmenides' denial that 'is not' is either sayable or thinkable: 'the other [sc. path of enquiry], that it is not and must not be, I tell you is an utterly inscrutable path, for you can neither know what is not, for that is impossible, nor indicate/speak of it [*phrasais*]' (Coxon fr. 3). Philosophers from the time of Plato have wrestled with the problem of whether this and similar denials phrased along the lines of 'one cannot speak or think of what is not' (immediately) refute themselves, by virtue of containing the words 'what is not', or some equivalent. It is already difficult to see that only on an inadequate conception of thought and speech would merely uttering or thinking these words trap one in contradiction; at least certain expressions, such as 'what is not', make *sense* only on condition that they do not *refer* to anything, although specifying how they achieve meaning in the absence of reference is no easy matter. It is even more difficult to develop a theory which goes on to explicate what happens when our thoughts include such non-referential components.[17] But whatever stance one adopts on this issue, and however he himself understood Parmenides' prohibition, there is no doubt that Gorgias is flying in the philosopher's face, and wants us to recognise that he is.

What might have been the point of this? At this date Parmenides' deduction was the paradigmatic, almost unique, example of logical progression and elimination, as manifested in Gorgias' conditional sentence (although the concessive structure is Gorgias' own). In the previous section we saw that when the goddess insists that what she says be judged by *logos*, she is, at least by implication, invoking a new, logically demanding criterion of persuasive adequacy. This does not mean that before Parmenides, Greeks did not argue rationally. Interpreters who disagree on almost everything else agree that what lends Parmenides his paramount importance in the history of philosophy is that he engages in second-order enquiry: that is, his historical position is central not just because of his argumentation, but rather because his argument concerns what can be an object of thought, and so, ultimately, what can be argued about. The goddess teaches that anything we enquire about must meet certain conditions; so far the discussion is formal, it applies unrestrictedly to any possible

16

object of enquiry. But anyone following through the grand deduction preserved in fr. 8 learns to their considerable astonishment that this second-order investigation has the most explosive repercussions. The goddess argues for the conclusion (among others no less radical) that whatever is to be thought about is single and absolutely changeless; this is a characterisation of reality itself, not limited to how we might conceive of reality. It follows that since our most basic apprehensions of the world state (or imply) that it changes in all sorts of ways, we are all basically mistaken; furthermore, and perhaps worse, the perfect unity of what really is entails that there cannot be any discriminable 'us' to be in error about 'it'. How could anyone believe that? So when Gorgias declares that reality is not, is he any less credible? If both thinkers marshal deductions to reach contradictory but equally incredible conclusions, what becomes of Parmenides' theme that conviction unfailingly accompanies truth?

'Even if things are knowable,' runs the beginning of the third section,

> how could someone, Gorgias says, reveal them to another? For how could he say in *logos* what he has seen? Or how could a thing the listener does not see become clear to him? For just as vision does not recognise sounds, so neither does hearing hear colours, but rather sounds; and the speaker speaks, but does not speak colour or the thing.
>
> (980ª20–ᵇ3)

Presumably when speakers speak, by definition they utter *logoi* (the verb 'to speak', '*legein*', is cognate with '*logos*'), so we can understand the conclusion as meaning that *logoi* are different from colours etc. Gorgias is assuming that the sense modalities exclusively apprehend their own objects: a heard *logos* cannot convey anything not aural. Since this section concedes (hypothetically) that things are knowable, we might assume that what has been seen is known to the seer, although he cannot impart such visual knowledge through *logos* (the word translated 'seen' is a form of the verb which in the perfect means 'know', and the Greeks were alive to the connection of vision with knowledge). But by the same token, it ought to be the case that Gorgias here concedes that what has been heard is known to the hearer; and then, since auditors hear *logoi*, why do they not know them just as they know any other sounds they hear?

In this passage the word I have translated by 'sounds', *phthongoi*, can mean 'speech' in particular; I have preferred 'sounds' because the

17

special object of hearing is surely sound in general, not limited to speech. So we confront a dilemma: suppose 'sound' is the right rendering. Then, on the one hand, hearers *should* know *logoi* no less than they know any other sounds they perceive, in which case communication does occur. On the other hand, Gorgias might have tried to meet this objection as follows:

> *logoi* are not just any old sounds: recognising a bird-call, for instance, is not like apprehending *and understanding* 'that's a wood-pigeon'. A dog can hear 'that's a wood-pigeon' as well as (quite possibly much better than) a person; but only a person can grasp what is said. Therefore I can concede (for the nonce) that sounds are known, without thereby allowing that *logoi* are.

This is, however, simply the other horn of the dilemma rather than a way out for Gorgias because any such reply itself relies crucially on the premiss that there is more to the comprehension of *logos* than simply hearing it – it must be interpreted. This premiss implies that *logos* requires interpretation because, unlike mere sound, it has semantic content, it means something. At the barest minimum, attributing semantic content to *logos* commits one to the proposition that it represents what it is about: very roughly, that it says something *about* its topic. If this does nothing to rule out the possibility that a *logos* might *mis*-represent its topic, even totally, the possibility also remains that some representation might be accurate – in which case Gorgias cannot explain why it is wrong to expect that, for instance, I might successfully tell you what I have seen (and thus know) but you have not. So *logoi* do, it seems, occasionally manage to transmit knowledge, and communication does occur. (We should not worry that Gorgias unfairly represses the possibility that a *logos* might communicate something less than knowledge, since his willingness to describe what has been perceived as known shows that the sense of 'knowledge' in play is very relaxed, and unlikely by itself to eliminate plausible candidates for communication.)

Gorgias now identifies *logos* as the tool with which we fruitlessly attempt to convey our thoughts to one another:

> when a person does not have something in his thought, how will he acquire it from another through *logos* or some sign different from the thing, if not, when it is a colour, by seeing, when it is a noise, by hearing? For to begin with, the speaker says neither noise nor colour, but *logos*; so it is not possible to

18

have either colour or noise in thought, only to see the one,
hear the other.

(980ᵇ3–8)

(Notice that the mere act of hearing or reading and understanding
what Gorgias says is enough to show that this cannot be true.) Two
features of this argument against successful communication are
particularly worthy of attention.

First, a sign is necessarily different from its object (the conclusion
of the previous passage quoted we took to mean that *logoi* are
different from colours etc.). As experience must (it is assumed) be
direct, all symbols, which are by definition different from what they
represent, inevitably fail to signify. Now Gorgias never denied that
there are *logoi*, only that they could transmit knowledge: so the
incommunicable *logoi* locked away in our thoughts, since they
cannot be signs *of* anything from which they differ, must also be
non-representational. I can no more retain a private *logos* representing
in memory what I once saw, but no longer see, than I can tell you
about it. Naturally, this fails to make any sense, since the notion
of *logos* bereft of representational content is itself nonsense.[18] The
assumption that experience must be unmediated by any representation is crucial to the argument, but the assumption is not even
explicitly formulated, let alone plausibly defended. However difficult it may be to achieve true, or good, or successful, or authentic,
or, for that matter, persuasive *logos*, such difficulty, no matter how
formidable, is not the product of the difference between word and
object; if words did not differ from their objects, they would not *be*
representations: that is, they would not be *words*.

Second, the word I have translated 'sound' in this passage is no
longer '*phthongos*', but rather '*psophos*'. Unlike '*phthongos*', '*psophos*'
cannot mean '(articulate) speech' as well as mere 'sound'; the best
translation of '*psophos*' is 'noise' pure and simple. So we can draw
the interesting conclusion that at this juncture Gorgias plumped for
the first horn of the dilemma outlined earlier, according to which
logoi are perceived as all 'sounds' are; and this holds whatever inde-
terminacy he might have wanted to retain in the other passage where
he used '*phthongos*' instead.[19]

Gorgias' model of communication assumes that were one person
to transmit knowledge to another, the first would somehow get a
thought to the second; and, if there is not be to a misunderstanding,
it had better be the very same thought which gets across: 'but how

will the listener have the same thing in mind? For it is not possible that the same thing be simultaneously in a number of things which are separate, since then the one thing would be two' (980^{b}9–11). One might speculate that here Gorgias surreptitiously goes far beyond the third negative proposition, that even were there something knowable, it would be incommunicable. For he now purports (feigns?) to establish that *whatever* is spoken of, knowable or not, speech cannot transmit one and the same (object of) thought. We have seen that Gorgias nowhere denies the existence of *logos*. So perhaps the suggestion is that of course one person speaks to another, and in so doing (mysteriously) evokes a *logos* in the mind of the auditor, but the evoked *logos* is not identical to the speaker's; it cannot be, because a *logos* is, or is like, a unique physical object incapable of bilocation or cloning. But this model would, of course, then dictate that communication is impossible: which is precisely the desired conclusion.

Now there is nothing *per se* objectionable in the proposition that thoughts either are, or are necessarily instantiated in, physical objects, although materialistic philosophers continue to encounter stiff resistance. And a materialistic philosopher could also consistently share Gorgias' assumptions about communication, by supposing that when one person through speech evokes a *logos* in the mind of another, although the *logoi* in the speaker's and the auditor's minds are indeed distinct physical *objects*, these distinct objects are nevertheless tokens of the *same* type, where the type is semantic – thus the model of communication as thought-transmission is satisfied. (I am referring to theorists who are 'materialists' so far as the philosophy of mind is concerned, not extremists who would not countenance talk of 'types' at all.) Consequently Gorgias must deny that thoughts, physical or not, are tokens, that is to say instances, of the same type.

In a sense this materialist argument is something of a red herring. For what is distinctive about these tokens is that they are also symbols or representations; that *physical* objects in particular cannot represent, and so must be meaningless, and so cannot effect communication, of itself adds little. Precisely because whatever has meaning thereby represents, whatever has meaning must be a token of a *semantic* type; but tokens (instances) are necessarily reproducible (in principle, if not in practice). The argument is easy to misconstrue. On my reconstruction, with considerable supplementation, its *deep* structure is not: if we communicate through *logoi*, then they must be transmittable from one mind to another; but, being physical, one and the same *logos* is not so transmittable; therefore we do not communicate through *logoi*, but rather: *logoi* are not tokens or symbols of anything, so they are unique physical objects; but unique physical objects can only be in one place at a time; so, given Gorgias' presumptions about communication, communication is impossible.

Subsequently Gorgias is willing, for the sake of argument, to concede the possibility that one and the same object of thought might be communicated (980ᵇ14–15). But this is not the huge concession it might at first appear, because he at once insists that differences between the two parties to the (putative) communication always preclude its *appearing* the same, even if (*per impossibile*) it were the same (thus this tactic reduplicates in miniature the overall concessive structure of *On What Is Not*). Communication is impossible '[1] on account of things not being *logoi*, and [2] because one person does not think the same thing as another' (980ᵇ18–19). [1] is met by the point I have already stressed, that *logoi* had better not be the things whose *logoi* they are, on pain of ceasing to be *logoi*. There is another possible analysis of what is going wrong so egregiously here. One might crudely suppose that words deputise for their objects, and that, since no substitute matches the original, we should never be satisfied with the pale imitation of reality which is the best *logos* can ever achieve, but should rather hold out for the real thing: if the more accurate a copy is the better it is, then by the most stringent standards things must 'represent' themselves. And that, of course, cannot be.[20] [2] goes nowhere until two conditions are satisfied: the existence of representation must not be repressed, and the manner in which representations are discriminated in thought must be assessed.

COULD THIS BE PHILOSOPHY?

What are we to make of these amazing propositions? Parmenides' philosophy issues in the 'rational' conclusion that all that is is a unique, changeless, homogeneous, timeless entity, but does not explain how he can then engage us in dialogue. In parallel, Gorgias' exercise in argumentation, a reaction to Parmenides, suggests that successfully *saying* that communication cannot occur must lead to self-contradiction and paradox.[21] If *On What Is Not* is a perfectly acceptable piece of philosophy, and if this is its message, then philosophical *logos* will by itself carry precious little conviction, despite Parmenides' attempt to monopolise persuasion.

But *is* it philosophy? Or is it merely a cerebral joke?[22] A joke of which I am the butt, for having just acted the part of a dismally dull philosopher breaking a 'sophistical' butterfly on the wheel. One might have thought that nothing would be easier than telling apart real (and thus serious) philosophy from jokes of any kind. But this chapter's epigraph from Wittgenstein can help us to understand that recognising philosophy as such might very well prove anything but easy. Wittgenstein is preoccupied with a problem in modern epistemology: whether declarations of faith in the truth of certain peculiarly fundamental propositions ultimately make any better sense than the expressions of radical scepticism they were designed to counter. The meaning of the quotation is opaque: Wittgenstein may either be saying that the philosophical context endows an otherwise crazy remark with (acceptable) meaning, or, on the contrary, hinting that the pretence of philosophy deludes us into imagining falsely that nonsense makes sense. For our purposes the opacity is acceptable: the lesson we should take away from Wittgenstein is that within the appropriate philosophical context, *On What Is Not might* be serious – or at any rate no less sane than at least some philosophy ever is (who could be crazier than Parmenides, implying that he himself does not 'really' exist?).

What are the choices? One might be inclined to favour a 'straight' reading, according to which Gorgias intends to convey a truth about the nature of communication to us. He has decided that we would learn best from an object-lesson, however: a deliberately self-refuting message whose actual, if concealed, import is that it is futile even to try to think or communicate in a way which denies the very possibility of thought and communication. His indirectness is not perverse, because the intention is to compel us to work through, and thus truly understand, the paradoxes for ourselves. There is no such thing as successfully saying that communication is an impossibility, as *On What Is Not* pretends to do, because that success would of necessity paradoxically entail failure. This could be construed as an elliptical critique of Parmenides' philosophy. Parmenides asserts that what is is a changeless, unique entity, but (as we saw) signally fails to explain how then he can engage us in dialogue. Gorgias indicates the contradiction between the philosopher's metaphysical principles and his practice by explicitly demonstrating, or rather enacting, the (im)possibility of communication on the basis of distorted, *quasi*-Parmenidean premisses. This option is 'straight' in the sense that it suggests that Gorgias is working critically within the philosophical tradition, albeit indirectly.

We cannot dismiss *On What Is Not* as a mere game just on the evidence of the grave argumentative flaws I have only partially catalogued, since by that standard a large proportion of early Greek philosophy would disappear from the canon. In any case, an advocate of a 'straight reading' might speculate that the mistakes, particularly the more flagrant ones, are intentional. On several occasions in the analysis, especially when unpacking Gorgias' presentation of *logos* as non-representational, I have hedged my bets on whether suppressed but crucial assumptions might not have been deliberately planted by Gorgias; 'straight' readers would enthusiastically welcome such a possibility, although they would be wise not to inflate it into more than that.[23]

On the other hand, one might be attracted by a 'parodic' reading. When Gorgias rejects Parmenides, as we all must, he concludes that so far as rigorous ratiocination is concerned, we have no grounds for faulting him. But if Parmenides' logic is impeccable, then engaging in an abstract logical exercise according to the rules set down by philosophy produces a result bearing no relation to what we *know* is real (the words 'know' and 'real' are now employed in a belligerently anti-philosophical sense). This type of reading demands that Gorgias' inferences be capable of withstanding at least an initial examination (in his own eyes, of course), since otherwise we could simply attribute the outrageous conclusions of *On What Is Not* to faulty reasoning, rather than to the nature of philosophical speculation itself. It must be initially plausible to suppose that things develop as bizarrely as they do not because these particular *logoi* are defective, but rather as a consequence of what any content-free, formalistic, philosophical *logos* must be like of its own nature. This option permits no unqualified answer to the question of whether *On What Is Not* is 'philosophical' or not.

Finally, we might consider a 'ludic' reading: *On What Is Not* is a sort of joke. It guys the pretensions of the deductive format without thereby declaring any far-ranging view on the ultimate validity of the philosophical enterprise, Parmenidean metaphysics, the capacity of pure reason, etc. This would not mean that the treatise lacks all significance: not all jokes should (or *can*) be enjoyed thoughtlessly.

How to decide between these strategies for reading Gorgias? Working out whether it 'really' is philosophical requires analysis of its arguments (or pseudo-arguments). But perhaps this analytical response presupposes just what we want to find out. Many scholars have claimed that *On What Is Not* formulates a *theory* of *logos* which liberates both rhetoric and literature from the supposed constraints of representational discourse: if language is not *about* the world, then poets and orators are free to influence us in disregard of the inaccessible facts.[24] This sadly mistaken reading overlooks the most obvious consequence of Gorgias' *paradoxologia*: his message refutes itself, and in consequence, so far from constituting a theory of *logos*, it confronts us with a picture of what language cannot be, with what it cannot be assumed to aspire to be.

I propose instead that the enduring significance of *On What Is Not* resides in our very uncertainty over whether Gorgias is in earnest (whatever that might mean in this context), in our final inability to decide between the strategies proposed for reading him. As emerged so strongly in our reading of Parmenides, philosophy pretends to an impersonal authority deriving from *logos*. But the fact that any attempt to answer the question 'does Gorgias' text have the status of "authentic" philosophy?' seemingly presupposes an affirmative answer to that question, suggests that its actual genre is only to be discovered in the intentions and pretensions of its author, and not in or from the *logos* itself. That is to make the decision a very personal, contingent matter indeed, and thus to dissipate the philosophical drive to find authority beyond the personal. *On What Is Not* seriously threatens philosophy because philosophy cannot tell whether to take it seriously without dangerously compromising its commitment to a reason which is no respecter of persons. Was Gorgias a part-time or erstwhile honest, and honestly deluded, Parmenidean philosopher? Or was he the sophisticated 'sophist' constructing an intellectual pitfall? If so, with what motivation? Without answers, in a quite serious sense we simply do not know what *On What Is Not* is saying. My suggestion is that this vertiginous uncertainty is itself the primary message (better, *non*-message?) of the text. To indulge in metaphors: it is not that Gorgias is offering us a ladder we must somehow throw away after we have climbed it, it is not even clear that we are not just stepping out into thin air. Or again: Gorgias is deliberately transmitting a message which consists largely of noise; in so doing he gets us to think about what any act of communication must be like, and about what philosophers claim their messages are like.

24

2

IN PRAISE OF FALLEN WOMEN

Gorgias' *Encomium of Helen*

Helen: Is it possible to respond with *logos* that if I shall die, it
           will be unjustly?
Menelaus: It was not for *logos* that I came, but to kill you.

(Euripides, *Trojan Women* 903–5)

WHO WAS HELEN?

Who was Helen? In the Greek world (and thereafter) she epitomises
sexual passion, an archetype whose cultural significance cannot be
exaggerated. Wife of Menelaus, lover of Paris, she is the irresistible
bad woman, an adulterous and infinitely desirable counterpart to
the eternally faithful Penelope, wife of Odysseus. Even in her first,
Homeric, incarnation, she arouses profoundly ambiguous feelings.
Although in the fourth book of the *Odyssey* she initially appears as
a wife reinstated in her old home and entertaining Odysseus' son
Telemachus with stories, Menelaus recounts an unsettling anecdote
which casts a shadow over her verbal skill. At the moment of
maximum danger, when the Achaean warriors were concealed within
the wooden horse, she mischievously imitated the voices of their
wives to lure them out (*Odyssey* IV.274–89).[1] But her association
with *logos* is implicit from the beginning: she yielded to the verbal
importunity of Paris, and she herself possesses a bewitching, deceptive tongue, imitating, with pointed irony, the seductive voices of
absent wives, exploiting the separation of husband and wife when
she is herself the glaringly, culpably absent wife whom the Greeks
have come to retrieve.

Or is she? As we shall discover, even in Homer there are at
least embryonic suggestions that her guilt might be extenuated.

25

Furthermore, from very early times there existed a literary tradition alternative to Homer's. Stesichorus, a lyric poet of the early sixth century BCE, supposedly struck blind for maligning Helen, is said to have recovered his vision on composing his famous *Palinode*, which cleared her of wrongdoing. This alternative tradition culminates in Euripides' *Helen*, which completely undercuts the Homeric story by asserting that only a phantom, not Helen herself, went off to Troy. Still, a sizeable gap remains between exoneration and commendation. If the celebrated – or notorious – feminine ideal put in Pericles' mouth by Thucydides, 'to be least spoken of, for good or ill, among men' (II 11.2), is taken seriously, then the mere fact of Helen's universal fame is sufficient to make her deeply unfortunate, regardless of whether she is to blame or not. Of course, the invisibility, in terms of social discourse, to which proper Athenian women are meant to aspire cannot be a norm automatically applicable to a legendary, semi-divine being; thus both positive and negative reactions to the figure of Helen will not be unproblematic.

So what would it mean to speak in *praise* of Helen? We can be quite certain that this is Gorgias' intention: although the title by which his work is known, 'Encomium of Helen', might of course not be his own, there is plenty of internal evidence that (part of) his purpose is to extol her virtues. In the technical handbooks rhetoric came to be divided into three main genres, forensic (speeches of defence or accusation before a lawcourt), deliberative (political advice to a legislative or executive body) and epideictic (speeches in praise or blame of some individual or institution). The *Encomium of Helen* ostensibly falls into the last category. Now despite plentiful claims that Gorgias himself and other rhetorical pioneers composed such handbooks (e.g. Buchheim test. 2), there are good grounds for scepticism about not only the character and scope, but even the very existence of these so-called *technai*. In particular, we lack firm grounds for supposing that Gorgias or his contemporaries were familiar with the tripartite generic classification as such. It gained general currency and eventual canonical status by virtue of Aristotle's endorsement in his *Rhetoric* (I 3), but there is no reason to think that the formal division antedates him by much, even if Aristotle himself did not invent it. One might indeed push the sceptical argument further by exploiting a later text. Isocrates in his own *Helen* upbraids Gorgias on the score of generic impropriety, asserting that despite his express intention, Gorgias actually wrote not an encomium, but rather a defence of her (*Helen* 14), while the occasions and topics of apology and encomium are actually incompatible (15). The sceptic might infer that to cry up his own product Isocrates, Aristotle's contemporary, is anachronistically drawing upon a conception of generic propriety which was not yet in force during the previous century.

Such historical scruples should not inhibit us, however, from wondering about what type of speech the *Encomium* might be. If there are good grounds for doubting the existence of a pre-Aristotelian handbook tradition articulating the tripartition of types of speech, by the same token there are none for suspecting that fifth-century thinkers would have found that tripartition at all esoteric or counter-intuitive. The classification became dominant, not just because of Aristotle's authority, but rather for the excellent reason that it makes splendid sense: as Aristotle says, speeches really are distinguished according to speaker, auditor and subject-matter, and with reference to ancient Greek institutions these criteria yield precisely the categories of forensic, deliberative and epideictic oratory. Therefore one might speculate that even if the classification of rhetoric had not been explicitly articulated by theoreticians during the period of Gorgias' activity, he might nevertheless have designedly played off (still relatively informal) generic expectations. This speculation has two components. First, to praise Helen, given what people expected of the subject of an encomium, at least verges on *paradoxologia*. But second, perhaps Gorgias stymied conventional expectations in a more complex fashion, by deliberately crossing the boundaries marking off the (nascent) genres. Isocrates could have supported his charge that the *Encomium* is more accurately described as an apology with a citation from Gorgias' text: we read that Gorgias plans 'to free the slandered woman from blame and to show that those who blame her are lying' (§2). This sentence not only makes clear that Gorgias' purpose is to defend as well as to praise: it might even employ vocabulary of special significance in this context, for the verb translated 'show' is *epideixai*, from which the generic label 'epideictic' is derived. Thus Gorgias' choice of diction might already be hinting that in the *Encomium* praise and defence are surprisingly combined.

One might complain that quite apart from the highly speculative character of this hypothesis, it seems pointless: why ever should Gorgias have been interested in generic confusion? Would it not merely signal the clumsy lack of expertise which Isocrates apparently wishes the reader to contrast with his own skilful *Helen*? But perhaps scholars have too readily accepted Isocrates' criticism at face-value.[2]

Evidently Isocrates should in all consistency write an encomium, and the encomium must, of course, be of Helen. But Isocrates' *Helen* does not in fact answer to this description. True enough, it is a speech of praise, but Helen is only the ostensible topic. The real object of praise is the figure of Theseus, that is, the city of Athens itself through its illustrious mythological representative:

> if the man who did these things had been a nobody rather than someone very distinguished, it would not yet be clear whether this *logos* is an encomium of Helen or an accusation of Theseus [because he raped her]; but as it is, although we shall find that other men of good reputation are deficient in courage, wisdom or some other such part of virtue, Theseus alone lacked not even one of them, but had achieved perfect virtue. And I think it is fitting to speak about him at even greater length; for I believe that if I can show [*epideixai*] that those who loved and admired Helen were themselves especially admirable, this will be the greatest assurance for those wishing to praise Helen.

> (*Helen* 21–2)

Isocrates is indirectly telling us that at the heart of the *Helen* is neither an encomium of Helen nor an accusation of Theseus, but rather an encomium of Theseus' city. If this is so, then Isocrates' apparent criticism of Gorgias conceals an *hommage* to his teacher, albeit one for the discerning reader only. While feigning dissatisfaction with Gorgias' supposed failure to do what he promised, Isocrates really emulates him. Yet again, to what end? I shall argue that although as concerns Helen, Gorgias' text is truly forensic – a speech for the defence – it crosses genres by mounting this defence within the framework provided by its overriding epideictic purpose, the glorification of (not Helen, but) *logos*. But if so, one might continue to complain, why not simply praise *logos* without muddying the issue in this way? The answer is to be discovered in the *Encomium* itself. It declares that for a *logos* to arouse pleasure, it must avoid the dully obvious, so that a devious approach recommends itself from the outset. Moreover, a running theme of the *Encomium* will be the force and attractions of deceit: how better to convey them than by the text's own partial occlusion of its central topic and true genre? By mimicking this indirection in his *Helen*, Isocrates declares – to the cultivated and knowing reader – that he too is able to please by making as if to deceive: he pretends to criticise Gorgias in order to

reveal, if hardly in plain language, his allegiance to the Gorgianic
programme of pleasurable confusion.

Although scholars today better appreciate that epideictic oratory
played a prominent rôle in the construction and maintenance of
civic identity in the Greek city-state,[3] a casual attitude towards the
Helen still prevails: Helen herself is no more than a figure from
mythology, so a composition about her can only have been a display-
piece intended to advertise Gorgias' expertise, and perhaps a model
for students as well.[4] Underlying this deprecatory attitude is an
implicit conviction that epideictic cannot be important because it is
not serious. It is designated by the Greek noun *epideixis* which, like
the cognate verb *epideixai*, refers to showing, an act of display. But
while every upright citizen knows that what goes on in the lawcourts
and the political arena is important if anything is, display, especially
showing *off*, suggests frivolity rather than weight.

Whatever the worth of this presumption nowadays, it is patently
unsound for the ancient Greek world. After all, despite serving as
vehicles of aesthetic pleasure, tragedies were *displayed* at civic festivals where Athenian political values and policies were subjected to
the most profound scrutiny and debate.[5] And there is a specific
reason for querying this dismissal in the case of Gorgias. We have
already learnt that *On What Is Not* might well work most seriously
and effectively against philosophical pretensions in the very act
of appearing to collapse into a philosophical joke; it would be quite
unwise to infer that if the *Encomium* is (in some respects) not serious,
it therefore is not an important text. In fact the *Encomium* master-
fully complements Gorgias' manœuvre in *On What Is Not* to
wrest the *logos* from philosophical control, and it also further develops
his challenge by uncompromisingly opening up the political dimensions of rhetoric. The subtlety of Gorgias' procedure can only be
appreciated by detailed and sequential analysis.

COSMETIC TRUTH

At the outset of the *Encomium* Gorgias announces: 'the *kosmos* of a
city is good quality in its men, of a body, beauty, of a *psychē* [conven-
tionally translated 'soul'], wisdom, of a thing,[6] excellence, of *logos*,
alētheia' (§1). Since he immediately assures us that 'one should
honour with praise what is worthy of praise, but attach blame to
the unworthy', the purpose of the opening sentence is evidently
to enumerate across a wide range of cases what might properly be

the subject of an encomium. If so, then Gorgias' abstract designation of what deserves admiration is *kosmos*. But '*kosmos*' was, we will remember, a key-word in Parmenides: although the core-meaning of the word is 'order' or 'harmony',[7] it extends to cover *speciously* attractive, imposed arrangements, as in meretricious make-up, or, in later rhetorical jargon, the 'ornaments' of speech. Parmenides was anxious to oppose deceptive *kosmos* to *logos*-as-argument. Will Gorgias too seek to persuade us by means of logical reasoning, even by means of logic alone? And does *alētheia* here, the *kosmos* of *logos*, signify unvarnished 'truth', with the implication that Gorgias' *Encomium* in particular can achieve the excellence of *logos* only if it tells us a *true* story? If *kosmos* can regularly connote ornamentation and artifice, the danger is that a cosmetic *logos* may disguise rather than represent reality. Does the orator, however, simply discover objective values in the world and faithfully match his *logos* to them? That would seem to be the implication of the assertion that 'it is an equal defect and act of ignorance to blame the praiseworthy and to praise the blameworthy'. The bland reassurance that praise and blame must be apportioned to *deserving* subjects excludes the unnerving possibility that what makes something an exploitable topic for acclamation or denigration might be a matter to be decided by the orator, on the basis of whims and personal interests. Thus, at least at the outset, Gorgias soberly affirms that *kosmos* does not function as mere ornamental artifice, as opposed to what really is: his wish is 'to show the truth' (§2).[8]

Gorgias complains that people who have listened to the poets (he ignores Stesichorus) have been misled about Helen; his stated objective is to offer a 'refutation' ('*elenchos*', the word used by Parmenides' goddess in fr. 7) of those who have slandered Helen, and to do so by 'adding a *logismos* to my *logos*' (§2). *Logismos* denotes ratiocination, so the claim is that the 'refutation' will take the form of reasoning or argument. We know that the goal is supposed to be truth, and that the poets have uttered falsehoods; but is there a further, implicit claim here that poetical conviction (beliefs either shared or imparted by poets) is not only false, but also irrational? Or might the message be milder, that the traditional, false verdict on Helen is (at least partially) based on defective reasoning, rather than on none at all? One might rephrase these questions by asking whether Gorgias is simply confronting an undifferentiated poetical tradition which he condemns as false, or mounting a more formidable challenge by laying claim to a special method or expertise inaccessible to that tradition. In other words, will he elect to discriminate between *logoi* on grounds more substantial than their naked truth or falsehood, by giving *logismos* a distinctive sense not found in the poets? When they do not simply ignore Gorgias, historians of philosophy pay exclusive attention to *On What Is Not*; but these questions indicate that the *Encomium* might well repay equal study.

IN PRAISE OF HELEN

Following the customary laudatory pattern, Gorgias goes on to assure us that Helen's illustrious parentage is 'not unclear to even a few' (§3). How so? Her genealogy emerges from the mythological and poetical tradition whose accuracy Gorgias has just impugned. And if, according to that tradition, it is 'clear that her mother was Leda', her paternity, at least initially, is made anything but 'clear': 'her father was a god, but was said to be a mortal, Tyndareus and Zeus, of whom the one seemed to be her father because he was, while the other was shown up [a form of the verb cognate with '*elenchos*'] because he said he was'. If 'was said to be' is tantamount to 'merely reputed to be' in contrast to 'was', the fact remains that both claims to paternity, mortal and divine, form part of the traditional mythology on which Gorgias' *logos* draws. How could one break through the reportage to verifiable reality, especially when what is at issue is parentage? It is the wise child who knows its father, but as yet we fail to break out of the circle of words. And notice that, in this particular instance, since Zeus is (supposed to be) the real father, what might have been anticipated as the less plausible claim turns out to be the correct one. But if divine parentage is relatively implausible, how is it that Zeus 'seemed to be her father because he was'? Elsewhere (Buchheim fr. 26) Gorgias warns that reality does not automatically make itself apparent: 'he said that being without seeming is unobvious, seeming without being is weak'. The answer is to be found in 'the other was shown up because he said he was'. This is a wonderful stroke. What one expects is something like 'the god seemed to be her father on account of reality, but the man seemed to be her father on account of reputation'. Instead, Gorgias daringly inverts the description of Tyndareus: so far from his appearing to be her father because he said so, he was revealed *not* to be her father because he said so. The idea, presumably, is that so brilliant is the sight of Helen's 'divine beauty' (§4) that it immediately suffices to give the lie to the mortal's pretension: we can clearly see that her beauty is 'divine' in the strict sense of the word. The truth is so vivid that we need not fear deception or delusion; falsehoods have only to be uttered to be 'shown up', to suffer refutation.[9] Of course we ourselves cannot see Helen; we must put our faith in Gorgias' *logos* when it reports how the sight of divine beauty affected the vision of her contemporaries, just as we must take the word of Homer's Priam and his elderly companions that Helen is 'marvellously like the immortal goddesses to look upon' (*Iliad* III 158).

'With one body she brought together many bodies of men' (§4). The Greek for 'brought together' has a specialised, hostile sense, 'joined in battle', and the suitors are already contending for her hand, just as her one body, conveyed to Troy, will, as Faustus will say, 'launch a thousand ships'. Helen's divine beauty is admirable because by means of it she collects – and erotically subdues – men who themselves merit renown for their various gifts and accomplishments, including 'the power of acquired wisdom'. Where power or capacity – *dynamis* – is really to be found, and how it works, will develop into the master-theme of the *Encomium*.

PLEASURE

Gorgias now excuses his passing over the familiar events leading up to Helen's departure for Troy with the claim that 'to tell those who know what they know carries conviction, but conveys no pleasure' (§5). 'Conviction' was the word used in §2 for the misguided faith people have in the poets' calumny of Helen. So 'conviction' in and of itself is simply confidence or assurance, not necessarily right or wrong; it all depends on the source of conviction. Gorgias' excuse is also a tangible compliment to his audience; while the poets' auditors are gullible, those who read or listen[10] to *him* must be spared boredom because they are knowers. Since this is an enjoyable piece of flattery, the excuse does not merely ward off tedium with the promise of future delight, it also itself surreptitiously conveys pleasure. But is there any reason to suppose that this flattering conviction is well-grounded? It is pleasant that Gorgias takes our wisdom for granted, but perhaps he is deceived in so doing – or intends to deceive us.

Plato's Gorgias will concede that the orator *cannot* communicate knowledge, and that his utterances carry no conviction whatsoever for knowers. Here, in contrast, the real Gorgias declines to retail common knowledge on the grounds that it brings no pleasure: if his *logos* is to be pleasing, then at the very least it must be novel. Granted, novelty is hardly incompatible with truth – otherwise it would be impossible to find anything out – but commitment to the principle that what will be said will be selected (at least partially) in order to please surely renders problematic Gorgias' other commitment, that to *alētheia* (only certain philosophers would even pretend, most implausibly, to take pleasure in the truth alone). To avoid boredom, Gorgias will omit the episodes we all know; his expression ('skipping that former time with my *logos*') signals the power of *logos* to interrupt or disrupt the chronological continuity of narration. Such continuity might have proved wearisome, but it could also have prevented rhetorical distortion of the plain truth for the sake of a delightful, cosmetic effect. Long after Gorgias' impact had been felt, Aristotle would resoundingly declare in the *Metaphysics* that 'all men naturally desire to know' (989A21). If that is true, and one cannot know falsehoods, then people have an innate appetite for the truth; and it makes sense to assume that fulfilment of innate appetites is intrinsically pleasurable, so that it would follow that there is a universal delight in truth. But even if one were to accept this Aristotelian conception of humanity, it would not follow that anyone, with the theoretical but very unlikely exception of an ideally committed philosopher, would take more pleasure in the truth than in anything else. We are endowed with a host of rival appetites which almost inevitably come into conflict; so we have little antecedent reason to believe that both commitments – to truth and to pleasure in *logos* – can (routinely) be met.

CAUSES AND EXCUSES

What Gorgias proceeds to give us are causes making Helen's behaviour *eikos*. Perhaps the single most important word in Greek rhetoric, *eikos* can be rendered as 'likely', 'plausible' or 'probable', often, as here, with the positive, normative connotation of 'reasonable'. It is a commonplace of later rhetorical theory that the orator's task of instilling confidence in the likelihood, reasonableness or plausibility of his case depends on achieving a verisimilitude which might, but need not, coincide with the facts. It is because the orator occupies the ineliminable gap between the likely and the true that he can serve flexibly *pro* or *contra*. Thus Gorgias' intention to deliver a 'likely' *logos*, in conjunction with his promise to please, distances him yet further from *alētheia* in Parmenides' sense of truth/reality.

33

Gorgias will exculpate Helen by running through each of the possible causes for her elopement with Paris, and suggesting in each case that she cannot be held accountable; thus, if the catalogue is exhaustive, her defence will be successful (it is perhaps this methodical procedure which he means by the *logismos* added to his *logos*). 'Helen did what she did through either the wishes of chance and the intentions of the gods and the decrees of necessity, or because she was seized by force, or persuaded by *logoi*, or captured by love' (§6). At this stage Gorgias presents force and persuasion as categorially distinct, but his rhetoric will erode this already hallowed distinction.

We begin with the first cause in the list: divine intervention. Gorgias proclaims that in this case Helen's innocence is manifest, since mortals cannot withstand gods, and it is 'natural' for the stronger to control the weaker. Perhaps the case is not quite so unproblematic as he pretends, since there is plentiful evidence, at least for earlier times, that Greeks tolerated an overdetermined scheme for the explanation of behaviour; one and the same act might be attributed to both a human agent and the intervention of a supernatural being, without divine influence necessarily freeing the human agent from the consequences of his or her action.[11]

Gorgias' tactics increase considerably in interest when he turns to the second possible cause, rape by way of brute force.

How would it not be *eikos* for a woman forced, deprived of her country and bereaved of her family to be pitied rather than reviled in *logos*? He acted terribly, but she suffered; thus it is just to feel sorry for her, but to hate him.

(§7)

Here *eikos* must have normative force, as a plea for a *reasonable and just* reaction from the listener or reader to the victim's plight. But this *reasonable* response is *emotional*; does this mixture of compassion and indignation also afford us the promised pleasure and, if so, does our judgement remain unclouded? The Greek translated 'how would it not be', in the optative mood (used for what might or would be the case), indicates some lack of commitment to what is expressed, and does so for a variety of reasons. Employment of the optative mood of the verb here is perfectly in order, since what we are contemplating is the *hypothesis* that Paris raped Helen, and thus our reaction is itself hypothetical. But there is an ambiguity in the words which follow, 'thus it is just to feel sorry for her, but to

34

hate him': the phrasing does not reveal whether this conclusion remains within the scope of the preceding optative, and so is properly hypothetical as well, or has shifted to the indicative, which is used for what is actually (supposed to be) the case. And of course it is notoriously easy for an imagination to be manipulated (notice the metaphor) into experiencing feelings indistinguishable from those aroused by the corresponding real situations: while there is consideration of hypotheses falling well short of belief, there is no analogous hypothetical 'quasi-feeling', as it were. So if Gorgias is playing on ambiguity of phrasing here, he is deliberately encouraging us to indulge in feelings which exceed what *logos* in the sense of reason should permit. Gorgias portrays Helen as the archetypal *pathic*, a pre-eminently beautiful body which is defenceless before Paris' onslaught. The opposition of 'he acted, she suffered' invokes a second fundamental polarity, that between action and passion, to set beside that of 'force/persuasion'; when the latter subsequently comes under pressure, the rôle of sufferer will enlarge to threaten us as well.

IN PRAISE OF *LOGOS*

The heart of Gorgias' text is to be found in §8: 'but if *logos* persuaded and deceived her *psychē*, it is also not difficult to construct a defence against that'. Helen went to Troy: if this action was not inherently bad, its consequences indubitably were. A conventional piece of forensic rhetoric would plead compulsion on Helen's behalf; if she were forced to go with Paris, she deserves to be exonerated, maybe even pitied. What one therefore anticipates is an argument that she did *not* yield to persuasion. The standard polar opposition between force and persuasion entails that succumbing to a merely verbal seduction is altogether blameworthy. Instead – and here, surely, we find the most illuminating example of the *paradoxologia* to which Philostratus attributed Gorgias' fame – he unnervingly collapses the polarity.

The process is begun by simply juxtaposing 'persuasion' and 'deception', as if persuasion too by its very nature 'takes in' its victims,[12] and by introducing the concept of the *psychē* into the argument, a tactic with the most far-reaching consequences. But, we object, even if everyone persuaded is 'taken in', does that mean that persuasion necessarily and of itself victimises those who succumb to it? One of Gorgias' most telling fragments suggests otherwise. On the subject of Athenian tragedy, Plutarch attributes this remarkable discovery to him:

> tragedy through its myths and feelings [*pathē*] furnishes a deception, as Gorgias says, with reference to which the one who deceives is more just than the one who does not, and the one who is deceived is wiser than the one who is not. For the one who deceives is more just, because he has done what he promised, and the one who is deceived is wiser, for what is not insensible is easily captured by the pleasure of *logoi*.
>
> (Buchheim fr. 23)

Now this view does not commit Gorgias to an aesthetic presupposing that tragedy aims at naïvely realistic representation; even a superficial acquaintance with the conventions of Athenian theatre would positively discourage any move towards such a theory. Rather, what he is saying is that tragedy, to have its characteristic effect, must generate a theatrical illusion in order to captivate the audience both intellectually and emotionally: members of the audience must react *as if* what happens on stage were indeed happening, if they are to enjoy the tragic experience. For this to occur successfully, the playwright must produce an imaginary world, but the audience must also imbue it with reality, by means of 'the willing suspension of disbelief'. Thus the tragic spectacle demands a sort of collusion in pretence, which provides Gorgias with the opportunity for more, audacious *paradoxologia*: we should conceive of the theatrical experience as a sort of contractual deception, relying on cooperation between the deceptive tragedian and the receptively deceived audience.[13]

The potential ramifications of this insight are fascinating, but we must proceed with great caution in tracing them out. For example, one should avoid leaping to the conclusion that this very special phenomenon of deceptive connivance regularly occurs outside the theatre, for that would have the curious consequence that in the case which immediately concerns us, Paris *justly* seduced Helen and Helen was *wisely* seduced. Gorgias' analysis depends on the fact that the theatre is an institution regulated by cultural conventions which define and guide its fictions; he can refer to the deceiver's 'promise' only because some of those conventions constitute an undertaking on the part of the playwright to create an illusion at which we connive for the sake of instruction and pleasure. No such conventions obviously obtain beyond the aesthetic sphere; in fact, it is precisely the operation of such rules of pretence which marks off the fictional.

Nevertheless, it does not follow that the doctrine of tragic deception has *no* bearing on the workings of persuasion in general. First, fr. 23 attributes the superior wisdom of the deceived audience to its sensibility to 'the pleasure of *logoi*'. We already know that Gorgias himself subscribes to the principle that the successful *logos* is one which is enjoyed, and clearly all sorts of *logoi* are to be found outside the theatre. Furthermore, sensitivity to 'the pleasure of *logoi*' cannot be ours only when we attend a play; if we are susceptible to the charms of deceptive *logos* within the bounds of fiction, why not in general? One might protest that such susceptibility is conditional on our *willing* connivance at deceit – which is to say that we are not 'really' deceived. But this objection overlooks the very real possibility that we are all too easily 'taken in'; perhaps undetected deception is the norm, and our awareness (which in any case need not be more than subliminal) of it in self-proclaimed fiction is the rare exception. The implication is that Helen might have enjoyed Paris' verbal seduction; in fact, it was precisely the pleasure she took in his *logos* which caused her to yield. Again one might protest that it would be disastrous for Gorgias to suggest any such thing, since if she not only gave way to temptation, but also actually *enjoyed* her fall, then she must be the worst of all possible wives, contrary to what Gorgias seeks to establish.

Fr. 23's second important message supplies the answer. It will not do to assume too readily that the fictional is everywhere and always easily and unambiguously separated from the real; we literally enter into and depart from the theatre, but the status of other *logoi* might be none too clear. In particular, what of the *Encomium* itself? Might it not be a piece of fiction? If it is, recognition of its fictitious character will be seriously impeded by Gorgias' commitment in §2 to truth-telling, since realising that a denial of pretence is actually a sort of second-order pretence demands quite a sophisticated response from the reader or auditor. So were the *Encomium* a fiction, we – supposed 'knowers' – would turn out to have been pleasurably and deceitfully persuaded of Helen's innocence; but then we could hardly take exception to her falling prey to the words of Paris, since we ourselves have been seduced by Gorgias. Perhaps, in the last analysis, we who are persuaded are all more or less willing victims of persuasion; at the very least, the degree to which we cooperate in deception might remain permanently obscure.

'*Logos* is a great *dynastēs*, which accomplishes divine deeds with the smallest and least apparent of bodies; for it is able [*dynasthai*][14] to stop fear, remove pain, implant joy and augment pity' (§8). Yet a further traditional Greek polarity is that between word and deed: the superhuman performance of *logos* erases it. We have already been informed that Helen's 'one body brought together many bodies of men' (§4). But while she may possess 'divine beauty', *logos* easily surpasses her achievements by accomplishing 'divine deeds', overwhelming her visibly attractive body with its invisible one.[15]

The ringing affirmation of §8 brings home the political implications of Gorgias' rhetoric. *Dynastēs*, like *tyrannos* (applied in §3 to Zeus),[16] need not carry sinister, 'tyrannical' overtones, but it certainly can. The rallying cry of Athenian democratic ideology was *isēgoria*, 'free speech': a citizen is supposedly free precisely in that his access to political power is limited only by his ability to persuade his fellows in the Assembly, not by brute force, or by the handicaps of low birth or poverty.[17] There is certainly an entrenched Athenian contrast between 'private individuals' (*idiōtai*) and magistrates or political leaders (*politeuomenoi*), but these latter must not be assimilated to professional 'politicians', in the modern sense. While our 'politicians' can be recognised by their party affiliation, selection as representatives, etc., Athenian *politeuomenoi* were at least as frequently designated as '*rhētores*' or '*hoi legontes*', that is, just as 'speakers'. To speak well was *ipso facto* to wield political power; the power to persuade in the Assembly was the alpha and omega of political success (so that a standard slur on an opponent is to call him *deinos legein*, 'clever/dangerous ['*deinos*' means both] in speaking').[18] We learn from Pausanias (I 22.3) that a deified *Peithō* (the goddess Persuasion), whose statue stood near the Acropolis, was even worshipped in Athens.

But if *logos* confers 'dynastic' power, the chief mechanism for the maintenance of a democratic state may actually turn out to subvert it. If the *Encomium* articulates this paradox and the danger it poses to ancient democracy, there is plenty of evidence from Athens that the threat was felt as a real one.[19] This passage from Demosthenes is especially emphatic testimony: 'formerly the Assembly was master of the politicians . . . Now, on the contrary . . . you, the Assembly, have become a sort of servant and subordinate of theirs' (III 30 ff.). The apparently masterful *dēmos*, the politically empowered people of Athens, represented as actually hoodwinked, and so dominated, by those who seem to flatter it, the 'speakers', is a commonplace in both Aristophanes (e.g. *Wasps* 654–724) and Plato (e.g. *Republic* VI 488D ff.).[20]

Gorgias' list of the divine accomplishments of *logos*, which presumably exemplify persuasion/deceit, all relate to emotional rather than intellectual change, while ability to instil *rational* conviction is not even mentioned. An almost universal inclination in Greek thought conceives of the emotions as *pathē*, states which happen to us, before which we are passive (the corresponding Greek verb '*paschein*', 'to suffer', is related to the word 'passive'). In retrospect we realise that Gorgias' own *logos* (which enjoined us, at least conditionally, to 'pity' Helen at the end of §7) may already have exerted an impact on our *psychai*, in which *logos* can 'augment pity'. If Paris seduced the hapless Helen, by the same token we, in responding emotionally to Gorgias' rhetorical seduction, are equally passive, equally impotent before his active, divine, power.

POETICAL EFFECTS

Gorgias' first species of omnipotent *logos* is poetry, which he famously defines as '*logos* with metre' (§9): its auditors literally experience 'sympathy' with literary characters when poetic *logoi* cause their souls to 'suffer'.[21] The receptive individual undergoes an emotion identical to the feelings which are portrayed on stage or in verse, or at any rate consonant with the events depicted. Thus poetry essentially involves the deliberate arousal and training of emotion through words; and the realisation that this holds good for rhetoric itself dawns on the perceptive reader of the *Encomium*. Later traditions in literary criticism will tend to discriminate amongst various poetical (especially theatrical) devices, while *not* attributing to *logos* as such the chief, let alone exclusive, responsibility for moving the emotions. Gorgias' monistic conception of *logos*, in contrast, should warn us that his definition is not intended to suggest that the emotional power of poetry resides *extrinsically* in the metre; while Parmenides was at pains to separate superior *logos* from deceptive 'words', Gorgias strives to fuse all aspects of *logos*, irrational as well as logical, into a single overwhelming force.

In the previous chapter we reflected on the poor reputation which Gorgias' style, condemned for both its *outré* diction and its extreme figures of speech, was to acquire. In particular, Gorgias offended the most basic generic proprieties by making use of devices which were later deemed appropriate only for poetry, not prose. Some critics have attributed these purported stylistic defects to Gorgias' early date: he was one of the first pioneers in prose, writing at a time when the vast majority of models available to him were verse. But the definition in §9 of the *Encomium* suggests a much more positive assessment of his technique. The earliest expression for 'prose' of which we are aware is '*logos psilos*' (perhaps occurring first in Plato's *Menexenus*, 239C), which means 'bare *logos*' – bare, that is, of metre. This makes perfect sense: if all *logoi* were originally verse, then one naturally thinks of prose as lacking a feature one would expect to find. But Gorgias' definition typically reverses the expectation: for him, the metre is an optional extra. Gorgias, then, may not have failed to perceive such generic boundaries as already existed, but rather may have chosen to disregard them, on the strength of the credo that if persuasive power is all, the persuader is free to exploit whatever resources will increase his success.[22]

'Fearful *phrikē* and tearful pity and mournful desire enter those who listen to poetry' (§9). '*Phrikē*' is primarily 'shuddering', and 'tearful' may similarly import a suggestion that poetical *logos* stimulates physical manifestations of the emotions. We have already seen that in §8 Gorgias blurs the distinction between word and deed (*ergon*), and the manœuvre is important for his purposes. This is not because Greek culture set a low value on language; the best Homeric heroes, Odysseus foremost among them, display both martial and verbal talents, and without the glamour of fame, which only glorification in song can provide, *erga* ('deeds', viz. 'heroic exploits') would lose much of their appeal. The fact nevertheless remains that in archaic culture *logos* is valuable inasmuch as it furthers, inhibits or memorialises the performance of *erga*. Thus the chief significance of the mention of physical symptoms in §9 might be to strengthen the impression that *logos makes things happen*, as we can directly corroborate by monitoring the palpable effects of poetry on ourselves and others.[23]

MAGIC

The second species of *logos* is magic, which also has the ability to change feelings:

> inspired spells working through *logoi* are attractors of pleasure and repellents of pain; for by coming together with the opinion

of the *psychē*, the power [*dynamis*] of the spell enchants and persuades and moves it by wizardry.[24] Two arts [*technai*] of wizardry and magic have been invented, errors of mind and deceptions of opinion.

(§10)[25]

The pleasure and pain caused by incantation include bodily sensations, but it by no means follows that the effects produced by poetry are emotional as distinct from physical: Gorgias' descriptions import no such dualism. The words 'coming together' and 'moves' strengthen the picture – not to be exaggerated into a 'theory' – of the soul as a quasi-concrete object open to manipulation. That spells work 'through *logoi*' makes them uniquely effective *tools*, but any potential distinction between *logoi* as meaningful, persuading by their meaningful content, and *logoi* as instruments, shaping by their 'impact', is blurred by the collocation 'enchants and persuades and moves', which fuses the semantic/persuasive and instrumental/coercive conceptions of *logos*.

The reason for this is clear: if a spell contains a linguistic message, it is one addressed to the god or demon whose aid is being sought, not to the intended beneficiary or victim, on whom the spell works. That, after all, is why it is sorcery. Are the *logoi* which serve as vehicles of enchantment exactly similar to the *logoi* which we employ in non-magical situations? Gorgias says nothing to discount the possibility that *all* words are capable of direct action, as it were. By so artfully intertwining physical and semantic features, he refuses to admit categorical differences between species of *logos*. Words simply make us do things, and even the distinction between the impact of a tool and the force of an argument drops into insignificance.

It is no mistake that oratory itself is missing from Gorgias' catalogue. He is at work on systematically obliterating distinctions between *logoi* which are all alike emotionally manipulative, and different only in mode of operation and, presumably, effectiveness; the whole family of *logoi* constitutes rhetoric, of which Gorgias is master. He made the transition from §8 to §9 by declaring that 'I shall show that this is so; and one must show it to the hearers by means of opinion'. Now that we have read (or heard) §10, perhaps the phrase 'coming together with the opinion of the *psychē*' will lead us to realise that Gorgias himself is operating on us as, if not *just* as, incantation works on those the sorcerer wants to bewitch.

41

SLIPPERY OPINIONS

'So many men have persuaded and do persuade so many about so many topics by shaping false *logos*!' (§11). How abrupt is the break with the preceding? It is hardly obvious that what goes wrong with poetical or magical *logoi*, when something does go wrong, is their *falsity*, as opposed to their inefficacy. What gives *logos* its potential for deceptive persuasion? Gorgias explains that if everyone had comprehensive memory of the past, insight into the present and foreknowledge of the future, *logos* would not be what it in fact is. As it is, recollection, investigation and prophecy pose formidable difficulties, so that in most cases the majority 'present opinion as adviser to the *psychē*', even though opinion is 'slippery and unstable'.

A first impression that this section is relatively transparent, peddling a doctrine of epistemological modesty, soon disappears. Just what 'recollection, investigation and prophecy' is meant to convey is far from clear. It might be unwise to restrict 'recollection' to strictly factual memory, since it could well include literary memorialisation (Helen's name has become 'a memorial of calamities' in the poetic tradition, §2). 'Investigation' could cover anything from the most casual visual examination to esoteric theoretical enquiries. 'Prophecy' denotes so difficult an area of expertise, the preserve of privileged people favoured (or cursed: remember Cassandra) by the gods, that the significance of ranking it with the other two is hard to evaluate: is Gorgias assuming that prognostication is surprisingly easy, or that knowledge of the present (if not the past) is surprisingly difficult?

Gorgias depicts opinion as a *pis aller*, forced on us by our general (he does not say universal) limitations. The contention that opinion is an unreliable adviser might seem to offer at least the pretence of an epistemological theory in the making. But, crucially, *logos* is not put at the service of memory, insight and foreknowledge in order to bolster feeble opinion, as the philosophically minded might anticipate. Instead, *logos* uses opinion to attack the deceived *psychē*. Such a position is sustainable only because Gorgias has so adeptly highlighted the instrumental aspect of *logos*.

FORCE AND PERSUASION

In §12 comes the crisis of the text, where Gorgias explicitly denies the difference between force and persuasion, indeed actually identifies them, to complete his defence of Helen and praise of *logos*. Most unfortunately, the first part of the text is irremediably corrupt, but the basic idea still emerges unmistakably:

> ... has the same power [*dynamis*]. For *logos* in persuading the *psyche* it persuaded forced [*anankazein*, related to '*anankē*', Parmenides' word for 'necessity'] it to obey what was said and approve what was done. Therefore in persuading, that is forcing, he commits injustice, but in being persuaded, that is being forced by the *logos*, she wrongly has a bad reputation.

In the original Greek, because '*logos*' is grammatically masculine, '*psyche*' grammatically feminine, an immediate transition can be made from the asymmetric relation between *logos* and soul to that between Paris and Helen: the 'he' and 'she' in the last sentence refer indifferently to *logos*/Paris, soul/Helen.[26] Grammar is being used not only to persuade us to apply the model to this particular instance of compulsion, but also to associate characteristics of a single mythological case with the persuasive/compulsive situation in general.

All the verb forms of which '*logos*'/'Paris' are subject are active, while all the forms of which '*psyche*'/'Helen' are subject are passive, as we have come to expect. But further, the deliberate femininisation of the *psyche* plays on the Greek cultural assumption that the female as such is a passive object shaped at will by a dominating, masculine force.[27] Thus, perhaps, every male citizen who yields to rhetorical *logos* is comparable to a man who suffers the physical violence of another, and whose masculinity is thereby humiliated:[28] the successful orator performs psychic rape.

It would be difficult to exaggerate the repercussions of this collapse, engineered by Gorgias, of *the* fundamental structural polarity in the culture of ancient Greece, the presence of which can be detected in a host of central texts. When the Andrians refused to contribute money to the Greek side during the Persian Wars, Themistocles appealed to them 'with this *logos*, that the Athenians had come having with them two great gods, Persuasion (*Peithō*) and Necessity (*Anagkaiē*)' (Herodotus VIII 111.2): attempts at political persuasion will be backed up by threats of force. In one of the best-known episodes in the *Iliad*, Aphrodite whisks Paris away from the onslaught of the vengeful Menelaus on the battlefield and brings Helen to him. First, disguised as an old woman, the goddess tries to persuade her to join him by describing his erotic charms (III 390–4), and succeeds in stirring her up (395). But Helen immediately recognises her temptress' true identity, and reproaches the goddess for seeking to trick her into shameful deeds (396–412). The furious Aphrodite will, of course, brook no opposition, and Helen finally capitulates in fear (413–18). It is almost as if Gorgias discovered his entire catalogue of potential reasons for which Helen might be blamed in this one passage. She is made to do what she does by a god, whom no mortal can withstand (§6), moreover by the goddess of love (§19). Helen almost yields to deceit (§8), and does give way – emotionally – before the intimidation of divine anger and prospect of overwhelming force. But, crucially, Aphrodite resorts to enraged threats only when her initial effort at seductive persuasion has failed; the force/persuasion polarity is intact. Hesiod provides a further instance of divinised Persuasion when he describes the construction of Pandora: 'the divine Graces and queenly Persuasion[29] placed golden necklaces on her skin ... and Pallas Athene fitted all ornament [*kosmos*] to her' (*Works and Days* 73–6).

When Gorgias abolishes the distinction between force and persuasion, he undermines the foundation on which rested the basic Greek division between ways of getting people to do things. Why does this matter so much? It is not as if that culture does not permit itself recourse to violence; rather, as the quotation from Herodotus illustrates, civilised Greeks do (or rather should) fall back on it only as a last resort, and only when circumstances justify the use of force. Greeks, and democratic Athenians first and foremost, are civilised rather than barbarian in part because they try to channel violent tendencies into the persuasive, if competitive, negotiations permitted by *logos*, and thereby to dissipate the danger of massive social disruption posed by conflict between individuals and between groups. If he raped Helen, then Paris is 'a barbarian who undertook a barbarian undertaking' (§7); but if we too unavoidably 'in persuading, that is forcing, commit injustice', then our use of psychic compulsion makes us no less savage than barbarians who engage in overt physical violence.

LOGOS IS *LOGOS* IS *LOGOS* . . .

Gorgias adduces further examples of *logos* 'moulding' the soul as it wishes: 'one should notice first the *logoi* of those who study the heavens [*meteōrologoi*],[30] who by removing one opinion and establishing another, make what is incredible and unclear appear to the eyes of opinion' (§13). 'Moulding' both summons up a mechanical rather than rational model of persuasion[31] and contributes further to the portrayal of the *psychē* as something entirely passive, since the word suggests that it is worked like wax or clay, taking the impress of the *logoi* without any resistance. Scientific controversy or debate comes across as sheer indoctrination ('removing', 'establishing'). Earlier, Gorgias had personified opinion as a fallible psychic 'adviser' (§11); now he seems to install it as a gullible homunculus not easily distinguishable from the *psychē* itself, which is brought to see – and so believe – 'what is incredible and unclear'. This is a richly ambiguous phrase. Given the very nature of the subject, these scientists are obliged to make the obscure appear before the mind's eye – that is perhaps even the condition of their achieving explanatory success.[32] But the wording lends itself to an unflattering construction, according to which the creations of the scientific imagination delude us: when *logos* makes us 'see' the 'unclear', it seems clear, but remains intrinsically 'incredible' – although we have been fooled into believing the unbelievable.

In the second place, we should notice 'necessary contests through *logoi*, in which a single *logos* written with skill, not uttered in truth,[33] pleases and persuades a great crowd [*ochlos*]'[34] (§13). These 'necessary' conflicts are legal battles, and 'necessary' in both a passive and an active sense: such speeches are delivered under compulsion by defendants, but they compel the jury to yield.[35] The opposition of a single *logos* to a great crowd will be turned against rhetoric in Plato's *Gorgias*; and now Gorgias' promise to retail pleasure rather than (known) truth appears to reach disconcerting fruition in the statement that persuasion results from a misleading pleasure induced by rhetorical skill inimical to truth. Granted, the specific reference is to the jury, and we are at liberty to distance ourselves smugly from their ignorance, just as we 'knowers' are not the gulls of the poets (§2).[36] But by this point, if we have been heeding the message which is gradually emerging from the text, we shall no longer feel so confident that there is all the difference in the world between the 'great crowd' and us; the pleasure afforded by the *Encomium* is perhaps tinged with the pain of insecurity.

The list continues: 'third, the conflicts of philosophical *logoi*, in which swiftness of judgement is also shown to make the conviction of opinion readily changeable' (§13). In making philosophical argument just another species of *logos*, Gorgias is deliberately ignoring Parmenides' insistence that deductive *logos is sui generis*: all varieties of *logos* are alike displays of persuasive contention; despite its pretensions, philosophy does not establish stable, well-founded judgement, but only demonstrates the mutability of passive belief as now one, now another participant in philosophical contests gains the upper hand. Greek philosophy certainly occupies an aggressive dialectical format,[37] but the word 'conflicts' (*hamilla*)[38] slyly imports a suggestion of unbridled competitiveness with no regard for what is actually the case. Scientists, speakers in court and philosophers are alike purveyors of persuasion; rhetoric is a global phenomenon. Gorgias' choice of illustrations is definitely pugnacious, maybe cynical; none of the (very loose) groupings enumerated would happily accept his description of their practice, and some would reject it indignantly. But since they are all mentioned to illustrate psychic 'moulding', the very terms in which Gorgias introduces his examples would preclude a representative of any of the categories from claiming an exceptional rank on the basis of the *mode* of persuasion employed. There is only the unitary model of *compelling* persuasion.

PSYCHOTROPIC DRUGS

The power [*dynamis*] of *logos* has the same relation [*logos*] to the order of the *psychē* as the order of drugs has to the nature of bodies. For just as different drugs expel different humours from the body, and some put a stop to illness, others to life, so too some *logoi* cause pain, some pleasure, some fear, some induce confidence in the auditors, some drug and bewitch the *psychē* with a certain bad persuasion.

(§14)

This passage assimilates *logos* to an irresistible drug administered either to heal or to harm at the whim of the practitioner, and assimilates the drug to an occult agent. The same *logos* which as white magic gives pleasure creates pain in the guise of 'bad' persuasion/compulsion, but in either case the defenceless *psychē* is drugged, not offered a rational invitation to react;[39] and, consistently with Gorgias' irrationalist programme, the psychic drugs make their victims feel things, not believe them. Gorgias elicits an analogy between rhetorician and doctor, *logos* and chemico-magical agent:[40] Plato will both insist on a sharp distinction between healing doctor and amoral wizard, and deny that the rhetorician deserves comparison with the doctor *properly* understood. Several hundred years later, Cato the Elder, that inveterate opponent of the wiles of Greek rhetoric, will also insist that the Greeks 'have conspired amongst themselves

46

to kill all the barbarians using medicine, and they do this very thing for money to make people trust them and to get rid of them easily' (Pliny's *Natural History* XXIX 14) – a fantasy whose synthesis of xenophobia with paranoid distrust of expertise is worthy of *Der Stürmer*.

EROTIC VISIONS

Gorgias' consideration of *logos* as a potential cause for Helen's elopement is now complete, and he turns to the fourth and final possibility, that love for Paris took her to Troy. In fact, love as such occupies him very briefly: if divine, then the factors already cited in §6 excuse her behaviour; if a merely 'human illness and ignorance of the *psychē*' (§19), then she is equally to be absolved from blame.[41] Instead, the idea that the sight of handsome Paris might have occasioned Helen's overmastering erotic passion leads him to discourse in general on how vision affects us: 'for the things which we see do not have the nature which we desire, but rather the one which each of them actually has; and the *psychē* is moulded even in its character through vision' (§15). The recurrence of the 'moulding' vocabulary in this new context reinforces the impression that the *psychē* is purely passive; the perceptual model evoked is one according to which the visual organs are mere channels permitting the ingress of images which *strike* the *psychē* without its reacting rationally or purposefully. Any claim these images may have to the label 'information' is in doubt, because our passivity before them entails that we are powerless to process or evaluate them.

Since this tyranny of vision might seem implausible in the usual course of events, Gorgias draws our attention to shocking sights which cause us to lose control of ourselves. The fearsome spectacle of a hostile army disturbs the passive vision which in turn actively disturbs the *psychē* (§16). Although nothing could be more shameful than casting down one's shield and fleeing in panic, 'the disregard[42] of convention, brought in as a colonist[43] by the fear which arises from vision, is strong'. Once more, just as the deeds of *logos* were all emotional rather than rational, so too sight attacks the feelings, and apparently the feelings, at least violent ones, are inimical to thinking: 'fear extinguishes and expels thought' (§17). The deserter is the primal male wrongdoer in Greek martial society, the counterpart to Helen, the faithless wife. What Gorgias now says about the man who breaks ranks is easily as subversive as his previous defence of the woman seduced by *logos*. His example might suggest that the very worst citizen, the military coward, in analogy with Helen, is *helplessly* overcome by the terror he sees. Gorgias unsettles his audience by convincing them to exculpate the actions of people ordinarily condemned as the most heinous criminals. He does so by denying them any measure of control; but, since what renders them powerless are circumstances which frequently threaten us as well, his rhetoric steadily erodes our own autonomy.

'Thus vision engraves images of things seen on the mind' (§17). The mind (*phronēma*), inasmuch as it is likened to a tablet in which pictures are inscribed,[44] is no less passive than the wax-like *psychē* moulded by *logos*. This is an artificial metaphor for a natural process, but Gorgias also explicitly includes pictorial and sculptural artefacts within his list of objects giving rise to shocking or seductive sights: 'when painters perfectly render one body and shape out of many colours and bodies, they please vision, and the making of statues and the production of figures supplies the eyes with a sweet sickness' (§18). The eyes are 'sick' because they are deluded, they 'see' what is not really there, that is, whatever the work of art *represents*; the sickness is 'sweet' because, of course, we delight in the visual deception.

'And many frightening things are omitted, but they are similar to those discussed' (§17). Is this a throw-away line, merely rounding off the section? Not at all. How 'like' an image can a verbal representation of it be? Words are not pictures; but, by depicting a fearful scenario in his *logos*, Gorgias is himself stimulating his listeners' or readers' visual imaginations, and thus at one remove managing to imprint images on their minds, images to which we involuntarily react. We had to take Gorgias' word for Helen's 'divine beauty' (§3); but no assertion that she was ravishingly beautiful, no matter how unqualified, no matter how emphatic, could possibly rival the look of her. Gorgias presents one and the same passive psychological mechanism as the basis for the functioning of both *logos* and vision; could this ground the assumption that there is, or could be, a 'rhetoric' in pictorial or plastic *media*, or an architectural 'rhetoric'? There is certainly historical evidence of such a belief: in antiquity, Cicero and Quintilian produced influential correlations between rhetorical and pictorial styles (*De Oratore* III 25 ff.; *Inst. Rh.* XII 10.1 ff.), and Vitruvius performed a like service for architecture (at *De Architectura* I.2 he informs us that architecture comprises '*taxis*', '*diathesis*' and '*oeconomia*' – terms taken directly from Greek rhetorical theory (e.g.

De Sublimitate I 4)). But disappointingly, the application of evaluative criteria originally formulated for the assessment of verbal rhetoric to the visual arts and architecture most often delivers platitudes at best. At worst, seemingly authoritative, substantive descriptions couched in a 'rhetorical' vocabulary turn out to be utterly vacuous.[45] The historical reality was that advocates of painting, sculpture and architecture were eager to capitalise on the prestige 'technical' rhetoric had earned. By associating themselves as closely as possible with one of the best-established branches of '*technē*' or 'art', they hoped to ensure that their callings too would be accorded the status of *technai*, a status which they did not yet firmly possess.

Apart from history, how should we gauge the independent merits of the proposal that we extend the concept of 'rhetoric' beyond verbal *logos*? An instance of this extension might be a claim to the effect that some public building 'tells us' that the government is both powerful and venerable. The building communicates institutional power by way of its imposing size, dignity by way of its incorporation of classical motifs. The example is fairly trite, but the simplification of detail does not make it simplistic, in comparison with standard 'rhetorical' approaches to architecture. If this trivial 'message' is the best that buildings can do, then architectural 'rhetoric' does not begin to bear comparison with verbal persuasion. Of course, the proper conclusion to draw is that neither buildings nor non-verbal works of art compete with *logos* as a vehicle of persuasion. The reason is not far to seek: *logos* alone can convey propositions to beguile or rationally engage an auditor or reader. This is not to deny that both pictorial iconography and architecture (e.g. the classical 'orders') involve highly elaborate semiotic systems; rather, the point is that they do not encode symbols, icons or symbolic connections in linguistic form, or anything like it. To suppose otherwise is profoundly to underestimate the capacities of the visual arts to move us, by radically misconstruing how they do so.

So much for the demonstrable inadequacy of the 'rhetorical' conception of visual artifice. Whatever its merits, why might Gorgias be at pains to suggest a single mechanism for *logos* and vision, which at least suggests the possibility of non-verbal 'rhetoric'? One might hazard the guess that Gorgias is moving to exclude the possibility that the power of persuasion which *logos* possesses might be awe-inspiring, but inferior to the direct force of images. Were it so, he as master of *logos* would be less powerful than a painter, sculptor or architect of genius.

There is an interesting connection between this admittedly speculative line of interpretation and Euripides' Gorgianic play, *The Trojan Women*.[46] Hecuba applauds Menelaus' intention to execute Helen, but warns him to avoid the sight of her, 'for she captures the eyes of men, destroys cities and burns homes; such are the spells which she possesses' (*Troades* 892–3). In the lines which form this chapter's epigraph, Helen beseeches Menelaus for the opportunity to defend herself with *logos*, but to no avail, until Hecuba paradoxically intercedes on her behalf. Not that she is Helen's champion: on the contrary, she wishes to debate with Helen, verify her guilt beyond doubt and ensure that 'the *logos* fully constructed will kill her' (910). In the event Helen defends herself ably, to the chagrin and disquiet of the chorus (966–8), but it is not her verbal dexterity which gets her off; Menelaus declares that Hecuba has persuaded him of Helen's full culpability (1036–41). We who know the story realise that in mythical time, after the drama's conclusion, Helen will survive to return to the conjugal life in Sparta described in *Odyssey* IV. Hecuba was reckless to place her confidence in the persuasive power of *logos*; as she originally feared (and continues to fear: 'let her not embark on the same ship with you', 1049), all the force of her *logos* evaporates in the radiance cast by Helen's 'divine beauty'. The irony is that in the play which owes so much to the inspiration of the *Encomium*, Euripides so elegantly – and silently – implies that in the last analysis, *logos* is not omnipotent.[47]

We have hardly plumbed the riches of this maddeningly attractive text, but, in conjunction with the results of our investigation of *On What Is Not*, enough material has now been assembled to permit meaningful comparison with Plato's *Gorgias*, in order to reconstruct the challenges that rhetoric and philosophy presented to each other in ancient Greece. The *Encomium* fingers itself as a perfect specimen of underhanded persuasion. We tend unreflectingly to share the conviction that good *logos* addressed to our active, discriminating minds is altogether different from bad or at any rate dangerous *logos* shaping our passive emotions, that rhetorical language can be isolated, analysed, understood as such, and so robbed of much of its menacing appeal. The assumption that Gorgias somehow argues or merely proclaims that this difference between *logoi* does not exist is unacceptably sloppy; rather, like any supremely competent rhetorician, he shifts responsibility for the problem on to his audience. The text ends: 'I wished to write the *logos* as an encomium of Helen, but as an amusement for myself' (§21). Too many pedestrian critics take refuge from Gorgias by understanding this sting in the tail as a simple disclaimer: it is all just a harmless joke.[48] But when we recall how *On What Is Not* dislocated philosophy by obstinately hovering between 'serious' and 'playful' intentions, we can recognise that the *Encomium*'s joke is on us. When we ourselves are made to pity Helen and execrate Paris, are persuaded (perhaps) that persuasion is manipulation, enjoy the deception with which Gorgias amuses us even as we discern it, we feel in our own souls the seduction of rhetoric.

3

IN DEFENCE OF REASON
Plato's *Gorgias*

All philosophers present themselves as if they had discovered and
reached their actual opinions through the self-development of a cold,
pure, divinely unperturbed dialectic . . . while at bottom an anticipated thesis, a notion, an 'inspiration', mostly an abstractly contrived
and sifted dearest wish, is defended by them on grounds sought after
the event.

> (Nietzsche, *Beyond Good and Evil*,
> 'On the Prejudices of Philosophers' 5)

RHETORICAL FEASTING,
PHILOSOPHICAL PLAIN FARE?

Plato's response to Gorgias in his dialogue the *Gorgias* is to present
us with the most emphatic reaffirmation of the Parmenidean ideal,
a scheme of philosophical dialectic utterly distinct from and immea-
surably superior to rhetoric, which is fiercely castigated as nakedly
exploitative emotional manipulation. The terms of the contrast
are of course by now thoroughly familiar; what Plato does is to
reinstate systematically all the great polarities which Gorgias just as
studiously, if with profound ambiguity, occluded. One running
theme of our investigation has been the skill with which Gorgias
paradoxically encourages us to place his very own words within the
scope of his rhetoric about rhetoric. In consistency we must ask how
the *Gorgias* itself fares according to its author's strictures on the use
and abuse of language. Gorgias insists that his *logos* constitutes no
exception to the way words work, because they all work to the same
purpose; but Plato's writing is informed by an incomparably higher
degree of tension, because his Socrates claims that there is all the
difference in the world between a philosopher and a rhetorician.

To avoid damning incoherence, this had better not be just another rhetorical claim.

Nevertheless, much circumspection is called for in evaluating the *bona fides* of a Platonic dialogue, precisely because it *is* a dialogue. No doubt had Plato elected to communicate various doctrines in a series of treatises, he would still rank as one of the greatest philosophers who have ever lived, such are the profundity and originality of his thought. But what makes him unique is the dialogue form, which he created, perfected and remains alone in employing effectively. There are various manners and degrees of error in attempting to cope with Plato's unparalleled philosophical artefacts. Naturally, most disastrous of all is the simple refusal to make the effort, that is, the direct attribution of the 'good' arguments (usually Socrates', of course) to Plato himself, which are then subjected to whatever scheme of interpretation and criticism is deemed appropriate. On such an approach it is inevitable that adoption of the dialogue format is at best a matter of distracting ornamentation, at worst, and most usually, a dangerous obfuscation which must surely call into doubt Plato's intellectual honesty. But less obviously reductive attitudes to the dialogues will still fail to do them justice, if they more or less surreptitiously cling to the conviction that the Platonic writings contain – if all too often only by concealing – Plato's 'philosophy'. Were that so, it would remain the case that he deliberately, and thus perversely, baffles his audience. If Plato has a philosophical message to convey, the general principle that direct communication of information is vastly superior to indirect immediately dictates that the dialogue was a bad vehicle for his purposes.

Evidently the conclusion to draw is that Plato has no message, no 'philosophy' to impart. Yet how can this be, when so many and such distinguished thinkers down the ages have identified themselves as adherents of Platonism? The beginning of an answer is to be found by considering an obvious analogy. No literary critic of any sophistication would dream of attributing the words or sentiments of a character in tragedy to the tragedian himself. True, there were those in antiquity and later ready to convict Euripides of advocating faithlessness because his Hippolytus protests against the necessity of keeping a fatal promise, once its implications become clear to him; but they thereby succeeded only in convicting themselves of a basic misunderstanding of drama. Analogously, no philosophical critic should contemplate attributing to Plato himself what any interlocutor, including Socrates, expresses. The only course open to readers aspiring to take Platonic dialogues with the seriousness they deserve is to regard them as fiction; and to produce fiction is not merely a way of smuggling in a coded message, whatever its detractors might suspect.

Immediate qualifications are called for. If a Platonic dialogue is fiction, it remains fiction of a distinctive, indeed unique type: the philosophical. This means that what the interlocutors are typically represented as uttering are *logoi* in the philosophical sense, arguments; and, as we shall see, some of the most significant of these utterances are self-reflexive and methodological. Therefore the appropriate response to the arguments we read in Plato must itself be argumentative: how do the arguments fit together, and are they any good? But – and the qualification is all-important – these arguments are not *Plato's* arguments, any more than Hippolytus' speeches are Euripides'. Philosophical fiction is philosophical inasmuch as its dominant *logoi* are recognisably argumentative; but by the same token it is fictitious inasmuch as the *logoi* are not asserted by Plato, and only people, not characters in a dialogue, are capable of assertion.

If these inferences are at least roughly correct, why would Plato have elected to forgo assertion? The very nature of the problem entails that he does not *tell* us the answer; but highly suggestive indications emerge from an attentive reading of the dialogues. Socrates is repeatedly depicted as vehemently attacking the pretensions of would-be educators who claim to teach lessons of great value by imparting a body of information or inculcating a skill; his invariable reaction is to subject such teachers to dialectical examination, and they are invariably depicted as failing the test more or less miserably (in the *Protagoras*, the *Hippias Major*, the *Euthydemus* and the *Gorgias* itself). The implication would seem to be that only something like Socrates' own activity is worth pursuing; and Socrates notoriously refuses to impart answers and sticks to the rôle of questioner. Thus if Plato represents Socrates as teaching, what he teaches is not a doctrine, but rather a technique, a way of learning; and that technique is philosophical, by way of argumentative *logos*.

The conclusion that the writing of treatises is inevitably a self-stultifying endeavour does not follow; nothing excludes the possibility that the readers of the treatise will react to the arguments asserted therein as they should, by assessing them critically on the basis of argumentative criteria themselves subject to philosophical appraisal. But the very real and very great danger remains that even the most vigilant readers will occasionally slip into slack acceptance of what

54

they are told; and that would be to frustrate philosophy's central purpose. The author of philosophical fiction effectively guards against this danger, on condition that its readers continuously bear in mind the cardinal fact that the *logoi* they confront belong to the dialogue's interlocutors, not to its author.

The most interesting moral to be drawn from this understanding of Plato is intimately related to the investigation at the heart of this book. Our interpretation of the paean to *logos* in the *Encomium of Helen* emphasised its pathological psychology: the *psychē* suffers *pathos* before the omnipotent onslaught of *logos*. Now if Plato deliberately forgoes assertion so as to discourage any temptation to accept passively what is said, then one might go so far as to contend that the Platonic dialogue is designed specifically to frustrate the overweening pretensions to which the *Encomium* gives voice. Plato is doing what he can to ensure that in giving heed to philosophical *logos*, his readers are not just seduced by it.

Because they are attributed to fictional characters rather than asserted by real people,[1] the arguments proliferating in Platonic dialogues cannot be taken at face-value. If we know what we are about when we encounter such an argument, our impulse will never be to accept the argument's conclusion automatically; we should instead react by critically assessing the represented argument, and endorsing it only if it reaches our logical standards. Thus while the dialogue makes no assertions, it nevertheless invites us to do so. When we critically reconstruct a Platonic *logos*, we thereby commit *ourselves*, we actively take responsibility for the philosophical work we have been prompted to perform. This is to say that Plato demands a special sort of 'active' reading which should in a way come close to the act of writing.

The ideal Platonic reader is constantly questioning, and at the limit this questioning generates a mental dialogue of one's own, for which the actual dialogue is no more than a template. Now evidently all this is perfectly consistent with the reasonable belief that certain problems monopolise Plato's attention, and even that the recurrence of certain argumentative patterns, especially when attributed to the chief interlocutor in most of the dialogues, Socrates, is a strong signal that Plato himself sees much to recommend in them. So if 'Platonism' means the philosophical tradition whose adherents share Plato's view of where the important problems lie and how they might promisingly be attacked, then the denial that Plato makes philosophical assertions can at once easily acknowledge the existence of 'Platonism' and account for its argumentative vigour. What an advocate of the hermeneutic approach to Plato advocated here must flatly reject is both the notion that endorsement of so-called 'Platonic' doctrine on its own could suffice to make someone a *real* Platonist, and any interpretation which reduces the character Socrates to Plato's mouthpiece.

The pertinence of these methodological remarks to evaluation of the *Gorgias* should be fairly clear. If our response to a Socratic attack on rhetoric is profound, perhaps violent, disagreement, this should not be translated into dissatisfaction with Plato's attack on rhetoric; for, since Plato makes no assertions, *a fortiori* he makes no assertions critical of rhetoric. We have no reason, at least so far, to presume that (well-reasoned) dissatisfaction with Socrates would prompt anything but satisfaction in Socrates' creator. This is not to suggest that Platonic dialogues are invulnerable to criticism. If, as we actively read, our mental dialogues diverge consistently and radically from the dialectical suggestions generated by Plato's template, then we must deem the dialogue a failure. But we must never forget that by renouncing direct communication with the reader, Plato thereby establishes the opportunity for philosophically challenging, indirect communication. On occasion in the dialogues the fiction of direct communication between interlocutors is subordinate to the reality of indirect communication between Plato and us. At such times what is communicated is not a doctrinal lesson, but rather a powerful encouragement to overcome our frustration at what is happening (or not happening) in the philosophical fiction by reaching beyond it to our own attempts at solution.[2]

The *Gorgias* falls little short of the *Republic*[3] in the continuous influence it has exerted on Western intellectual and political history, and it has stimulated a voluminous scholarship. Largely because in it Socrates propounds his celebrated paradox that 'no one does wrong willingly' and embarks on the psychological theorising which attains full expression in the *Phaedo*, the majority of its students concentrate on the second two-thirds of the dialogue, in which Gorgias is replaced as chief interlocutor first by Polus, and then by Callicles. We shall instead focus for the most part on the first portion, where Socrates asks Gorgias to teach him whatever it is he teaches, and where Plato most obviously addresses rhetoric in rhetoric's own terms;[4] even so, our analysis will be highly selective, omitting everything not directly germane to an appreciation of why Gorgias and Plato's reaction to him matter so much to the history of persuasion.

evoke provoke

Plato's Gorgias will be driven to the humiliating admission that the
master of oratory lords it only over those who do not know: ever
since, philosophers have approached the wiles of rhetoric with
circumspection, while its self-professed champions have indignantly
denounced Plato's defamation as a piece of shoddy rhetoric.

Socrates arrives too late: too late, that is, to hear Gorgias perform.
In the very first words of the dialogue Callicles quips that 'this is
how they say one should take part in war and battle' (447A1). But
as so often in Plato – a trait he shares with the real Gorgias – a
joke can have significant import. These opening words evoke violent
conflict; and if Socrates is too late for the performance, he is just
in time for (philosophical) 'war and battle', since his presence will
provoke extreme and protracted verbal conflict. Socrates responds to
Callicles with a metaphor which will not lie dormant, by asking
whether he and his companion Chaerephon have missed the rhetorical 'feast' (447A3). This notional 'feast' happens outside the *Gorgias*,
albeit only a little while before its fictional beginning (447A6): is
this a text from which rhetoric has been banished? Socrates explains
that Chaerephon is responsible, because he 'forced' (*anankasas*) them
to spend time in the marketplace (447A8): so the Gorgianic theme
of persuasion/compulsion is present in the dialogue from the outset.
Socrates is assured that Gorgias will gladly 'display' for him again,
epedeixato, 447A6; followed by *epideixetai*, 447B2, *epideixetai*,
447B8, *epideixin*, 447C3, and *epideixeōs*, 447C6. This piling-up of
'display' vocabulary creates a rhythm sharply punctuated by a single
word, *dialechthēnai* (447C1), 'to engage in dialectic', which Socrates
requests as a substitute for rhetorical performance.

Nothing could be more 'rhetorical' than the opening lines of the
Gorgias in the degenerate, vacuous sense of 'cunningly crafted, carefully and skilfully composed'. Since the dialogue is an unmediated
narrative, free of the complex multiple framing devices Plato deploys
to remarkable effect in such works as the *Symposium*, the *Gorgias*
simultaneously suggests the untampered-with immediacy of live
interchange and undercuts the suggestion by displaying systematic,
'rhetorical' elaboration. Rhetoric has already 'happened' in the
fictional time-scale, and now 'dialectic' confronts 'display', tempting
us to complete the metaphorical scheme by setting wholesome philosophical nourishment against rhetorical party-food. Not that this by
any means exhausts Plato's artistic repertoire: when Chaerephon
promises to put matters right, he says he will 'cure' the problem
(447B1), the first occurrence of the medical theme which will sound

so insistently in the sequel – or rather the recurrence of this theme, for those who come to the dialogue properly prepared by reading the *Encomium*. Might we even hazard the guess that the antecedent *epideixis*, unheard by Socrates the philosopher, is none other than the *Encomium* itself?

If these are inducements to belief, or at least persuasive devices designed to incline us favourably towards endorsing certain beliefs, they are emphatically not the argumentative agents of persuasion alone tolerated by Parmenides and those who follow him as champions of reason. If Plato's intention is to disguise his 'rhetoric' so that his readers are unconsciously taken in, his persuasion, if successful, will ironically enhance rather than destroy the message of the *Encomium of Helen*, since we shall have been deceived into the belief that philosophy abjures deception. But if, on the other hand, the rhetoric is there to be noticed, no such damaging conclusion follows. Not that the intentional employment of 'rhetoric' is unproblematic, so long as it is *intentionally* revealed; the *Encomium* taught us that the seduced *psychē* knowingly connives at its own deception. Nevertheless, if Plato writes as he does to make us ask whether and why we are persuaded, rather than to persuade us in advance of the philosophical *logoi* to come, we have been challenged rather than immediately fooled.

POWER REVISITED

Socrates specifies that what he is soliciting from Gorgias is a dialectical explanation of what the *dynamis*[5] of his *technē* might be, and what it is that he advertises and teaches (447C1–3). The repeated interrogatives herald the philosopher's concentrated insistence on rigorous, articulated, definitional knowledge. All the words in Socrates' statement are capable of bearing special Platonic connotations; in particular, it will emerge that an authoritative restriction of the scope of *technē* might well rob Gorgias of his claim to an authentic verbal specialism (already foreshadowed in Chaerephon's question, 'of what *technē* has he *knowledge*?', 448C2–3). Callicles is confident that Gorgias will readily agree, since he has been urging all and sundry to pose questions to which he will respond (447C6–8). This feature of the portrait of the accomplished sophist is evidently related to the boast recorded in Philostratus, that no question whatsoever exceeds Gorgias' ability to answer. But now we readers ask: when the context is philosophical exchange rather than rhetorical display, when the questioner is Socrates alone, bent on discovering the truth rather than one member of an audience collectively keen on entertainment, will Gorgias be able to cope? The substitution looked for is of a profoundly serious, philosophical conception of question-and-answer as an invaluable heuristic instrument for a thoroughly frivolous, sophistical conception of it as an occasion for amusement. Thus the *Gorgias* is largely about the forms, pretensions and powers of *logos* – discourse hortatory, investigative and argumentative.

Socrates encourages Chaerephon to put the question to Gorgias: 'who is he?' (447D1). But Chaerephon does not understand, and replies 'what do you mean [*legein*, cognate with *logos*]?' (447D2). Socrates clarifies that what he wants is an explanation of what Gorgias' claimed expertise permits him to do. Chaerephon is puzzled because the question posed by Socrates is verbally reminiscent of the formula a Greek would employ when asking for a simple identification; but everyone can identify the famous Gorgias of Leontini. Socrates is already speaking as a dialectician, that is, he is at once employing certain concepts in novel fashions, separated from their ordinary pragmatic implications, and trying to ensure mutual comprehension ('don't you understand what I mean?' (447D4–5)).[6]

Before the main protagonists grapple, Polus, Gorgias' disciple, intervenes to insist on taking his master's place. Chaerephon sceptically asks whether Polus imagines he can answer 'better' or 'more fittingly' or 'more finely' or 'more attractively' than Gorgias (448A9–10). The word in question, *kalon* (used in a comparative form here), is an extremely general term of approbation (already used by Callicles to characterise Gorgias' performance, 447A5); what we do not yet know – what we should be asking ourselves – is what 'fine' *logos really* is (just as words associated with *epideixis* were before, so now *kalon* and its derivatives are forced on our attention: 448B8–9, 448C8–D2, 448E8–449A1). Polus rudely brushes off the challenge with the dismissive reply that it makes no odds, on condition that what he says is sufficient for Chaerephon (448B1): but should we believe that the criterion for adequacy in discourse is thus relative to auditors or disputants? Polus' little party-piece (448C4–9) mimics Gorgias' easily guyed structure and diction to perfection. What Plato harshly achieves by placing this feeble example of *epideixis* in this context is a revelation of its trite near-meaninglessness. Although Socrates drily compliments Gorgias on his pupil's 'fine' (*kalon*) equipment in *logoi* (448D2), it is apparent that (this) *epideixis* says nothing to Socrates' pressing concerns: it consists of empty words which fail to commit their utterer to much of anything.[7]

Socrates explains that he would prefer Gorgias himself to Polus as respondent because 'even from what he [Polus] has said he seems to me to have had more exercise in so-called rhetoric than in dialectic' (448D8–10),[8] although at this juncture we are not given much help in understanding where the difference between them might lie. Socrates' dissatisfaction with Polus arises from his failure to answer the question posed: asked what Gorgias' *dynamis is*, he has said what it is *like* (that is, praised it to the skies, produced an 'encomium' of it, 448E3). Socrates seems especially keen on brevity (448E8–449A1); presumably he regards it as a virtue in discussion not *per se*, but rather because it keeps the interlocutor to the point. The clash between lengthy speechifying and dialectical brevity forms an important episode in the *Protagoras* (335A), where the most august of the sophists is ungraciously chivvied by Socrates into submitting to dialectical questioning. The purported ground there for Socrates' preference is that forgetfulness makes him lose the thread in a protracted monologue, while Protagoras' professional dignity obliges him to accept Socrates' disingenuous expression of confidence in his, Protagoras', mastery of both continuous exposition and philosophical interrogation (335A1). Gorgias takes the same tack here: yet another of his boasts is that 'no one can say the same things more briefly than I' (449C1–3). Socrates takes him at his word, requesting that Gorgias make a 'display' of his brevity, and indeed in the immediate sequel Gorgias' lines are almost comically curt. If we have every reason for suspicion that the difference between dialectic and rhetoric is far more than a superficial matter of quantity, Gorgias himself is as yet represented as betraying no sign of such recognition.

Gorgias has identified his *technē* as 'rhetoric' (449A5), and further committed himself to the claim that he is 'capable' (*dynaton*) of passing on his expertise (449B1). Since '*dynaton*' is cognate with '*dynamis*', Plato's phrasing of Socrates' question serves to remind us both that the original query (447C1–2) was phrased in terms of rhetorical *dynamis*, and further, presumably, that the *Encomium* glorifies the threat of a *dynamis* of persuasion hostile to the philosophical enterprise. Socrates asks what rhetoric is 'about' (449D1–2), and Gorgias answers that it is 'about *logoi*' (449E1). As it stands, Socrates' question is quite indeterminate, and thus unexceptionable. But if it is premissed on the assumption that, to count as a *technē*, a candidate skill must meet certain standards, including the requirement that what it is about, what it makes, etc., must be unitary and belong to it alone, Gorgias is bound to get into trouble. The real Gorgias implied that *logos* is *logos* is *logos*, and the Platonic Gorgias' simple response, 'about *logoi*', would seem to suggest that he is meant to share this conception. But when Socrates demands clarification, and elicits the admission that *logoi* concerning matters of health are the exclusive preserve of the doctor, the physician *rather than* the rhetorician (449E2), Gorgias is made to concede at once that the scope of rhetorical *logos* cannot be universal (449E4): Gorgias' specialism has already been distinguished from that of his doctor brother, Herodicus (448B5), disposing of the comparison in the *Encomium* between global *logos* and a physician's enchanting drug. Socrates' objection hangs on a view of expertise which the Platonic Gorgias never resists, that *knowledge* alone confers mastery of a given domain.

Gorgias attempts to rescue his position with the proposition that while other skills involve handicraft to a very great extent, rhetoric uniquely confines itself to *logos* (450B9–C1). But Socrates points out that, while this distinction does define a certain class of skills, those proceeding largely or exclusively through *logos*, it fails to isolate rhetoric itself within this class. A stickler for *logoi* (450E7) might ask Gorgias whether he sees no difference between arithmetic, for example, and rhetoric, but Socrates himself does not resort to such tactics – or so he says, having neatly silhouetted Gorgias' clumsiness in a recognisable 'rhetorical' figure. Socrates' list of skills which stick to *logos* (450D6–7) is open-ended, and includes humble pastimes like draughts, but his extended demonstration of how to answer correctly employs only mathematical examples. A Platonic philosopher would not necessarily judge these to be instances of knowledge, but would consider the disciplines from which they are drawn good candidates for improvement which might well earn them the status of true theoretical knowledge. Since such epistemological investigation and reformulation has everything to do with producing philosophical *logos* in argument, the polemical implications of Socrates' apparently innocent exposition are considerable – for the alert (not passive) reader.

Under increasing pressure to explain what rhetoric is about *in particular*, Gorgias finally makes the grandiloquent pronouncement that its *logoi* concern 'the greatest and best of human affairs'

IN DEFENCE OF REASON: PLATO'S *GORGIAS*

(451D6–8). Socrates objects that this claim is doubly contentious: there is disagreement over what is greatest and best, and there are rival claimants for the rôle of providing it, specifically the traditional contenders for the supreme good, health, beauty and wealth, and their matching specialists, the doctor, the trainer and the money-maker. But to make his complaint Socrates assumes a variety of dialectical *personae* within the question-and-answer format: the rival experts themselves, rather than Socrates *in propria persona*, are made to appear to challenge the rhetorician, just as the stickler for *logoi* has done. So this is not, or not just, a fight between philosophy and rhetoric.

Or is it? Socrates' mode of expression permits Plato to deploy against Gorgias the conventional, fiercely competitive values of the Greek city to which Gorgias himself subscribes (e.g. 447C5–448A3), without thereby obliging Socrates himself to endorse those values. His reply is a subtle reworking of the real Gorgias' *logos*, but one endowed by Plato with a newly explicit political emphasis; for rhetoric now imparts freedom to the man who can wield it, together with control over everyone else in his city (452D6–8).[9] The Platonic Gorgias thus aggressively enunciates the anti-democratic possibilities incipient in '*logos* the great *dynastēs*'. Rhetoric is the *dynamis*, 'capacity' *and* 'power', to persuade with *logoi* people assembled in any *political* gathering whatsoever; it makes 'slaves' of all the other experts to the expert empowered to persuade 'the masses' (*ta plēthē*), who appropriates their products and profits (452E1–8).

Within the non-philosophical discourse of the day, the phrase 'the greatest and best of human affairs', pompous or not, requires no gloss: it is immediately comprehensible as 'power politics' (one might compare how Meno expresses his obsession with political supremacy in the dialogue named after him, 71E1–5). But Socrates feigns not to understand: he refuses to recognise the phrase's obvious idiomatic implications, just as with his unusual use of the question 'who is he?' earlier.[10] Part of the philosopher's technique is to use, and affect to understand, language in an almost infantile way, robbing expressions of even their most obvious unspoken connotations. This phenomenon is of considerably greater interest than Socrates' more familiar penchant for 'humble' examples from the handicrafts. Is this 'infantile' philosophising just a disconcerting rhetorical ploy? Philosophers answer 'no', on the grounds that they speak as they do because in a certain sense *everything* must be said: no unargued assumption should be allowed to pass undetected and untested.

62

Of course, Plato as author of philosophical fiction does not *tell* us this; but perhaps through his Socrates he *shows* us.

It is hard to imagine a threat more dangerous to Athenian democracy than the Platonic Gorgias' affirmation of persuasive power. That democracy claimed to depend on guaranteed 'free speech', *isēgoria*; but Gorgias' verbal *dynamis* frees the rhetorician only by putting him in control of his auditors. The *Encomium* presented people gathered together as passive 'masses' fully open to artful persuasion. The distinction of the category of free citizen from both autocratic and servile status is vital to democratic ideology; but the expert persuader enslaves his would-be competitors. This brings to the surface an important historical issue concerning the nature of Athenian rhetorical competition. In that society, the orator's audience will also be (potential) competitors, whether voters or jurors. This crucial difference from more familiar rhetorical situations must be borne in mind: jurors today are not (usually) even potential barristers; MPs are speaking to us, not just to their fellows. Even ancient Roman courts allowed representation by lawyers drawn from a relatively closed political élite. But *isēgoria* cannot be vindicated by replying that any member of the Athenian gathering is entitled to exploit the same persuasive *dynamis*, since that *dynamis*, if Gorgias is right, is inherently exploitative.

Surely Plato was Gorgias' most attentive reader. Socrates expresses satisfaction with the completeness of Gorgias' disclosure, and quietly encapsulates it in the definition which has echoed down the centuries: rhetoric is 'the craftsman of persuasion' (453A2);[11] the power of rhetoric is 'to produce persuasion in the *psychē* of the listeners' (453A4–5). Socrates will demolish 'Gorgias' by taking issue with the Gorgianic conceptions of both persuasion and psychology.

FOR THE SAKE OF THE *LOGOS*

Before pushing the argument a stage further, Socrates interjects a methodological aside bearing directly on his attempt to prise apart philosophical dialectic and rhetorical display. Socrates has 'persuaded himself' that he, if anyone, is anxious to know what a dialectical *logos* is about, and trusts that Gorgias shares his eagerness (453A8–B3). We have already on several occasions remarked on what begins to emerge as a highly characteristic move in Plato's 'rhetoric', the artful use of ostensibly casual vocabulary which, however, has rich and strong resonance for the careful reader. We have just read that Gorgias' expert speaker profits by his persuasion to the disadvantage of others. Socrates' words now remind us that we freely talk of self-reflexive 'persuasion', 'I persuade myself of . . .'. Of course, nothing has been said to establish that such language does not mask conceptual incoherence; while philosophers might take a cue from linguistic hints, talk can provide them with nothing more than apparent, defeasible testimony as to how things are. Nevertheless, the 'rhetoric' is reminding us of a possible alternative which we might otherwise overlook. We must both be alert to its suggestions, and withstand any temptation to convert the possibility into a certainty; but the 'rhetoric' itself does not pretend to be argumentative *logos*, nor does the responsibility for too easy a conviction lie anywhere but with ourselves.

Socrates insists that more clarification come from Gorgias, rather than himself, 'not for your sake, but for the *logos*, so that it will advance in the fashion best able to render what is under discussion clear to us' (453C2–4; cf. 454C1–5, and *Charmides* 166C–D). Gorgias had represented rhetoric as an asymmetric, exploitative relation: the active individual uses *his logos* to enslave the passive multitude. Now, while Socrates does not shift to concern for his interlocutor as an individual – his procedure is not for Gorgias' sake (alone) – the dialectical *logos* does not fall within the scope of a personal pronoun. It progresses through the phases of argumentative development to the intellectual benefit of questioner and answerer together. Dialectic is ultimately for the sake of knowledge. If it appears either to attack or to spare the interlocutor, that is a mere appearance. The *logos* itself is not only our chief but our sole concern: we interact with our partners in the investigation only because and insofar as they contribute to it. By the same token we do not care about our own dialectical fate as such, that is, whether whatever fragment or figment of truth emerging from the discussion is 'ours'. Truth on this Socratic conception is not a commodity accessible at some points within a hierarchy at the expense of the occupants of other positions; all participants in the discussion share the truth communally.[12] Socrates' expression of impersonal allegiance to the *logos* is presented as a comment on method made in preparation for the further investigation of rhetoric; in reality it constitutes the starkest possible contrast to Gorgias' description of his *dynamis* as clever manipulation for the sake of personal political power. Plato compels rhetoric to submit to the rigours of philosophical definition, but allows philosophy the freedom of self-demonstration.

64

CROWDS

Socrates suggests that the definition 'craftsman of persuasion' is successful only if rhetoric is unique in producing conviction; as a matter of fact, however, all expertises, simply by teaching, persuade us of matters falling within their specialities, so that the distinctive variety of persuasion to which rhetoric lays claim still remains obscure. Gorgias insists that specifically rhetorical persuasion is aimed at 'crowds' (*ochloi*), and adds that it concerns what is just and unjust, a topic apparently embracing deliberative politics as well as legal conflict (454B5–7).[13] His earlier reference to 'the masses' (*ta plēthē*, 452E8) could, but need not, carry pejorative overtones: 'crowds' most definitely does.[14] Plato puts in Gorgias' mouth a word which would exacerbate any democrat's suspicions of that indispensable but dubious ally, the orator. Or, to be more precise, Plato borrows this inflammatory word from the real Gorgias to bring home the full, damning repercussions of the 'compulsive' model of persuasion: 'a single *logos* written with skill, not uttered in truth, pleases and persuades a great *ochlos*' (*Encomium of Helen*, §13). 'Democracy' means 'rule of the *dēmos*', and '*dēmos*' neutrally means 'the common people', as opposed to the affluent and aristocratic few. Only an enemy of the people would designate them 'the crowd', a term of opprobrium at home in oligarchic polemics.

This is not to pretend that the Platonic Socrates is by any means a democratic champion; in the last portion of the dialogue, he will contentiously disparage the achievements of the greatest Athenian heroes, and astonishingly reserve for himself the title of the city's only authentic politician, albeit in his own special sense. Socrates is not at all concerned to deny that the Athenian civic body is a 'crowd'; his aim is to demonstrate that Gorgias' advertisement for the omnipotence of rhetoric is indeed justified within a democratic political structure, and thus to damn rhetoric, rather than defend democracy. But to jump to the conclusion that he therefore stands revealed as the enemy of freedom would be highly premature. If – a very large 'if' – his vision of dialectic as enquiry aimed at shared truth can be sustained, then liberty, if not unqualified equality, is to be found within the limits of philosophical *logos*, and perhaps there alone.

Socrates now exploits, lethally, Gorgias' earlier admission that teaching issues in persuasion. He extracts the agreement that learning and conviction are distinct; there is false conviction as well as true,

transcendant truth
epistemology

but knowledge is always true. Therefore there are two species of the genus persuasion, one convincing with knowledge, the other without it, and Gorgias volunteers that rhetorical persuasion falls within the latter (454E8–9).

> Then neither is the speaker capable of teaching juries and other crowds about justice and injustice, but is only capable of persuading them; for certainly he could not teach such great matters to so many people in a short time.[15]
>
> (455A2–6)

'Such great matters' recalls Gorgias' phrase 'the greatest and best of human affairs', but Socrates has made the stuff of power politics into subjects demanding, if not receiving, the most serious ethical and political education. Philosophical insistence on knowledge as opposed to mere fallible belief shows that the Gorgianic identification of his *logos* with power is at least partially falsified by the rhetorician's incapacity to convey knowledge within his special context, that of adversative debate on political and legal matters before the masses. The *Encomium* had not ignored philosophers; but there they were yet another type of fighter contending in the battle of *logos*, compelling rather than instructing the souls of passive auditors.

The question of abiding interest to us is not whether this, the most scathing critique of Athenian participatory political and judicial practice, is warranted,[16] but rather more worryingly, whether the category 'persuasion without knowledge' has validity today. Socrates' denigration of democratic decision-making relies on two presuppositions about which we moderns might feel rather differently. The first is the supposed impossibility of 'true' education on a mass scale. If anything, subsequent history has given us far greater reason for profound pessimism on this score (as well as about there being one 'true' education for all). But the second is the proposition that there is, or could be, 'instructive persuasion' in politics. Anyone who claims to possess political 'expertise' (unless they mean Gorgias' anti-democratic power politics) must believe that there is. Thinking democrats, on the other hand, should insist that, although there is a recognisable sphere of public interest, it does not define a corresponding specialist; no one individual is *authoritative* about justice. Plato has Protagoras expound how this could possibly be so in his eponymous dialogue.[17] If we wish to resist the second assumption made in the *Gorgias*, we must be prepared to explain how modern democratic ideology is compatible with the political 'expertise' which its inaccessible institutions encourage and the propagandistic manipulation which they invite.

IN DEFENCE OF RHETORIC

Socrates goads Gorgias into delivering an extended defence of and panegyric on (not Helen this time either, but) omnipotent rhetoric, by making a deliberately naïve claim about the Athenian manner of implementing public programmes: surely the advice of the relevant expert, the architect, say, will prove persuasive, rather than that of the rhetorician? 'For it is clear that the most accomplished expert [*technikōtatos*, from *technē*] must be chosen' (455B4–5). Socrates maddeningly pretends that in pursuing this dialectical line he is actually looking out for Gorgias' interests:

> for maybe there happens to be somebody inside who wishes to become your pupil – I perceive there are some, indeed quite a few – who perhaps would be ashamed to interrogate you. Suppose that in being interrogated by me, you are also interrogated by them . . .
>
> (455C6–D1)

Itinerant sophists are on the lookout for affluent young men to whom they might offer expensive political tuition. Just as Protagoras in the *Protagoras*, so here Gorgias is brought before the Athenian civic bar: what profit will accrue to his associates, and about what will they be enabled to advise the city (455D2–3)?

This passage continues to emphasise the political implications of rhetoric. Gorgias had maintained that the rhetorical persuader can dominate every political 'gathering' (452E3); now the word recurs (455B3), referring specifically to a gathering for the choice of putative experts. Since the Greek for 'gathering' is *syllogos*, we can think of the associated active verb *syllegō*, 'gather up – viz. choose'. If we are more and more worried about what remains of democratic political empowerment when expertise makes itself felt, then perhaps Socrates' evocation of the people as (passively) gathered together to gather up (actively?) their advisers might allay our fears. Socrates' mention of possible embarrassment amongst Gorgias' potential pupils opens yet another of the dialogue's motivating themes. It is a commonplace of criticism of the *Gorgias* that the sequence of Socrates' interlocutors, Gorgias–Polus–Callicles, is a progression

particular type of gathering convened to make particular types of choices based on [...]

culture

in 'shamelessness' (or, to be less *parti pris*, in 'candour'); but at this point Socrates, by his own admission, is without shame – on behalf of others, and in pursuit of the truth.

'I shall attempt to reveal the whole *dynamis* of rhetoric to you, Socrates', says Gorgias (455D6–7). Why does persuasive power require uncovering, revelation? Is it a special, guarded mystery, open only to initiates?[18] Or can it not express its true nature frankly in public advertisement for ideological reasons? Gorgias retorts that as a matter of verifiable historical fact, it was Themistocles and Pericles who through rhetoric were responsible for Athens' imperial projects. He insists that if a competent orator such as himself were to compete against a doctor or other knowledgeable specialist in convincing a recalcitrant individual to submit to painful treatment, or for a civic medical position, the orator would invariably win – 'for there is nothing concerning which the orator could not speak more persuasively than any other craftsman among the masses' (*en plēthei*, 456C6, cf. 457A6–7: the damning word 'crowds' has now discreetly disappeared).[19]

So much for panegyric. Gorgias' apology on behalf of rhetorical experts, which is not obviously consistent with the implications of his former characterisation of rhetoric as the means for tapping ultimate political power, rests on the plea that in itself it is a neutral *dynamis*, a capacity. It can be exploited for good or ill, but that is a decision for the individual skilled speaker, not his rhetorical teacher.[20] Rhetoric is intrinsically an amoral weapon. This position is inherently unstable, since Gorgias classes rhetoric together with the martial arts as a *combative* skill (456C8); surely this entails that it is also intrinsically aggressive.[21] The defence is culturally specific and wholesomely conventional. Greek society enthusiastically cultivated expertise in all sorts of competitive physical combat. It is of course no part of the job of the physical trainer to encourage his student to unleash that deadly expertise against friends and family: Gorgias piously assures us that analogously rhetoric is to be used justly, that is, only defensively against enemies and wrongdoers (456E3–4); the worthy rhetorician could but would not rob the physician of his reputation (457B1–4). 'But those who pervert rhetoric use its strength and *technē* incorrectly' (457A1–2). Interestingly, it is only at this point, where Gorgias has felt obliged to retreat moralistically, that for unitary, global *logos* he substitutes the pair, capacity and skill.

Gorgias now pretends that the proper exploitation of rhetorical power is invariably morally correct – words for ethical injunction and prohibition run right through his speech. He nowhere specifies what this actually means, but given his repeated appeal to conventional mores, he must intend to rely on the popular Greek conception of right and wrong, familiar from the *Republic*, that right action benefits or protects members of one's 'own' group, not outsiders; harm to enemies is positively encouraged. The connection between the dialogues here is very close: since Polemarchus contends that justice is the *technē* which renders benefit to friends and family, injury to enemies (*Republic* 332D4–6), we might conclude that proper use of rhetoric in accordance with Gorgias' prescriptions must be 'just' by definition; indeed, that the *technē* of justice and the *technē* of rhetoric are ultimately one and the same. But these palatable conclusions would follow only were Polemarchus' conventionalism defensible, and it swiftly comes to grief in the dialectic of *Republic* I. Moreover, a Greek's sense of his affiliations, the ground for even minimal moral consideration on the Polemarchan conception, was notoriously fluid and easily capable of generating unresolvable contradictions; most Athenian political dissension was the direct result of individuals pursuing the ambitions of their 'own' clan or class against those of the larger body politic. Thus Gorgias' proviso guarantees very little. It leaves the potentially lethal orator free to speak against the interests of anyone beyond what might prove a desperately narrow social limit. Furthermore, his reference to disciples who pervert rhetoric of course concedes that the uninhibited, selfish exertion of rhetorical power is a fact of *Realpolitik*.

PHILOSOPHICAL COMPETITION

Before returning to the attack, Socrates interposes a further declaration of the essential distinction between philosophical and rhetorical conflict. He begins by soliciting Gorgias' agreement, as a colleague well versed in *logoi*, with the observation that interlocutors 'cannot [*ou dynantai*] easily, by defining for each other, and learning and teaching themselves, what they are attempting to engage in dialectic about, conclude their meeting in this way' (457C5–D1). Despite the courteous appeal to Gorgias, the reference is to dialectical exchanges of which he has apparently had little experience. Rhetoric is a *dynamis* promising easy victory over victims to be subjugated: dialectic is a practice fraught with difficulty, typically marked by frustration rather than ease of achievement. But, in complete opposition to the masters

69

and slaves created by rhetoric, dialectical interlocutors are partners, they do what they can 'for each other'. Again, if dialecticians *learn and teach*, then this is the species of persuasion which convinces with knowledge, in contrast to rhetoric which sways the ignorant 'crowd'. And a further vital component of Socrates' description of how to philosophise is present. So far we have compared and contrasted the orator manipulating a foolish gathering with, say, a doctor educating his pupils. While this instruction will convey an understanding lacking in the rhetorical case, we have been given no reason to believe that the medical students will be any less passive before their instructor than are the members of the gulled mob before their deceptive persuader. But dialecticians learn from and teach *each other*: according to Socrates, philosophical education occurs in a process of mutual enlightenment, wherein active and passive rôles are not to be distinguished.

Socrates admits that the absence of an easy . *dynamis* which characterises dialectic all too often misleads its practitioners into 'taking it personally', as we would appropriately say. Disgruntled interlocutors imagine that objections are levelled against them in 'competition' (*philonikountas*, 457D4, cognate with the *erōtos philonikou*, 'contentious love', of *Encomium* §4), rather than in joint pursuit of the topic for investigation in the *logos*. The mutual vituperation and acrimony can reach such a pitch that the audience becomes ashamed at having listened to such abuse – a far cry it seems both from Socrates' own 'shamelessness' in dialectical questioning, and from Gorgias' admission at the close of the digression that it would be 'shameful' for him not to persevere dialectically, when he has promised to answer any question (458D7–8). Or is it? If '*philosophia*' means 'love of wisdom', '*philonikia*', 'love of victory', in dialectical practice, where the questioner strives to refute, the respondent, to avoid refutation, is there so very much to choose between them? After all, as I have said, Socrates is pausing before renewing his *attack*. He explains that he has digressed because he suspects that Gorgias has been guilty of inconsistency, and 'I am afraid to push through my examination [*dielenchein*] of you,[22] lest you suppose that I am speaking in a competition to clarify the issue not with it, but with you' (457E3–5). By his own admission, Socrates *is* competing; but, all-importantly, he competes for the truth, and not against Gorgias. It is against the recalcitrant subject-matter that Socrates struggles, in competition with obscurity. More precisely, perhaps, if he competes against Gorgias, that is only because, if the refutation is valid, then Gorgias' defeat is a victory not for Socrates, but for truth.[23]

'I am one of those who would gladly be refuted on saying something not true, gladly refute someone else uttering falsehood, but bearing refutation no less gladly than administering it' (458A2–5). How can this equal pleasure be squared with Socrates' confession of *philonikia*? By understanding that Socrates always and only means winning (through to) the truth. In the *Encomium* Gorgias had undertaken to refute Helen's slanderers, but his exaltation of a *logos* which pleases and deceives left no room for construing refutation as anything other than personal defeat. Socrates' reaffirmation of truth as the supreme good, falsehood as the ultimate evil (458A8–B1), at once implicitly condemns Gorgias' sweet deception and promises to open a space for unselfish 'competition', where dialectical 'victor' and 'victim' alike share in the spoils of discovery.

IGNORANCE

Socrates' renewed onslaught addresses the implications of the idea that the audience (once again a pejorative '*ochlos*', 458E7) in the rhetorician's sway is ignorant: if a speaker is more persuasive in this context, that is only because a person who does not know has the advantage over one who does among the equally ignorant. Socrates allows himself the confident assumption that an orator could shine only before the *ochlos*, 'for certainly he will not be more persuasive than the doctor among knowers' (459A3–5). Having conceded the distinction between teaching on the one hand and conviction without instruction on the other, the character Gorgias is in no position to challenge Socrates' assurance, despite the delightfully deceptive novelty which the real Gorgias offers to 'knowers' (about Trojan events) in the *Encomium*. As the real Gorgias had proclaimed, rhetorical power consists in deception, since it has found out a 'device of persuasion' which causes it to *appear* more knowledgeable than expertise – to the foolish (459B8–C2). The Platonic Gorgias is made to seize the poisoned chalice with both hands and fatuously extol the convenience of besting legitimate experts without the inconvenience of learning anything but meretricious rhetoric (459C3–5).

This is the philosopher's damning representation of Gorgias' boast that he can extemporise with equal facility on any topic whatsoever thrown at him in public display. It is mere display, because only the readiness of the ignorant 'crowd' to be amused by the equally ignorant blandishments of rhetorical *logos* assures rhetorical success. Now a basic strategy of the real Gorgias in both *On What Is Not* and the *Encomium* had been playfulness: are these texts *jeux d'esprit*, and any the less effective for it? High Platonic seriousness will brook none of that. But notice how Socrates' indictment turns on a rationalist presumption which comes all too easily to thinkers, such as Parmenides and perhaps Socrates himself, for whom the supposed fact that '*logos* [the ratiocinative variety] is a great *dynastēs*' entails that logic must be omnipresent in discourse and in reality. Of course a *manifest* fool would be unpersuasive in political debate; but that is no reason to conclude that rhetorical authority uniquely appeals, or even pretends to appeal, to the intellect.[24] Political discourse need not mimic ratiocination, as the authentic Gorgias indicated in his global catalogue of *logos*; only in Socrates' wholly rational world would even fools require specious *knowledge* to be impressed.

MORAL EDUCATION?

In a single powerful, lengthy and finely articulated sentence, Socrates, using only materials supplied by Gorgias himself in the dialectical exchange, constructs the first horn of a dilemma which will produce Gorgias' complete discomfiture. The first uncomfortable alternative is that the rhetorician's relation to the moral and political values about which he speaks so persuasively (to the ignorant) is precisely the same as to any other subject: he possesses a mere pretence of knowledge about them (459C8–E1). The second alternative is that he does, exceptionally, know about values. Socrates immediately redescribes and complicates the options in a fashion designed to maximise the pressure on Gorgias: either the prospective rhetorical student arrives in full possession of moral knowledge (459E1–3); or, if not – now the alternative splits further – the sophist, whose function is not moral edification, lends him the hollow semblance of moral knowledge and goodness (459E3–6); or, incapable of instructing in rhetoric a man ignorant of ethical truth, sends him away (459E6–8); or . . . ? Socrates winds up with a renewed appeal to Gorgias to make good on his promise to 'uncover' the *dynamis* of rhetoric, and Gorgias himself not only supplies, but also endorses, the final disjunct: he claims to teach the morally ignorant student morality (460A3–4).

The consideration crucial to evaluation of this interchange is the pervasive and extreme intellectualism critically exploited by Socrates and fatally tolerated by Gorgias. Taking the brunt of the dialectical attack, the sophist would have had great trouble in confessing that he belongs to the set of, produces or even associates too closely with, moral idiots (who could each be well described as 'one who does not know what good or bad or fine or ugly or just or unjust is' (459D4–5)). But remember that Socrates is famous, or notorious, for maintaining that everyone is ignorant, ignorant about what matters most – values. If philosophical knowledge of definitions is an extremely rare and difficult attainment – there are no examples of it in the 'aporetic' dialogues – then we can say with Socrates, of ourselves and our entire acquaintance, that 'we do not know what good is'. The words in our denial of knowledge are perhaps no longer employed in their customary senses; an 'infantile' dialectician, however, might contend that they are nevertheless used in their *proper* sense. But then, since the Platonic Gorgias is motivated almost entirely by conventional aspirations and inhibited only by conventional prohibitions, he perhaps slips into damaging compliance with Socrates' line of questioning because he cannot see that from the Socratic perspective, moral idiocy is both rife and unavoidable, unless we avoid both our fellows and ourselves.[25] Yet again, if this interpretation is valid, it hardly entails that Plato is cheating, or that he is representing Socrates as playing the sophist. Plato cannot deceive a fictional character, and Socrates is not portrayed as attempting to do so. Instead, we are shown a Gorgias who misses far too much of importance, that is, is given (but muffs) the opportunity to gain an active recognition of what is truly at stake.

Socrates has already consistently coupled moral knowledge/ignorance with virtue/vice; now he fully articulates one of his most radical and counter-intuitive hypotheses, that knowledge is sufficient for virtue:

Socrates: Thus according to this *logos* someone who has learnt just things is also just?
Gorgias: Absolutely.
Socrates: And of course the just man performs just acts.
Gorgias: Yes.
Socrates: So is it necessary for the rhetorician to be just, and for the just man to want to act justly?
Gorgias: At least it seems so.

Socrates: Then the rhetorician will never want to commit
                injustice.
Gorgias: At least it seems not.

(460B6–C6)

Even were knowledge sufficient for virtue, it would not follow
that the just man unfailingly performs just acts, unless further
momentous assumptions are silently made about how material and
social circumstances promote or hinder human action.[26] But if
Gorgias manifests some slight reluctance ('at least it seems so/seems
not'), he certainly does not resist the conclusion that if he imparts
values to the aspiring rhetorician, and does so successfully, this
ensures his students' probity. Why is this? Gorgias seems in part
simply not to gauge the significance of Socratic rationalism, in part
to subscribe himself to an aggressive intellectualism. But even were
he fully alive to the import of the sufficiency of knowledge thesis,
Gorgias might still not admit to an incapacity to make people good.
His refusal would not be a matter of logic, but would rather arise
from his championship of *dynamis*: the man who claims supremacy
as speaker and teacher is not going to concede that his *logos* is powerless to reform values.[27] This finally yields the threatened incoherence:
Gorgias' defence of himself as an upright teacher hinged on the
concession that his students might turn the weapon of rhetoric to
perverted ends; but now, inconsistently, it emerges that a trained
rhetorician cannot abuse his *dynamis*, given that his training ensures
that he knows proper values (and so acts on them) (460E8–461A2,
461A4–7).

FORCE AND PERSUASION REVISITED

The refutation of Gorgias is complete. But the examination of
rhetoric is not: Polus indignantly jumps in, protesting that his teacher
has only succumbed as a consequence of excessive shame. The
ensuing discussion brings up much to ponder about the nature of
pleasure and its inducement, the limitations on political and rhetorical *dynamis* as vulgarly conceived, and the bearing of knowledge –
especially self-knowledge – on the satisfaction of (true) desire. All
this is of immense independent interest. We shall nevertheless pass
over these stages of the dialectic, despite their relevance to Socrates'
formulation of a view of persuasion entirely antipathetic to Gorgias',
because they rely on substantive philosophical presuppositions whose

74

analysis is best pursued with the help of the commentaries on the dialogue. We shall instead restrict our attention to those passages which speak directly to the issue of persuasive power; our concern will be not so much what Socrates has to say first to Polus, then to Callicles, as what he has to say about *how* he says it.

In response to the slur that he secretly concurs, but keeps up a merely verbal disagreement, Socrates protests that Polus is indulging in rhetorical refutation, which works by sheer weight of numbers, piling up against the opponent hostile witnesses of good repute (etymologically, 'those who *seem* good' (*eudokimous*), 471E6). But such refutation is worthless for truth:

> I alone do not agree [*homologō*]; for it is not that you are applying force to me [*anankazeis*], but that by presenting many false witnesses against me you are attempting to expel me from my property and the truth. But if I do not present you alone as a witness agreeing with me about what I say, I think I have accomplished nothing of any account [*logos*] in what the *logos* concerns.
>
> (472B3–C1)

What sort of 'force' is in question here? As a dialectician, Socrates is obliged (and content) to give way only when the force of argument delivers good reason to do so.[28] Plato has begun the gradual process of reanimating the Parmenidean imagery of logical necessity, the necessity which Gorgias in turn had subsumed within a uniform persuasion exerted on the altogether yielding *psychē*.

On a first reading, Socrates' declaration might simply strike us as anti-democratic; after all, he scornfully rejects the notion that majority rule could contribute to the discovery of truth. But his preference for dialectical over rhetorical *elenchos* also manifests a perfect allegiance to a type of personal intellectual liberty and integrity. Rhetorical compulsion is eminently personal; but if it is reason which impersonally compels our assent, then this logical necessity might paradoxically enhance our intellectual freedom, as Descartes would claim: to be confined within the limits of truth is not to be imprisoned. Socrates encourages Polus to 'submit himself to the *logos* as if to a doctor' (475D5–7, cf. *Theaetetus* 191A4), as if the rigours of dialectic free us from the malaise of false belief.

But in yet another sense, dialectic might seem highly personal, in a manner to which rhetoric, democratic or not, cannot hope to aspire. Socrates denies that he is a 'politician' (as Polus and others understand the word) because dialectic cannot be undertaken with a group (474A5–B1). The difficulty is technical and fundamental, and has nothing to do with any élitist attitude towards the many.[29] Since dialectical examination inspects an interlocutor's beliefs, but different believers may well have discordant commitments, plural *elenchos* is an impossibility.[30] Thus within the dialectical situation the beliefs of anyone apart from one's interlocutor and oneself are of no interest whatsoever. No one will pay more serious attention to my beliefs than my dialectical partner; but again this is a curiously impersonal sort of intimacy, since they are of overwhelming interest not because they are mine, but because they are currently the only resource we have available for mutual progression towards the truth.

And this should heighten our appreciation of just how injurious to the deepest aspirations and central ideology of Athenian democracy Socrates might well have proved. In that democracy citizens confirm their fundamental identity as citizens by participation in civic discourse, speaking as one of many among the many. Socrates not only indulges in a mode of philosophical discourse which necessarily excludes the Athenians as a collectivity, he also insists that everything worth having is accessible solely by its means. It is as if he were continually forming transient philosophical city-states in the marketplace or the Lyceum, intellectual communities whose membership cannot exceed two, rather than, as he claims in the *Apology* (31C5 ff.), not engaging in politics at all. How could Athens not regard itself as a host to philosophical parasites? If his mission was to minister to the Athenians, this could only be done by appealing to the *psyche* of each Athenian taken singly. Socrates admits to minimal participation in the life of democratic Athens; in reality his dialectical activity foments revolution.

Following Polus' eventual discomfiture, the final interlocutor, Callicles, intervenes, expressing a bewilderment at Socrates' anti-conventional arguments which swiftly boils over into outrage at what Callicles regards as Socrates' unseemly behaviour. Socrates' initial rejoinder is to ascribe responsibility for what is said to his 'beloved', philosophy (482A3–4), a personification of his impersonal, rational activity, but Callicles is not appeased:

> you seem to me to be swaggering youthfully in *logoi* like a true demagogue ['*dēmēgoros*', one who addresses the *dēmos*]. And

now you are indulging in this demagogy when Polus has suffered [*pathos*] the very thing which he was accusing Gorgias of suffering at your hands . . . that because of this agreement [*homologia*: viz. that he would teach justice], Polus said, Gorgias was compelled [*anankasthēnai*] to contradict himself, and this is just what you like.

(482C4–D5)

That the 'infantile' dialectician deliberately 'misunderstands' and places special, philosophical constructions on language has so far been an interpretation of the text, rather than evidence emerging directly from it. Now Callicles launches one of his principal attacks on philosophy, the accusation of immaturity (admittedly adolescent hooliganism rather than childish prattle at this point). The accusation of low oratory, playing to the crowd, is nothing short of bizarre, in light of Socrates' dialectical concentration solely on the beliefs of his interlocutor. Already in this opening salvo Callicles' authentically Gorgianic orientation is strongly in evidence. He has a horror of *pathos* and being forced to submit to compulsion, and evidently regards the logical revelation of inconsistency as a humiliation visited on a dialectical victim by an inquisitor, rather than by a partner in examination: Polus in his turn 'because of this agreement again was himself shackled by you in *logoi*, and muzzled, since he was ashamed to say what he thought' (482D8–E2). Much is packed into Callicles' metaphorical analysis of Polus' coming to grief. First, he conceives of (argumentative) *logos* as a bond or chain, but reacts to the image negatively, as if it meant that the argument traps an individual, rather than positively, as if *logos* preserved the security of the truth. Second, he continues to emphasise the passivity of the dialectical victim, as he perceives him: Polus is the subject of a series of passive grammatical forms, and Socrates is the demeaning agent who restrains him as one might a slave or animal.[31] But third, Callicles believes that it was only disabling shame, not logic on its own, which handicapped Polus; does he then suppose that an interlocutor strong and confident enough to brazen it out could not be refuted by the *elenchos*?

MAGIC REVISITED

The *Gorgias* had such a profound influence on Nietzsche largely as a consequence of Callicles' impassioned protest against what he

77

dismisses contemptuously as the ignoble morality of the herd. Its feeble members combine to enslave the leonine man who should – by natural right – reign over them, endlessly and strenuously fulfilling huge desires guaranteed satisfaction by his *dynamis*. Callicles' refutation, which has been amply studied in the philosophical literature, cleverly takes advantage of a fatal lack of integrity in his attitude towards 'the many' (or the 'crowd'). On the one hand, his superman ideal encourages contempt for the *dēmos*, the people of Athens; on the other, his own rhetorical drive after *dynamis* in Athens demands at least the semblance of an accommodation with the masses, which should alone demean a truly powerful individual. It is this leonine ideology which holds the key to Callicles' otherwise puzzling condemnation of Socrates as a mob-orator. Because he views any morality which inhibits the promiscuous satisfaction of desire as the crippling of the naturally strong by the naturally weak (if conventionally powerful), he must consider the Socratic arguments which criticised Polus' glorification of tyranny and rhetoric as the philosopher aiding and abetting the mass enemy. Socrates is, as it were, the running dog of the slavish *dēmos*.

We 'mould the best and strongest among us, taking them from youth like lions, and by reciting magic spells and bewitching them we enslave them, saying that one should have equal shares, and that this is what is fine and just' (483E4–484A2, cf. 484A4–5). Callicles is dissecting what 'we' Athenians as a society supposedly do to ensure that the natural nobility is tamed by indoctrination in democratic ideology, but he clearly sees Socrates himself as pandering to the values of the many, squandering his time and talents on dialectical pursuits which serve only to reinforce by argument the bad magic which preaches self-denial. In the *Meno* (80A–B), Meno accuses Socrates in remarkably similar terms of reducing him to *aporia*, a state of intellectual numbness; but crucially, it is precisely rational argument which has brought Meno to this pass, not indoctrination. Callicles, of course, finds it hard, if not impossible, to distinguish the two. This puts us in a position to reopen a theme from the *Encomium*. Gorgias had likened the effect of *logos* to that of magic, or even assimilated the two; and he further drew an analogy between the administration of efficacious drugs for the body and of words for the *psychē*. As we have already remarked, Socrates was at pains to distinguish the ignorant rhetorician from the expert physician; in a passage we did not consider, he also denies the analogy between somatic medicine and psychic rhetoric, claiming that it is actually nothing more than 'flattery' (463B1), a 'knack' rather than a properly theoretical *technē* (465A2–6), and only the 'image' of a part of (authentic) politics (463D1–2).

We would therefore anticipate that Socrates would be depicted by Plato as eager to repudiate any likening of philosophy to magic, albeit content with medical comparisons. To an extent this expectation is not disappointed: from a negative perspective, passages which refer to the sinister magic of sophistry abound (e.g. *Euthydemus* 288B8), and positively, we have already noted Socrates' representation of *logos* as a therapeutic, purgative agent (475D5–7); his famous self-portrayal as a psychic midwife in the *Theaetetus* comes to mind as well.[32]

Nevertheless, the situation is considerably complicated by the great number of occasions in the Platonic corpus when Socrates himself is ascribed magical powers (perhaps the best-known is the passage just cited from the *Meno*): how is this to be squared with the anti-Gorgianic separation of medicine and magic? The most obvious reply is that such characterisations issue not from Socrates' own mouth, but rather from disconcerted interlocutors smarting under the effects of the *elenchos*.[33] But this straightforward exoneration of Socrates as a 'white' magician of philosophy, a wizard in a purely metaphorical sense, a rationalistic hero opposing 'black' sophistical enchanters, will not quite do. In the peroration of his encomium of *erōs* (the marked Gorgianic character of which Socrates remarks on, *Symposium* 198C1–5), Agathon declares that *erōs* is 'the *kosmos* of all gods and men, the finest and best leader, whom every man must follow singing in fine celebration, sharing in the magic song which he sings, charming the thought of all gods and men' (197E2–8).

Later, when Alcibiades bursts in and disrupts the proceedings by eulogising not *erōs*, but rather the extraordinary philosopher himself, he tells us what Socrates is like by comparing him to the satyr Marsyas. Alcibiades insists that the resemblance is thoroughgoing: not only is Socrates sexually impudent, he also is a supernatural flautist, and far more wonderful than Marsyas (215B8). For Marsyas would enchant (215C1) men with his audible music, but Socrates achieves precisely the same effect with bare *logoi* (215C7–D1). No other speaker – not even Pericles – can match the impact of Socrates' words on Alcibiades' *psychē*, even when reported indirectly and in distorted form (215D1–216A2). The message is that Socrates is *erōs* in his magical aspect.[34]

We ought to be reminded of the *Encomium*, with Socratic *logoi*
(corresponding to Paris' seductive words) throwing Alcibiades' *psychē*
(corresponding to Helen's) into complete emotional perturbation.
Much caution is called for. Alcibiades, to say the least, is no unjaun-
diced witness to the truth; in particular, he is so very upset by
Socratic 'magic' precisely because he lacks the strength of will to
abandon the ambitious pursuits which those *logoi* expose as so much
trash. Thus one might conclude that Alcibiades suffers Gorgianic
effects only because he lacks the resolution to live in consistency
with reason. A philosophical lover, one might speculate, would
experience no such conflict, valuing Socrates exclusively for his
magnificent contributions to dialectical investigations whose deliver-
ances the lover would easily accept. Still, the fact remains that Plato
leaves us with a portrait of Socrates the erotic magician whose ambiguities he does nothing to resolve. This lack of guidance is just what
we should expect from philosophical fiction; in the last analysis,
Plato issues no direct condemnation of the ambiguous, alluring
dynamis which he depicts as magic.

PARMENIDES REVISITED

Callicles explains that he has nothing against philosophy, so long as
it is kept to its proper place – or rather time, namely, a gentlemanly
smattering during boyhood. Extended beyond that limit, it ruins
good men by keeping them <u>inexperienced in the political realities</u>
of the city, including its *logoi* (484D3).

> For whenever I see a child, whom such discourse still befits,
> mumbling and playing, I am charmed, and it seems to me
> to be charming, free and fitting the age of a child ... But
> whenever someone hears a man mumbling or sees him playing,
> it seems ridiculous, unmanly and worthy of a thrashing. That
> is just what I, too, suffer with regard to philosophers.
>
> (485B2–C3)

Now, finally, we have some textual evidence for detecting an
'infantile' strain in philosophical discourse, albeit from a hostile and
disapproving source. To Callicles, for whom the only manly
occupation is the unbridled pursuit of political influence by means
of rhetorical *dynamis*, the language of dialectic must seem both
regressively naïve and falsely affected: these endless, footling discussions do not contain the words of power which confer a victory

80

worth having, over other adults. Is Socrates not 'ashamed to hunt after words' at his advanced age (489B7–C1; cf. 499B4–6)?

There is something quite disgusting in the prospect of a man of genuine endowments who 'flees the city centre and the marketplaces' (485D5) and wastes his life 'whispering with three or four boys in a corner' (485D7–E1). Apart from the obvious sexual suspicion, what should strike us most forcibly about this vivid evocation of nausea prompted by philosophical neoteny is its political aspect. As I have suggested in commenting on the remarkably subversive implications of dialectic, allegiance to philosophy is seen as a perverted withdrawal from public space – that is, the places where men talk politics. Socrates' deft reaction will be to invert Callicles' conventional assumptions about where maturity is to be found. Because rhetoricians please rather than benefit the *dēmos*, they are in fact treating the audiences they flatter like children (502E7–503A1); those who play the political game so earnestly are in reality no better than deluded children. A 'real' orator, one possessing a genuine *technē*, would be capable of improving the *psychē* of an auditor (504D1–E3) – but this 'real' orator is ideal, unless he is to be identified with Socrates himself.

Despite his vaunted candour, Callicles' refutation no less than that of his predecessors is precipitated by an access of shame. Socrates has been asking whether no bounds whatsoever are to be placed on the range and structuring of desires whose fulfilment Callicles regards as the natural good of the leonine man: what about an entire life of undiluted pleasure arising from scratching an itch (494C6–8)? After some resistance Callicles assents (494D6). But when Socrates proceeds to infer that since what one scratches cannot make any difference, Callicles should, in all consistency, agree that the life of a *kinaidos*, a catamite, should also be considered perfect, on condition that it affords him untrammelled enjoyment (494E4–6), Callicles answers: 'are you not ashamed to lead the *logoi* to such things, Socrates?' (494E7–8). One must realise that very special cultural factors are at work; Callicles is not being prudish, his 'shame' – projected on to Socrates – is not a matter of the social niceties. It is not homosexuality *per se* for which Callicles feels such pronounced repugnance; rather, what he cannot stomach is the idea that the catamite, who is supposed to be the passive sexual partner, could experience a pleasure which ought to be satisfied. The insuperable objection to such pleasure is just that it is passive: Callicles, who yearns to be a man among men through his active *dynamis*, cannot possibly accept such an inversion of value.[35]

An evolving theme of this book has been the admittedly paradoxical impersonality of the philosophical enterprise.[36] But if all the interlocutors in turn capitulate to shame, what could be more personal than this exploitation by dialectic of an individual's embarrassment? Why should anyone repose the slightest confidence in the results of *elenchos*, if its 'logic' is so easily vitiated by the intrusion of feelings which should rationally be disregarded? These damaging suspicions would be fully warranted, were it the case that 'refutation by shame' did come down to an embarrassed unwillingness to say what one *really* believes, a bullied refusal to enunciate one's hidden, internal commitments. (This is to simplify somewhat: if interlocutors are defined as such by their complexes of beliefs, some of these may be barely accessible to the believer as *beliefs*, rather than as 'irrefutable', unchallengeable truths.) But while embarrassment may be Polus' and Callicles' ready diagnosis of their predecessors' discomfiture, none of Socrates' interlocutors endorses any such judgement about his own fate.[37] Accordingly we have no reason to fear that hypocrisy will from the outset routinely disable the *elenchos* as an instrument for the detection of the truth. We are, of course, left with the disconcerting possibility that the best which dialectic might achieve is to work towards the elimination of inconsistency, without thereby approaching any closer to the truth, unless coherence somehow guarantees truth. But such uncertainty might simply be a consequence of human epistemological limitations, and so the unavoidable concomitant of human philosophy.[38]

Eventually Callicles becomes so alienated from the proceedings that he refuses (temporarily) to speak; since Socrates' philosophical method is essentially dialectic, he is constrained to question himself.[39] Before plunging into this strange solo question-and-answer, Socrates takes the opportunity to remind the assembled company of why there is an unqualified demand for philosophical perseverance:

> I for one think that we must all be competitively disposed towards knowing what is true and what is false in what we are talking about (cf. 515B5–8); since for this to become clear is a common good for all ... I search in common with you, so that if someone disputing with me is clearly saying something, I am the first to concede it.
>
> (505E4–506A5)

82

A more lucid commitment to the impersonal model of philosophical competition without a victim could not be desired, and its connection with Parmenides' original project is unmistakably signalled through re-employment of the first philosopher's best-known image:

> these things which appeared thus to us earlier in the previous *logoi* are – so I say – held fast and bound down, even if it is somewhat crude to say so, by iron and adamantine *logoi*: so at least it seems.

(508E6–509A2)

Perhaps the final phrase introduces a hint of a conditional – '*if* these *logoi* are indeed valid, *then* indeed the conclusions are immovable' – but even so, Socrates' faith that sound argument should fix belief unshakably is beyond question. His re-use of Parmenides' metaphor of compulsion revives the force/persuasion polarity which Gorgias had collapsed, and – most importantly – presents 'compulsion' as the liberating force of persuasive *reason*.

Callicles does not remain permanently alienated, and even makes a curious confession: 'I am not sure how, but I believe that you are speaking well, Socrates; yet I have undergone the same experience [*pathos*] as most people: I am not quite convinced by you' (513C3–5). Socrates answers: 'that is because the love of *dēmos* which is in your *psychē* opposes me, Callicles; but if we investigate these same things often and better, you will be convinced' (513C7–D1). Socrates optimistically predicts that repetition of the dialectical exercise would finally leave Callicles rationally persuaded, but does not indicate whether in that case his countervailing (irrational?) love would be totally eliminated; or simply overwhelmed by his newly strengthened rational convictions; or perhaps not extirpated, but organised harmoniously with reason.[40] The first two options would seem plausible only to a thinker supremely confident about the efficacy of reason in dealing with *pathos*. If a feeling is 'irrational' just in the sense of being mistaken, then repeated exposure to *logos* should indeed wipe it out; if it has more autonomy from the intellect, an extreme rationalist might nevertheless suppose that the second option is a possibility.[41] The radically rationalistic psychology which Socrates expounds here (and in the *Phaedo*) abets this optimistic attitude towards handling the recalcitrant *pathē* which the Gorgianic rhetorician manipulatively arouses or stills. But with the gradual complication of psychological theory introduced in later Platonic

83

dialogues, culminating in the *Phaedrus*, comes a new tolerance of rhetoric as emotional appeal, provided it is thoroughly subordinated to the rational control of the guiding philosopher.

A PHILOSOPHER IN POLITICS

Socrates is by no means through outraging Callicles' sensibilities. He proceeds to argue that Callicles' preferred examples of eminently successful Athenian politicians – Pericles, Cimon, Themistocles and Miltiades – were really abject failures. The criterion for the exercise of 'authentic' rhetoric is that it result in improving the citizens; but as these supposed political successes suffered lapses from popular esteem – indeed, some were banished – they could not even have enjoyed mastery of false, conventional rhetoric, since in that case their flattery of the *dēmos* should have protected them (516E9–517A6). The commentators generally take a harsh view of Socrates' argument,[42] but its evaluation requires very nice judgement. Are the factual details of Socrates' historical reportage falsified? Despite considerable scholarly suspicion, arising primarily from the dialogue's being our unique source for at least some of the political travail having been so severe, we possess no independent ground for impugning its testimony. Much more important, is the presentation of democratic motivation and decision-making nastily skewed? Is this rhetorical abuse of a political constitution of which Plato disapproved? Socrates' *logos* is simple and explicit: the good politician/rhetorician is so just to the extent that he both intends to make the citizens better, and succeeds. Since the improvement in question is moral, it necessarily follows that the citizens benefited will feel only goodwill towards their benefactors (on condition that they remain benevolent: but Socratic good men do not fall into corruption).

Since the Athenians adopted hostile measures towards these four historical leaders, they were not good politicians. All that could justify action taken against them would be 'real' – that is, psychic – harm which they did to the Athenians. If, as a matter of historical fact, they prosecuted Themistocles to protect their military interests against Persia, in the reasonable belief that he was plotting with the treacherous Pausanias, Socrates would hardly have been impressed. From the conventional perspective, whether Themistocles played the traitor for personal advancement might make a world of difference to the evaluation of Athens' treatment of him; but for Socrates, the difference between such treachery and loyal imperialism feeding self-destructive desires might pale into insignificance. Therefore the Athenians were plausibly without *Socratic* justification for their treatment of the four, and could not have been improved by them. Once more, Plato is making no attempt to deceive the reader: we are surely intended to be outraged; and then to reflect that that reaction only has a basis within the conventional system of values which Socrates repudiates. Finally, Socrates delivers the *coup de grâce*, the most perplexing and outrageous claim of all (to the Gorgianic rhetorician): he, perhaps alone of the Athenians, is a true politician (521D6–E1).

The conclusion is inescapable, given the preceding argument: Socrates is unique in his unwavering commitment to a *logos* which is capable of doing his fellow-citizens good. The ordinary world has been turned upside down. Regardless of his stated 'naturalism', Callicles actually cleaves to a conventional conception of the rhetorical route to political *dynamis*. Really it is Socrates who thoroughly subverts convention by legitimating the private, one-on-one discourse of dialectic as the only authentically political sort of talk. If Gorgias' idea of '*logos* the great *dynastēs*' made the rhetorical basis of Athenian democratic institutions questionable, Plato's presentation of philosophical politics is no less of a radical challenge – and no less astounding an instance of deliberate *paradoxologia*.[43]

If my understanding of Plato's philosophical fiction and reconstruction of Socratic procedure are tenable, then Nietzsche's Callicles-like dismissal of dialectic in the epigraph to this chapter as retrospective rationalisation can easily be resisted. Of course, I do not dogmatically maintain that they *are* tenable; but Gorgias' followers have no grounds for complacency. Plato's confrontation with Gorgias takes shape in the opposition of methods, display vs. dialectic, regardless of whether in this particular instance the philosophical method actually yields truth. Does Socrates 'bewitch' Gorgias, does Plato seduce us, into haplessly conceding that the *logos* which is proper argument logically compels a conviction distinct from the psychic impress of a brute force? Gorgianic psychology is bleakly reductive, Socratic psychology is overweeningly rationalistic; yet if we are not to accept a portrait of ourselves as so many passive Helens, persuasive power in all its guises cannot be allowed to reflect mere superficial variations in mode and effectiveness.

4

AFTERLIVES

Judge by *logos* the contentious test I have expressed.

(Parmenides, fragment 7)

In my eyes, he [Plato] was most an orator when heaping scorn on them.

(Cicero, *De Oratore* I 47)

'THE GORGIAS/*GORGIAS* PROBLEMATIC'

We have now arrived at a major turning-point in our exploration of the nature of rhetoric. At the outset we posed the question whether persuasion as such is 'rhetorical', whether persuasion, if successful, inevitably manipulates the auditor. In other words – the words of the *Encomium of Helen* – does persuasion compel? Should we conceive of rhetoric as the means to tap that least resistible power of all, the power of persuasion? Chapters 1 and 2 suggested that these pressing doubts are not just our modern reaction to the question of rhetoric: they are deliberately raised, but hardly settled, by Gorgias, who in so doing perhaps earns the title of inventor of rhetoric, as our cultural tradition understands it. Furthermore, we found that Gorgias' procedure delivered its full sense only when apprehended specifically as a challenge to Parmenides' insistence that philosophical *logos*, argumentative *logos*, makes a uniquely privileged appeal to our reason; that is why the *Gorgias* is overwhelmingly concerned to discriminate between dialectical *logos* and rhetorical display, as we learned in Chapter 3.

My intention falls well short of wanting to establish that Gorgias and the *Gorgias* constitute either the sole or necessarily the very best avenue to the appreciation of rhetoric; but I am, of course, committed to the thesis that together they are one of the best. The remaining

86

chapters and the Epilogue are meant to put the claim for Gorgias and Plato to the test. To the extent that their quarrel helps illuminate some key developments in rhetorical theory and practice, the main idea of this book will have been justified. The ancient figures to be considered do not all show equal interest in, or sensitivity towards, the quarrel; but they can hardly neglect it, so that even evasion of the central debate might prove significant. In fact, the great evaders, Isocrates and Cicero, initiate and continue the tradition of rhetorical autobiography which makes philosophy the pretentious dependant. So spectacularly successful did the grand evasion prove that most modern accounts of ancient rhetoric rest content with uncritical reportage of these earlier apologists and with facile exposition of fancy orations. The Epilogue, on gender in philosophy, is presented as an experiment in the application of the original terms of the rhetorical dispute to one of its latest, and most important, manifestations. We shall require some convenient label for the defining disagreement which Gorgias and Plato are supposed to have bequeathed to later dealers in persuasion; since I have been at pains to emphasise that this great formative encounter yields dissonance, not resolution, we shall refer to it as 'the Gorgias/*Gorgias* problematic'.

PROTAGORAS AND ISOCRATES: THE GENIUS OF EVASION

In the history of rhetoric Isocrates is a transitional figure of immense weight.[1] Indeed, one might with some justification regard him as *anti*-rhetorical: he tends to deprecate public speaking before the masses (e.g. at public festivals, *To Philip* 12: he lacks the assurance to front the *ochlos*, 81) and to discern decisive advantages in addressing *individuals* in the Greek world capable of implementing his ambitious pan-Hellenic policies (*To Philip* 13).[2] Doubtless he adopts this manœuvre in reaction to the sea-change in power politics which involved the gradual but irreversible decline in Athenian influence. In terms of rhetorical theory and practice, this means that Isocrates sedulously makes as if to maintain some of the forms and fundamental preconceptions of persuasive discourse, but actually operates in new terrain.

For example, *To Philip* is addressed to Philip because, so Isocrates claims, the Macedonian ruler is *uniquely* placed to implement the policies which could be the salvation of Greece (*To Philip* 15).

So Isocrates is openly confessing that he is trying to persuade a mighty *dynastēs* (to Athenians listening to Demosthenes, a 'tyrant' in the worst sense of the word); and, surely, the tone and devices of speech designed to curry favour with princes cannot be the same as those used to win round the *dēmos*.[3]

> You possess such quantities of both wealth and *dynamis* as does no other Greek, which alone are naturally suited both to persuade and compel ... and as persuasion will be beneficial with regard to the Greeks, so compulsion will be useful with regard to the barbarians.
>
> (*To Philip* 15–16)[4]

The traditional, defining polarity of rhetoric is invoked, and aligned, in the fully traditional manner, with the distinction between civilised Greek and savage barbarian; but these comforting, familiar commonplaces cannot disguise the brute fact that Philip's *dynamis*, which resides in Macedonian military power, immediately threatens Greeks, not Persians. To many in the Greek heartland, Philip himself is little better than a barbarian. It is all very well for Isocrates to affect to assume that Philip will persuade rather than force Greeks to do his bidding, but events had already revealed, and would again reveal, that pretence for what it was.

This is a momentous stage in the evolution (or, perhaps, degeneration) of rhetoric after its imperial Athenian heyday. The 'rhetoric', as it were, remains; but with the dislocation and disappearance of the democratic institutions in which the persuasive words were originally spoken, it takes on an entirely new cast.[5] The point is not that during some golden age of radical politics rhetoric possessed a purity and authenticity which it lost with the enfeebling, and eventual collapse, of democracy: after all, one of the basic lessons to emerge from our readings of Gorgias and Plato is how problematic the relation between rhetoric and democracy must be. Rather, the point is that the simultaneous erosion of democratic power and maintenance of rhetorical fixtures inextricably linked to democratic persuasion add a whole new dimension of complexity to 'the Gorgias/*Gorgias* problematic'. Isocrates pioneers the rhetorical strategy of accommodation with the domineering presence of monarchical power which can, much of the time, afford simply to ignore the humbled *dynamis* of *logos*.

If Isocrates so strikingly accommodates his persuasion to new political realities, how does he react to the problematic? To understand the ingenuity with which he evades rather than engages in the conflict between philosophy and rhetoric, we must review some details of the so-called 'great *logos*' which Plato puts into Protagoras' mouth in the *Protagoras*.[6] Hippocrates, a youth whose desire for self-improvement is more enthusiastic than discerning, calls on Socrates at the crack of dawn so that they might together seek out the celebrated Protagoras, who has come to Athens. Despite Philostratus' description of Gorgias as the father of sophistry, Protagoras' reputation as *the* master-sophist remains largely unchallenged, from antiquity to the present. His political stature was such that he drafted a constitution for the Athenian colony of Thurii in 443 BCE (Diogenes Laertius 9.50); he expressed views on theology and linguistic propriety, now unfortunately impossible to reconstruct with any assurance; and he formulated a notorious relativistic thesis – that 'man is the measure, of things that are, that they are, of things that are not, that they are not' – which undergoes sustained critical investigation in the *Theaetetus*.

But, despite the many-sidedness which comes to be one part of the concept 'sophist', Plato elects to construct the *Protagoras* around a single aspect of the expertise he claims. Hippocrates explains that he is so eager to pursue the visiting educator because according to the common opinion Protagoras is wisest (*sophōtatos* = 'most *sophos*') at speaking (310E6–7). This can hardly have been anything but deliberate, since elsewhere it is precisely the sophists' polymathy which comes under attack. In the *Hippias Major* Plato ridicules this ideal in the person of Hippias, who gleefully boasts that his skills extend from astronomy to tailoring the very clothes he wears. The *Sophist* gives almost canonical expression to the belief that the sophist, defined as a man-hunter going after rich young men for money, luring them with the semblance of education (*Sophist* 223B2–7), possesses a manifold *technē* (223C2). 'Sophists' are so designated because of their (pretence to) wisdom, *sophia*; the Platonic dialogues manifest an implacable hostility towards professional thinkers consistently depicted as possessing no more than the mere pretence of wisdom, and actuated by the most venal motives. The pretence is all the more pernicious because multiple, and so more apt to impress and confuse the unwary. 'Sophist' becomes a term of opprobrium because what is at stake is whether a conception of wisdom apparently inimical to the Socratic will continue to enjoy popular currency.

The character Protagoras expresses positive contempt for the manifold *technai* of Hippias (*Protagoras* 318E): everything will

stand or fall with his acceptance, explanation and defence of his
unparalleled reputation for wise speech. If the *Gorgias* represents
philosophy's struggle with rhetoric over what *logos* can and should
be, the *Protagoras* no less suggestively indicates that the phenomenon of the multi-purpose sophist, striking as it might be, pales
into insignificance beside the issue of who truly speaks well.
And, since the good speaker has the *logos* of real value, this is to
say that fundamentally the *Gorgias* and the *Protagoras* address a
set of shared concerns: ultimately we need not adjudicate between
the claims of the two great figures to sophistical pre-eminence, since
the dialogues named after them are actually complementary
contributions to the Platonic debate between philosophy and
rhetoric.

> And of those who followed behind, listening in on their
> discourse, the majority seemed to be foreigners. Protagoras
> draws these people from every city he visits, enchanting them,
> like Orpheus, with his voice, while they follow after his voice
> spell-bound.[7] But there were also a few native Athenians in
> the chorus.

(315A5–B2)

Socrates' description of his first sight of Protagoras holding court is
anything but innocent. Isocrates analogously muddied Gorgias'
reputation by commenting that he amassed fabulous wealth, ducking
the expenses incurred by stay-at-home citizens who support both
their *polis* and their children.[8] Protagoras is not only not of Athens,
his foreign entourage shows that he might well deprive the city of
promising young Athenians who succumb to his charisma. And the
Encomium has forced on our attention the vexed question of *logos*
whose power of attraction is, or can be likened to, magic.
Furthermore, an acute reader of the *Gorgias* will be immediately
alerted to the danger that if Protagoras' persuasion is a binding spell,
the conviction it induces will not be the outcome of rational
reflection. If Protagoras' formidable reputation as a speaker rests on
his powers of enchantment, then the diffuse popular belief in his
verbal skill may, when suitably focused, only damn him, from the
philosopher's point of view. He is 'wisest at speaking' where the
purpose and result are to overcome, to seduce, to bewitch: in a word,
his power is rhetorical.

Protagoras' very first words in the dialogue are doubly significant:
'do you want to speak to me in private, or in front of the

90

others?' (316B3–4). First, although the translation of Hubbard and Karnofsky is not to be faulted, their English rendering inevitably loses an important feature of the Greek. The original for 'speak' is '*dialechthēnai*'. Although the word can indeed mean no more than 'speak', it is of course the verbal form of the noun 'dialectic', in the sense of Socrates' proprietary philosophical method. We should not infer that Protagoras is here represented as *au fait* with dialectical technique; but competent readers will not fail to recognise the connotations of this ostensibly casual choice of word. Second, awareness of the resonance of '*dialechthēnai*' makes us more conscious of Protagoras' attention to the matter of with and before whom he speaks, to the neglect of *how* he speaks. When Socrates expresses his indifference to the presence or absence of an audience, Protagoras declares his preference for discussion before others, so as to avert the suspicions typically excited by sophistry (316C–317C). But Socrates wonders whether his true motive might not be the desire to make a display ('*endeixasthai*') before his professional rivals, Prodicus and Hippias (317C–D). Thus a deep thematic convergence with the *Gorgias* looks increasingly likely. Socrates' unflattering speculation, together with the use of '*dialechthēnai*', in effect replicate the very terms of the confrontation in the *Gorgias* of rhetorical display with philosophical dialectic.[9]

In response to the question what Hippocrates will gain, if he receives tuition from Protagoras, the sophist answers that he imparts a capacity for 'good planning both of his own affairs, to the end that he would best manage his personal estate, and of the city's', a capacity which would make Hippocrates 'most capable' ('*dynatōtatos*') of carrying out 'in speech and action, the common business of the city' (318E5–319A2). '*Dynatōtatos*' is cognate with '*dynamis*': that is, Protagoras is claiming the ability to endow his students with executive power. His formulation takes it for granted that personal advantage cannot conflict with the public interest, and Socrates accordingly chooses to understand Protagoras as saying that he purveys *aretē*, 'excellence', pure and simple. But this is not to let Protagoras off lightly. For Socrates now objects that he is in doubt whether *aretē* can indeed be taught, and he explains:

> you see, I, in common with all other Greeks, call the Athenians wise [*sophoi*]. And I observe that whenever we convene in the assembly, and the city has some business related to building, it is the builders who are summoned as advisers about the

91

buildings ... and the same for every other matter which they consider is capable of being both learnt and taught ... But when they come to deliberate political issues, then a builder can get up and give advice, or, equally, smith or cobbler, merchant or shipper, rich or poor, high-born or low, without distinctions.

(319B3–D4)

Socrates' explanation of his (purported) reasons for doubting whether excellence can be transmitted finally elicits the 'great *logos*' from Protagoras, in response to Socrates' challenge: 'so if you can show [*epideixai*] us more clearly that *aretē* is teachable, don't begrudge us, but do so' (320B8–C1).[10]

'Shall I show you by telling a story [*mythos*] as an older man addressing his juniors, or shall I go through a *logos*?' (320C2–4).[11] Once more the choice is left to Protagoras, who elects to give the *mythos* on the grounds that it will be 'more pleasant' (320C6–7: remember the dangerous possibility, raised in the *Encomium*, dissected in the *Gorgias*, that truth will be a casualty of the pursuit of verbal pleasure). Students of Plato have been perennially exercised by the question of the status Plato intends us to accord the *mythoi* which occur at prominent junctures in a number of central dialogues. Introduced by Socrates and other speakers of unimpeachable character, they can hardly be totally untrustworthy, entirely worthless *per se*. One recurrent and inherently plausible thesis is that the *mythoi* contain material for which Plato felt at the time of composition he could not generate adequate arguments ('*logos*' in the distinctively philosophical sense) to attribute to the dialogue's interlocutors. Or, more arrestingly, perhaps they retail doctrines to which he was committed but which somehow remained permanently beyond the range of argumentative support. Therefore the bald fact that Protagoras designates the 'great *logos*' a *mythos* cannot of itself undermine its status, since there is some reason to suppose that *mythos* is the chosen Platonic vehicle for the presentation of what might well be true, but (as yet?) cannot be argued for. However, Protagoras' motive for rejecting argumentative *logos* – that pleasure will thereby be increased – is quite different from any motive we might ascribe to Plato for including *mythos* in philosophical dialogues, since the evident implication is that a *logos* is available, but is not going to be formulated. His patronising reference to his seniority signals that, in marked contrast to the rigorous

92

egalitarianism of the dialectical encounter, Protagoras' relationship to his auditors (not interlocutors) is akin to the asymmetrical one of unique adult to throng of listening children. Competent grownups may not tell children unedifying stories, but the stories they do tell need not be true, or able to stand up to critical, adult scrutiny. At a superficial level Protagoras is saying no more than that we shall enjoy what we hear (more); by the same token, Plato is warning the reader not to trust the narrative too readily, precisely because it is told, in part, to please.

Protagoras' creation *mythos* relates how when the god Epimetheus ('Afterthought') leaves man unequipped and inferior to the beasts (321B–C), Prometheus ('Forethought') steals technical skills from Hephaestos and Athena. Consequently 'man articulated speech and words by *technē*, and discovered dwellings, clothes, shoes, bedding, and foodstuffs from the earth' (322A6–8).[12] But people continued to die in droves. Since they could only survive the attacks of wild beasts by forming viable communities, Zeus dispatched Hermes with the crucial gifts of justice and shame (322C). Finally, the distribution of these two properties is (unlike technical attainments) to be universal, in order to ensure political stability (322D). 'Having shown [*epideixamenos*] so many and such things Protagoras brought his *logos* to an end' (328D3–4).[13]

Socrates is answered – if not given an argument – insofar as Protagoras' *logos* shows how certain qualities might be found in everyone, because they are essential to the maintenance of the social fabric. Were 'smith or cobbler, merchant or shipper, rich or poor, high-born or low, without distinctions' not all alike competent in political deliberation, then – or so democratic ideology would have it – the *polis* would collapse into anarchy: the preconditions for political existence as such and for Athenian *isēgoria* reassuringly coincide. Socrates need not endorse this ideology *in propria persona*, and his falling in with the majority view that the Athenians are wise (319B3 ff.) quietly suggests as much. But since he mounts his attack on the teachability of virtue on the basis of Athenian political practice, Protagoras has every right to react with a *mythos* which appeals to cherished Athenian ideology. His story has the further advantage of suggesting how Athenian citizens might all be *sophoi*, yet nevertheless stand to benefit from the guidance of the sophist: if justice and shame are universal social attributes, they need not also be invariant, or incapable of skilled improvement. Protagoras' self-justification in *logos* thus insists that his distinctively political wisdom transcends the merely 'technical', by cultivating our common social endowment for the common good.

We are now at last ready to appreciate Isocrates' reaction to 'the Gorgias/*Gorgias* problematic'. Of course, the 'great *logos*' requires further study, at the very least because it remains quite unclear how its reassuring message, that sophistry improves common social virtues, might be consistent with its persistent, if masked, promise to confer political power; and much of the rest of the dialogue can be profitably read as a protracted, restless investigation of the unclarities hampering interpretation of Protagoras' *epideixis*. But fascinating as it is in its own right, we have broached the *Protagoras* only to gain illumination on Isocrates, and for that limited purpose we have enough.

In the *Nicocles* Isocrates delivers a remarkable paean to *logos* in general before expounding the details of his political advice to the Cyprian king who is the addressee of the treatise.

> With this [viz. *logos*] we both contend against others on matters which are open to dispute, and seek light for ourselves on things which are unknown; for the same proofs which we use in persuading others when we speak, we employ also when we deliberate; and, while we call eloquent [*rhētorikous*] those who are able to speak before a multitude [*plēthos*], we regard as prudent those who best discuss [*dialechthōsin*] their affairs in their own minds.
>
> (*Nicocles* 8)[14]

In praising *logos* Isocrates follows in the steps of Gorgias, if what is exalted in the *Encomium* is really *logos* itself, rather than Helen. Not that Isocrates merely replicates his great predecessor's achievement. It is of the essence of Gorgias' challenge that his attack on our complacency be covert: we must first be lulled into false security so that subsequently we can recognise ourselves as victims of all-powerful *logos*. Isocrates, in complete contrast, is concerned to develop an almost tediously transparent exposition representing *logos* as the common possession, not, to be sure, of everyone, but of a right-thinking, superior, 'we'. In fact what he is doing in these few, highly-charged lines, is beginning to effect a curious synthesis of the *Gorgias* with the *Protagoras* – a polemical combination to be thrown back at Plato.

The *logos* of Isocrates makes itself felt along the broadest possible front, which is just what we should expect from a follower of Gorgias.

But, while the *logos* of the *Encomium* is unitary because always and only an instrument of dominating power, *logos* as praised by Isocrates is universally *useful*. Furthermore, the departments in which its utility is shown to shine are not a haphazard assemblage. Disputation is obvious enough as the original matrix for rhetorical skill; but *logos* as heuristic tool and as aid in private deliberation are careful innovations on Isocrates' part, since they inevitably recall philosophical endeavour. What is important and original here is not, of course, the mere invocation of *logos* in its association with rationality. Isocrates' clever tactic is to insist throughout the passage on the absolute identity of *logos* for deliberation with *logos* for persuasion. In effect he is saying that one and the same *dynamis* has an internal, 'philosophical' aspect, and an external, 'rhetorical' aspect. Since which aspect manifests itself is entirely a matter of whether our unitary *logos* is engaged privately or publicly, the very idea of a quarrel between philosophy and rhetoric properly understood is incoherent: they are the same thing differently disposed. The philosopher *is* the orator who directs his 'proofs' ('*pisteis*', things creating conviction) at himself; rhetorical eloquence *is* the sound judgement of the man engaging himself in silent dialectic. It is no accident that Isocrates refers to internal discourse by appropriating the very word '*dialechthōsin*' which every reader of Plato will immediately recognise as reserved by Socrates for his special dialectic, ultimately inspired by Parmenides.

> If there is need to speak in brief summary of this *dynamis*, we shall find that none of the things which are done with intelligence occurs without *logos*, but that in all our actions as well as in all our thoughts *logos* is our guide, and is most employed by those who have the most intelligence.
>
> (*Nicocles* 9)[15]

The synthesis is complete. For Protagoras, simple verbal communication is just one more 'technical', *pre*-political attainment, since, according to the *mythos*, people achieved 'articulated speech and words by *technē*' before there were cities or the civilising political gifts necessary for their maintenance. Isocrates, in contrast, assumes a single *logos* at once internal and external, private and public, thereby making redundant any radical shift, however achieved, from a pre-political to a political society. The upshot is a world in which *logos* is indeed unitary – and as on this conception rhetoric is simply the externalisation of the faculty of deliberative persuasion,

AFTERLIVES

the Platonic Socrates was entirely misguided in his attempt to wrest
a distinctive, rational *logos* away from Gorgias. *Logos* is unified, but
is not to be identified with the threatening power of persuasion
which is championed by the opponents of the heirs to the
Parmenidean tradition. But this *logos* is not a great leveller. We *are*
all endowed with it: only some more than others; and the political
realm has lost its distinctiveness. Isocrates' compromise might well
be a mediocre evasion of a challenging debate, but in its skilful dead-
ening of the discomfort aroused by the 'the Gorgias/*Gorgias*
problematic', it is nothing less than a masterpiece of mediocrity. Let
Isocrates the expert on philosophy speak for himself (he is pretending
to be a latter-day Socrates, on the capital charge of corrupting his
pupils):

> In the matter of 'wisdom' [*sophia*] and 'philosophy' [*philosophia*,
> 'love of *sophia*' – Isocrates is playing on the original sense of
> the compound], it would not be fitting for people pleading a
> case on other matters to speak about these names (for they are
> foreign to all practical concerns), but in my case, since I am
> being judged on such matters, and since I declare that what
> some people call philosophy is not philosophy, it is appropriate
> to define and indicate to you what would rightly be consid-
> ered philosophy. My view of these things is quite simple. For
> since it is naturally impossible for human beings to acquire
> knowledge which would allow us to know what must be done
> or said, in the next resort I consider wise those who are able
> to arrive at what is best for the most part as far as their opin-
> ions go, but philosophers those who spend their time on things
> on the basis of which they will arrive at this sort of practical
> wisdom [*phronēsis*] as quickly as possible.
>
> (*Antidosis* 270–1)

So far from being an embarrassment, the almost heroic vapidity
of this 'definition' of philosophy constitutes the triumph of the
Isocratean speaker over the Platonic thinker: whatever 'some people'
might imagine, the only 'philosophers' we need acknowledge are
those who concentrate on getting their opinions in line with 'the
best'. Isocrates does not explain how we can achieve this goal while
safely abandoning the impossible quest for knowledge, but, since *real*
philosophers are not interested in such things, the question is quietly
shelved.

96

CICERO: THE IDEAL ORATOR

It was through Cicero that this anodyne resolution of the quarrel achieved an authority which set the seal on the status eventually enjoyed by rhetoric as universal culture. Cicero's *De Oratore*, in the form of a dialogue between celebrated political speakers of the recent past, is the lengthiest and most elaborate of the various rhetorical treatises which he composed, and it spans all the issues which might be thought to concern the aspiring orator, from the abstract theory of persuasion to the most technical minutae of diction and pronunciation. Accordingly Cicero does not neglect the general question of the relation between rhetoric and philosophy, and his engagement with 'the Gorgias/*Gorgias* problematic' is quite precise, since Gorgias' boast of fluency on any subject is a salient topic in the first book of the *De Oratore*.

> According to my opinion at least, no one will be able to be an orator, heaped with every sort of praise, unless he has achieved knowledge [*scientia*] of all great matters and all great arts; for his speech should bloom and overflow from his understanding [*cognitio*] of his subject-matters. Unless the matter is perceived and understood by the orator, his speech has a certain trivial and almost childish expression. Not indeed that I shall impose so great a burden on orators – especially on our own, tied up as they are in public and private affairs of such importance – that I think there is nothing they ought not to know; although the power of the orator and the very profession of speaking well seem to undertake and promise that any subject, whatever might be proposed, will be spoken of by him elegantly and at length.
>
> (*De Oratore* I 20–2)

Cicero prevaricates. First he summons up the image of the ideal orator, who is perfect in his omniscience (at least in what matters). The puzzling feature of this ideal is that it seems to presuppose an at least equally knowledgeable audience: for how could their praise be of discourse overflowing with genuine knowledge, if they could not recognise it? How can Cicero pretend that, in the absence of knowledge, rhetoric falls flat and risks appearing infantile? It is as if he were reacting to the argument of Socrates in the *Gorgias* that ignorant orators only impress similarly ignorant crowds by blandly assuming that the audience for rhetoric consists of

97

omnimaths. In the *Gorgias*, the *ochlos* can be likened to a mob of silly children duped by self-serving sweet talk; here in the *De Oratore*, at least in the ideal situation, it is rather the speaker hampered by ignorance who will be dismissed as childish. One cannot object that Cicero must mean something far less ambitious by (near-)universal knowledge than Socrates, since he would then have no reason to excuse busy Romans from the acquisition of complete knowledge. Not that Cicero's notion of *scientia* is itself crystal-clear. If his countrymen can plead the sheer weight of civic and private duties as an excuse, the implication would seem to be that, by contrast, the suitably gifted man of leisure (Cicero himself?) *is* in a position to achieve total *scientia*; and Socrates' point was not that what prevents orators from discoursing knowledgeably, as well as facilely, on all topics, is lack of free time.

But Cicero then qualifies his leniency towards his fellow-citizens and their busy lives with what must surely be an allusion to the Gorgianic profession of universal fluency.[16] The phrase 'the power of the orator' translates '*vis oratoris*', and '*vis*' is the Latin for '*dynamis*'; thus Cicero is, most probably, deliberately evoking Gorgias' persuasive power, immediately after paying lip-service to the Socratic demand for knowledgeable discourse. Furthermore, 'the very profession of speaking well' translates '*professio bene dicendi*', where the semantic range of '*professio*' more or less exactly corresponds to that of 'profession' in its old-fashioned sense, viz. from 'public declaration' to 'occupation' ('what I profess to do'). Thus we might hear in Cicero's Latin a translated echo of Gorgias' profession 'Give me a theme!' – which, so Philostratus informed us, he cried out 'to demonstrate that he knew everything'.[17]

There is, however, an interesting inconsistency here with the tradition about Gorgias, or at least an ambiguity. Cicero does not say that the very profession of oratorical skill seems to promise ability to discourse *knowledgeably* on any subject, but rather just to speak 'elegantly and at length' on it. Evidently the Loeb translator felt the difficulty, and sought to ease it by mis-translating 'every subject whatsoever ... will be treated by him with both distinction and knowledge'. True, Cicero has just asserted that ignorant speech will be all but puerile, so that one might argue that by implication the Gorgianic elaboration and abundance which he advocates cannot, in fact, be achieved without knowledge. If this is indeed Cicero's train of thought,[18] then apparently he retains the Gorgianic paradigm of the persuader on every topic; implicitly accepts a watered-down version of the Socratic demand that speaking well means speaking knowledgeably; and waters down too the philosophers' claim that it is impossible for a universal science to underpin rhetoric, by implying that this is not impossible, just very, very rare. In fact, as Cicero remarked earlier, the number of brilliant orators has been and always will be minuscule, even compared to the number of accomplished political and military leaders (I 8). He thus keeps alive the middle-brow Isocratean vision of the orator who at the limit indeed 'knows', but only because his knowledge is some sort of approximation to polymathic competence, rather than mastery of the all-demanding, all-conquering *logos* to which Gorgias and Plato alike responded with pure extremism.

The Isocratean connection can be made much tighter. Having delivered his own fulsome encomium of the power of persuasion, Crassus asks:

> therefore who would not rightly marvel at this [viz. rhetoric – but see immediately below], and consider that one should exert oneself to the utmost so as to surpass men themselves in that unique respect wherein they are most superior to the animals? . . . Which other power could have brought scattered men together in a single place, or led them away from a wild and savage life to this human culture and political condition, or, when communities had been constituted, could have delineated legislation [*leges*], judicial investigations [*iudicia*], and rights [*iura*]? But, not to pursue the numerous [viz. achievements of rhetoric], which are almost innumerable, I shall sum them up in brief: this is my solemn belief, that not only his own dignity, but also the welfare both of very many private individuals and of the entire state depend to the highest degree on the moderation and wisdom of the perfect orator.

Protagoras (I 33–4)

There can be no doubt that this is Cicero's version of Isocrates' reworking of Protagoras in reaction to 'the Gorgias/*Gorgias* problematic'. Just as in Isocrates, it is the power of speech itself, rather than the cooperative social virtues of respect and shame which figured in the 'great *logos*', which places man above the animals, and which utterly dominates the narrative of evolution towards the state of full civilisation.[19] In fact, when Crassus asks us to 'marvel at this', the 'this' is, in context, not rhetoric, but our power to converse and express our feelings in language; and it is not until we reach the reference to the 'perfect orator' that we realise that Crassus has assumed that excelling in language is simply doing rhetoric, and that the 'power' he eulogises is the power of oratory. This power continues to operate today in the characteristically Roman elaboration of judicial distinctions. It is essential that one realise that this substitution does not reduce to the truism that the ability to communicate is necessary for even the most primitive social existence, although it might well trade on it. The *vis oratoris* is the power of persuasion, not the mere capacity to communicate. If language raises us all above the bestial state, the master-speaker analogously transcends the ordinary human condition (despite Cicero's earlier assumption of an ideal audience to match the omniscient orator). Once again, victory for rhetoric is achieved by evasion and obfuscation. Socrates' reaffirmation of Parmenides insisted that, so far from encompassing cogitation and communication in general, authentic *logos* is sharply limited to rational argument. The Isocratean/Ciceronian response is surreptitiously to expand *logos*/*vis oratoris* to encompass the rational faculties construed as broadly as possible, and thus to credit rhetoric alone with all the blessings of our rational civilisation (note how Crassus' description culminates in a list of judicial institutions which anyone would recognise as falling within the scope of a narrow, and uncontentious, conception of rhetoric).

Crassus' ideal orator on whom the state itself depends is close to divinity, far beyond comparison with any merely human potentate. Just as Isocrates extolled the forms of democratic persuasion when they were rapidly losing their original political significance, so Cicero's deification of the perfect speaker coincides with the marginalisation of the Senate in the last days of the Republic (followed shortly by the installation of a *Princeps*, *primus inter pares*, posthumously accorded divine honours). Isocrates and Cicero are the two great compensating fantasists of rhetoric. Socrates' commonwealth of dialectic, in which every citizen is equally (un)privileged, remains a mysterious paradigm of a distinctively philosophical democracy; the ideology of his rhetorical opponents serves up impotent dreams of political domination, itself masquerading as benign civic service.

'Whatever the subject from whatever branch of learning, of whatever type, the orator, as if he has studied a client's case, will speak of it better and more elegantly than the discoverer and originator of the thing himself' (I 51–2). Crassus backs up this claim with the assertion, reminiscent of Gorgias' description of how *logos* affects the *psychē*, that the pre-eminent efficacy of rhetoric resides in emotional manipulation (I 53). He further maintains that this working on the emotions arises from a thorough knowledge of human character, which the orator takes over from the philosopher.[20] Thus in a sense this knowledge is *not* his own. But, relying on the model of Roman legal practice, in which, unlike the Athenian system, advocates spoke on behalf of clients, Crassus implies that just as the judicial advocate gets up his client's case, so too the oratorical exponent of philosophical doctrine will assimilate the philosophy which he puts into words at once proper and effective (perhaps proper *because* effective). It is glibly assumed that such assimilation will prove equivalent to thorough knowledge of the philosophy.

Subsequently Crassus commits himself to the strong thesis that 'no one can be eloquent about anything of which he is ignorant', but conjoined with the denial that 'anyone can speak eloquently about the very thing he knows, not even if his knowledge is perfect, if he is ignorant of how to make and polish an oration'; he insists that what Socrates used to say, that everyone is sufficiently eloquent on what he knows, is plausible, but false (I 63). In §§62 ff., we are given a series of Greek and Roman examples exemplifying this symbiosis of knowledge and persuasion which speak volumes to readers of the *Gorgias*. Crassus contends that Philo the architect did indeed speak ably of his work to the Athenians, but *qua* orator, not *qua* architect; and Asclepiades the physician, a skilful debater, is a parallel case. But were Antonius, one of the participants in Cicero's dialogue, to speak on behalf of Hermodorus the naval architect, *qua* advocate he *would* himself have knowledge of Hermodorus' business. We are immediately put in mind of Gorgias' gloating description in the *Gorgias* of hapless experts, prime among them a doctor, enslaved by rhetorical power. Here, in total contrast, knowledgeable but ineloquent clients rely on persuasive advocates in amicable cooperation. Yet Crassus does not go so far as to make the relationship symmetrical: the advocates are persuasive *and* knowledgeable, albeit indirectly, through briefing, not persuasive but ignorant, as the *Gorgias* had charged.

Cotta and Sulpicius have invited Crassus to venture an opinion on whether there is an 'art' of speaking. Since '*ars*' is the Latin for '*technē*', he is answering the question put to Gorgias by Socrates in the *Gorgias*, but what he says is initially perplexing:

101

What? Do you now set me a trifling little question, for me to
express my opinion about, as if I were some idle and chattering Greekling, if perhaps a learned and erudite one? When
do you think I paid attention to and mulled over those things,
rather than always laughing at the impudence of those men,
who, when they have settled in a school, command anyone in
a great throng of people to say if he has any question to ask?
Which people say Gorgias of Leontini was the first to do, who
seemed to undertake and promise something enormous, in that
he declared himself prepared for anything about which anyone
might want to hear. Afterwards, indeed, they began to do this
commonly, and do it today, so that there is no subject, no
matter how great, unforeseen or novel, about which they will
not promise to say everything which can be said.

(I 102–4)

How is this consistent with the endorsement we discovered earlier
of a diluted Gorgianic paradigm, supplemented by the assimilation
of borrowed philosophical knowledge? The tone is indignantly
dismissive, and the disconcerting message seems to relegate
to the status of super-subtle Greek silliness 'the Gorgias/*Gorgias*
problematic' which has apparently shaped much of the progress of
Book I of the *De Oratore*. Crassus is heaping scorn on the real-life
caricature of his ideal orator, a mountebank who performs his cheap
improvisational tricks in schools or amphitheatres rather than
the vast civic arenas in which the master-speaker shines. At one level
– the simplest – Crassus is exploiting the standard opposition
theoretical (and fecklessly idle) Greek vs. practical (and politically
accomplished) Roman, a wildly popular polarity (with the Romans).
But at another, Cicero is ensuring he will win the game for rhetoric
against philosophy by changing the rules.

So far we have traced his complex, confusing interventions in
continually modified versions of 'the Gorgias/*Gorgias* problematic'.
Now he does not so much retract his contributions to that debate
as suggest that, from a certain traditionalist perspective, it is
ludicrously beside the point. The advantage of this tactic is that it
permits Crassus *not* to take the figure of Gorgias seriously. Although
it is just possible that his mockery does not extend to the founder
of the practice of universal extemporising, the phrase '*seemed* to
undertake and promise something enormous' probably implies that
Gorgias no less than contemporary rhetorical showmen is a cheat.

Crassus implies that this limitless eloquence is a transparent fake. But if the impudent trick is so obvious, it is equally obvious that only a chattering Greekling – a philosopher? – would be so foolish as to take it seriously. Any philosopher who assumes that genuine rhetoric has a case to answer, because Gorgias does, has grotesquely mistaken the ideal orator for a tedious buffoon. And if Gorgias is not to be taken seriously, then neither is the *Gorgias*. Since Plato could hardly have fallen into so vulgar a confusion, we have confirmation of what we anyway knew all along – that the *Gorgias*, so far from being a real onslaught on rhetoric, is actually a magnificent piece of rhetoric.

The *De Oratore* never achieves a final resolution; Cicero endlessly vacillates between ill-defined positions on whether eloquence requires knowledge by playing endlessly with the scope and substance of 'knowledge'. At least in terms of historical influence, this evasive action could not be more impressive, since the increasing currency of the Isocratean/Ciceronian compromise with 'the Gorgias/*Gorgias* problematic' in the culture at large was eventually to lead to the virtual equation of enlightened education with rhetorical training, broadly conceived on Ciceronian lines.

My analysis could with some plausibility be faulted for exhibiting gross bias in favour of philosophy. Throughout, my critique has been premissed on accusations of begging the question and changing the subject. But a reader more sympathetically disposed towards Isocrates and Cicero might object that the enjoyable narratives they offer up are neither more nor less than what one should properly expect from a rhetorician who tells a story, who makes a display, rather than engaging in argumentative dialectic. The rhetoricians, so the objection runs, might not *prove* that Socrates is in the wrong, but their adaptations of the 'great *logos*' *show* how he might be. To demand argumentative engagement from them is really to insist unfairly that they concede the struggle by virtue of conforming to the standards of the rival practice, philosophy. The accusation is not easy to answer. Possibly the best that can be said for my critique is that it articulates, from within the philosophical perspective, what is objectionable in the evasive reaction to 'the Gorgias/*Gorgias* problematic', with no further claim to neutral adjudication between the philosophical and rhetorical rivals. But perhaps the fantasist ideology of political domination which I claim to have discerned in the rhetoricians might tip the balance, even for those who are not *parti pris* in favour of philosophy.

ARISTIDES: THE SPEECH FOR THE DEFENCE

Aelius Aristides was a prolific and enormously successful rhetorician who lived in the second century CE, a time, generally known as the 'Second Sophistic', of greatly increased literary activity in the Greek part of the Roman empire. In keeping with this movement Aristides makes every effort to emulate certain aspects of his revered models of classical Attic prose. One of his most unusual productions is the *To Plato: In Defence of Rhetoric*,[21] which seeks to reply to the *Gorgias* in the greatest detail, and consequently at vast length. We shall find that often the key to understanding Aristides, whose *Defence* caps the tradition of evasive strategies in response to the *Gorgias*, is to remember the disparity between his actual historical and political circumstances and the literary conventions he takes over from the vanished classical past.[22]

Replying to the accusation that orators aim only at the approval of the masses, Aristides protests that

> the predominant characteristic of the nature of rhetoric is at the outset not to permit the occurrence of what the multitude approves, nor do orators consider anything more than what is best, nor does it escape the notice of peoples [*dēmoi*] themselves that orators are their superiors in reasoning about affairs . . . For if Plato's charge were true, and orators did not lead the *dēmoi*, but rather belonged to them, first of all what reverence and honour would they have from the *dēmoi*? Where would they obtain precedence or extraordinary privileges?
>
> (*In Defence of Rhetoric* 178–9)

Aristides further insists that the orator's commonplace warning that he is uttering uncomfortable but necessary home truths is to be taken at face-value.[23] He seems not to understand – or perhaps chooses to ignore – that the *Gorgias'* attack on the integrity of rhetoric is considerably more subtle than the simple accusation that the orator clumsily panders to the crowd. The charge, rather, is that the speaker and his auditors achieve a seductive complicity relying upon tacit, mutual reinforcement of both positions, as the orator feeds the self-esteem of his listeners.

It is the massive alteration in political circumstances which permits Aristides to put his confidence in what appears a singularly feeble reaction to Plato. The *Gorgias'* portrait of sedulous collusion between *rhētor* and *dēmos* derives its critical force from the undeniable and ineliminable tension which must subsist between a *democratic dēmos* and a persuader anxious to wield power. But, according to Aristides, the people freely acknowledge the orators' deliberative superiority, which they mark with all sorts of special prerogatives. (Aristides does not specify these privileges further, and it is not clear whether he is simply lumping together forensic orators and public deliberators with performing sophists – who had wealthy patrons – and teachers of rhetoric – who were often exempt from taxation under the empire.) In other words, he takes a post-democratic situation for granted. Bearing in mind that Aristides writes under Roman hegemony, we might go further: what he is happy to represent as a political constitution in which orators aristocratically guide affairs for the public weal was in fact a strong autocracy which meticulously maintained all the trappings of rhetorical debate as a means of sophisticated social control.

Later we are assured that if orators 'were the servants of the mobs [*ochloi*] and spouted what the audience approved, it would never have been possible for them to have spoken freely [*parrēsiasasthai*], nor to be proud beyond other men' (188–9). Here '*parrhēsia*' functions not as the watchword of the radical democracy, the public speech freely available, in principle, to *all* citizens, but rather designates a liberty reserved for the leaders. Fitting names for the orator are 'ruler', 'overseer', 'teacher' (190): the relation of orator to *dēmos* corresponds fully to that of teacher to children (ibid.).

> The leader leads the chorus, the helmsman the sailors, the general the soldiers, the orator the *dēmos*. Thus all rulers are naturally stronger than those beneath them. If someone with authority *also* gratifies, by persuading rather than compelling, and in addition to preserving his own status also aims at the desires of those beneath him, he is the real political man.
>
> (192–3, emphasis added)

That is, the authentic politician is a benevolent, paternalistic emperor. Persuasive power, aiming at the *desires* of the ruled, is no more than an appendix to brute compulsive power.[24] Having independently hit upon the best course to pursue, in a position to implement his decisions regardless of the views or feelings of the populace, the ruler dispensing rhetoric merely gratifies them humanely when he can do so without any compromise to policy.

Following a now altogether familiar pattern, Aristides represents rhetoric as 'having the greatest share of *logos*, or rather as being entirely in *logos*' (204). But, as we have come to anticipate, recognition that it might be important to discriminate between *types* of *logos* is absent. He produces a variant of the genetic story. Men naturally fall into two classes, stronger and weaker. Originally, the stronger relied on their superior strength to exploit the weaker. Rhetoric, 'the amulet of justice and the bond of human life', developed to right this gross wrong, 'so that affairs should not be decided for anyone by main force, weapons, anticipation, numbers, size, nor any other inequality, but that *logos* should determine what is just in peace' (210–11).

Aristides also provides his own adaptation of the 'great *logos*'. In his version, as in Isocrates', humanity's salvation resides in verbal skill; but Aristides goes even further in his modification of Protagoras. In the beginning men perished in droves, prey to wild animals – and they perished *in silence* (395–6). Solicited by Prometheus, Zeus dispatches Hermes to mankind's rescue with rhetoric itself (396). But – and this is the most glaring 'correction' of the 'great *logos*', where justice and shame are universally distributed – he orders Hermes to dispense rhetoric selectively: he is 'to choose the best, the noblest and those with the strongest natures' (397). Consequently 'they discovered the beginning [or principle: *archē*] of community' (398). There follows a paean to *logos* (indeterminate *logos*, of course) highly reminiscent of Isocrates, in which it is predictably identified as the agent responsible for all further civic developments (398–9).

Evidently speaking of himself, Aristides acknowledges that opportunities for deliberative rhetoric have largely disappeared under the empire, but insists that were he even to speak to himself alone, he would nevertheless thereby 'have honoured the nature of *logoi* and the beauty in them' (430). And thus, ultimately, Aristides' lengthy answer to Plato is a 'defence of rhetoric' only inasmuch as his own voice has achieved a curiously unpersuasive loneliness, at odds with his glorification of *logos* as mythical creator of the human community. The orator does not truckle to tyrants, he is not beholden to any audience – but only because he lacks one. In the *Gorgias* Plato represents Socrates as so strongly wedded to the dialectical method that when Callicles refuses to cooperate in the examination of his views, Socrates is obliged to fulfil the rôles of both questioner and respondent. This marks a genuine breakdown in the dialectic, but the rupture is only temporary. In contrast, Aristides' striking representation of himself as perfectly autonomous, engaged in pure self-communion, purchases liberation from 'the Gorgias/*Gorgias* problematic' only at the cost of sacrificing all persuasive power. It is time to turn to an infinitely more ambitious, if no less contentious, effort at compromise between Gorgias and Socrates.

5

ARISTOTLE'S *RHETORIC*
Mighty is the truth and it shall prevail?

. . . and Aristotle challenged Isocrates himself . . .

(Cicero, *Orator* 62)

EPISTEMOLOGICAL OPTIMISM

Aristotle's *Rhetoric* is a deeply provocative, almost shocking text. It is rhetoric's near-total domination of both general and political culture in the West from the time of the Roman Republic down to at least the beginning of the nineteenth century which has dulled our appreciation of its polemical power; for it eventually achieved a position in the regiment of canonical handbooks equalling Cicero's in influence. How can the *Rhetoric* shock, when it so perfectly exemplifies our most venerable educational tradition? Only – or, at least, most effectively – by the shattering of that same tradition. If nowadays 'rhetoric' and its etymological kin in the Romance languages tend to suggest, in ordinary parlance, no more than the dissembling, manipulative abuse of linguistic resources for self-serving ends, we have assembled abundant evidence that the mere mention of 'rhetoric' in fourth-century BCE Athens would have evoked a host of similar, and similarly sinister, associations. Thus Aristotle was the immediate inheritor of the violent controversy over the nature and power of persuasion initiated by Gorgias and given enduring form by Plato in his *Gorgias*.[1] The pronounced contemporary tendency (to put it no more strongly) to feel disquieted by the mere mention of 'rhetoric' should help us to appreciate that if the *Rhetoric* was finally instrumental in forging the ruling cultural consensus on the legitimacy of persuasive training, no such consensus existed when it was constructed.

Even the most casual perusal of Aristotle's opening case for the legitimacy and utility of rhetoric in the first chapter of the first book

108

reveals that the *Gorgias*' argument with Gorgias set the terms on which Aristotle wished to see his own project assessed. The famous first words, 'rhetoric is the counterpart of dialectic' (1354A1), flatly reject Socrates' uncompromising thesis that philosophical arguments are *categorially* distinct from rhetorical pleas. And while the Platonic Gorgias had, embarrassingly, a struggle to demonstrate what rhetoric is about 'in particular', here rhetoric's very generality in grasping what is persuasive (and what is not) is just the respect – topic-neutrality – in which it so closely resembles dialectic; for dialectic is also of universal application in testing and sustaining argument (1354A4–6, 1355B8–9).

As for the utility of rhetoric, Aristotle contends that 'even the most exact knowledge' would not make persuading certain people any easier. Such knowledge is characteristic of teaching, which – apparently because of the orator's typical audience (a multitude, not a select gathering) – is impossible in the rhetorical situation (1355A24–9). Precisely that impossibility had, in the *Gorgias*, led to the lethal inference that rhetoric can be effective only to the extent that it trades on ignorance. Aristotle, in contrast, concludes that it proceeds on the basis of 'common' assumptions and beliefs, and so feels able to convert what, in Plato, had been a devastating criticism of rhetoric into an advantage. The effectiveness of Aristotle's manœuvre depends on the intrinsic interest and plausibility of his anti-Platonic presumption that the non-philosophical multitude is far from ignorant, if also far below the heights of penetration, accuracy and learning which only those who know achieve ('easy learning is naturally pleasant for all', 1410B10–11).

But by far the most audacious of all Aristotle's claims on behalf of rhetoric is the very first ground he alleges for its utility:

> rhetoric is useful because what is true and what is just are natu-rally stronger than their opposites, so that if legal judgements do not turn out correctly, truth and justice are necessarily defeated by their opposites, and this deserves censure.
>
> (1355A24)[2]

If losers are blameworthy – obviously, only those with justice on their side are to be considered here – that must be due to their stupidly squandering the advantage conferred on them by the rightness of their cause. It is rather as if 'the facts' automatically communicate themselves, so that if the wiles of our (unjust) opponents threaten to interfere with the true message, our rhetorical expertise does come into play, but only to serve the strictly ancillary function of countering interference from the other side. What Aristotle sees as the natural advantage enjoyed by the truth is hardly abundantly clear at this point, it must be admitted. He might mean that people tend, at least in normal circumstances, to recognise the truth, and that the reason for this tendency is something to do with their psychology.[3] Or – and the possibilities are not necessarily exclusive – he might mean that the truth is *intrinsically* more plausible, although people are cognitively neutral with regard to their reactions to truth and untruth. (One might similarly contrast having a test for gold with gold's being of such a sort that it is very hard to make something which looks just like it, but isn't.)

Nothing could be further removed than this benign vision from Gorgias' proclamation in the *Encomium* that 'a single *logos* written with skill, not uttered in truth, pleases and persuades a great crowd [*ochlos*]' (§13). At this juncture Aristotle approximates much more closely to Plato's reassuringly moralistic Gorgias, who insists that rhetoric *properly* deployed will never abet injustice (*Gorgias* 456E ff.). But Aristotle's position is actually even more extreme: the Platonic Gorgias merely asserts that rhetoric *should* not, not that it *could* not, go wrong, whereas Aristotle insists that the defeat of justice is blameworthy – and that must be because he supposes that, other things being equal, truth and justice will prove victorious, where 'other things' are the comparative levels of verbal skill of the contestants. Defeat of justice is to be deplored because victory for it is – 'naturally' – easy. So, although for the Platonic Gorgias rhetoric is an ethically neutral tool or weapon, and much the same holds good for Aristotle, the latter makes the significant addition that circumstances 'naturally' – and so routinely – favour the morally upright use, not the corrupt abuse, of the instruments of persuasion. Thus, for Aristotle, rhetoric *could* indeed go wrong – after all, what are our opponents up to? – but not very wrong, since the nature of things itself militates against persistent malpractice in the field of persuasion.

Aristotle's confidence that truth prevails readily accounts for the equanimity with which he deliberately concedes to the *Gorgias* that rhetorical 'teaching' is an impossibility. If truth is naturally more powerful than untruth, then presumably even people unfitted for full-scale knowledge, both intrinsically and as a consequence of their situation in an arena of public debate, might nevertheless 'naturally' incline towards correct verdicts, 'naturally' attain a state of true (if unjustified and perhaps unarticulated) belief.[4] So Aristotle's confidence that rhetoric defeats the accusation levelled in the *Gorgias* – that it succeeds only at the cost of pandering to ignorance – stems from an assurance that truth and justice are natural victors. But what are the precise implications of such epistemological optimism?[5]

This view that grasping the truth is a natural achievement is expressed elsewhere in the *Rhetoric*: 'to speak without qualification, what is true and what is better are always naturally easier to argue for and more persuasive' (1355A37–8). *Physics* II 8 teaches us that what is natural occurs 'always or for the most part'. Disputes in which truth is worsted by falsehood must, therefore, be somehow 'unnatural'. Two ways for truth to be defeated suggest themselves: our just cause may be defeated because we are ourselves 'unnaturally' puny in disputation, so that our audience falls prey to malicious rhetoric despite the persuasive edge truth lends us; or our political arrangements may themselves go against nature, in that they lessen the advantage those in the right ought to enjoy, and usually do. In either case, such aberrations cannot be plentiful. Again, the contrast with Gorgias' triumphant '*logos* is a great *dynastēs*' – over *both* right and wrong – could not be greater.

One final, crucial, quotation on this topic from the *Rhetoric*:

> to see both the truth and what is similar to it belongs to one and the same capacity, and at the same time people have a sufficient natural disposition towards truth, and in most cases they reach it; that is why someone likely to hit on reputable opinions is also someone likely to hit on the truth.
>
> (1355A14–18)

The notion that people are naturally disposed towards truth calls to mind perhaps the most celebrated declaration in Aristotle, the opening words of the *Metaphysics*: 'all men naturally desire to know' (989A21). This striking parallel forces us to look for light to throw on the epistemological optimism of the *Rhetoric* outside as well as within the *Rhetoric* itself. In fact, the optimistic pronouncements of the *Rhetoric* are obviously continuous with Aristotle's descriptions of his dialectical method, which are of such consuming interest to students of philosophical methodology: witness the *Rhetoric's* mention of the capacity to hit on 'reputable opinions', the raw material from which Aristotle ultimately refines his finished theories.[6] The proper approach must be to explore his portrayal of people as trackers of the truth both philosophically *and* rhetorically.

We should also carefully register the connection between Aristotle's rehabilitation of rhetoric on the basis of the remarkable prevalence of truth and Parmenides' original assurance that truth is in itself persuasive. Gorgias' reaction was to deny the distinctiveness of philosophical reasoning; his is a monolithic conception of *logos*, according to which would-be persuaders evidently differ only in the skill with which they attempt to manipulate their audiences. Plato's reaction to Gorgias was to reinstate the Parmenidean antithesis between *logos* as argument and 'mere' words. Finally, Aristotle's reaction to Plato's reaction hardly endorses the rejected Gorgianic extreme – persuading the many is *not* teaching them, rhetoric is *not* philosophy – but does perhaps speak of an ambition to reach a new conceptual unity: one which, unlike Parmenides' volatile combination, might survive the strains generated by the conflict between competing images of what persuasion is, and of how it might best be achieved.

INVALID PERSUASION

The issue we should now address can be formulated more sharply: a reader of the *Rhetoric*, properly impressed at the start by its expressions of epistemological optimism, would reasonably become troubled on discovering that more than a few of the persuasive techniques outlined in the sequel are at best neutral with regard to the truth, and on occasion downright misleading.[7] In parallel, a reader of the *Topics*, encouraged by the impression that this work offers instruction in the positive philosophical task of the construction and inspection of definitions, might very well be brought up short with a rude shock on coming to Book VIII and the *Sophistici Elenchi* ('*Sophistical Refutations*'): what has this intimidating catalogue of tricky procedure and fallacies to do with authentic philosophical dialectic? There are, of course, standard, dismissive responses to both problems: in the case of dialectic, that Aristotle's intention is purely prophylactic; in the case of rhetoric, that his refreshingly anti-Platonic realism induces him to grapple with political realities, including the murkier ones, even if this means that his hands get dirty while the detached philosopher's stay clean.

We should resist such pat reactions, investigating some of the evidence for Aristotle's tolerating, or even conniving at, invalid persuasion. By 'invalid' I intend something much less formal and more flexible than strictly logical invalidity, taking in whatever might properly strike us as we go along as at least veering towards argumentative impropriety, and 'impropriety' here applies to any feature of debate designed to occlude or suppress the truth for the sake of victory. (This might seem to beg an important question, by assuming that we will indeed be struck by what goes wrong, regardless of our background, or lack of it, in logic and dialectic. Evidently that is not so: we all do come to the task with some experience in the construction and evaluation of argument, and expect our performance to improve as we proceed.) Then we shall try to square our conclusions with Aristotle's commitment to the persuasive force of truth, always comparing and contrasting the rhetorical and dialectical material.

Alongside the issue of consistency, we shall also examine that of triviality – although in the nature of the case results here are bound to prove inconclusive. It would be grotesque to suppose that the description in the *Metaphysics* of *homo philosophicus* entails that everyone aspires to be, or has the capacity to become, a fully-fledged philosopher. The evidence Aristotle cites in support of his contention that the desire to know is universal is that we all take pleasure in the exercise of our senses (980A21–2); and presumably the proto-intellectual aspirations of some people never get beyond the satisfaction they take in perception. By the same token, in the rhetorical context our natural intellectualism means only that 'easy learning is naturally pleasant' (1410B10–11), not that abstruse, demanding argument will delight a mass audience. The examples of devices for captivating auditors in III 10, such as metaphor, come with the warning that, although we must avoid the flatly obvious, we should also not make things too difficult: 'quick learning' (1410B21) is the goal of 'smart' rhetorical language (cf. 'the function of rhetoric . . . lies among such listeners as are not able to see many things at once or to reason from a distant starting-point' (1357A1–4)).[8]

The issue of triviality is thus the worry that, despite its lofty Parmenidean associations, our natural appetite for the truth might be too easily sated (remember Gorgias' excuse for passing over the events leading up to Helen's departure for Troy): so Aristotle's deployment of the idea that we all desire to know can perhaps be seen as yet another prime but unrecognised component of his reaction to 'the Gorgias/*Gorgias* problematic'. But again, if Aristotle, unlike Gorgias, escapes the suspicion that the drives to pleasure and to knowledge conflict rather than combine, that might only be because the truth we all desire to know has been surreptitiously devalued, is a truth so mediocre that his response to the separation of rhetoric from teaching in the *Gorgias* sounds hollow.

LEGITIMATE FEELINGS

Still within the first chapter of Book I, Aristotle deprecates rhetorical appeals to the *pathē*: 'slander and pity and anger and such emotions of the soul have no bearing on the issue, but are directed at the juryman' (1354A16–18). Since Gorgias' *logos* had bragged that *logos* is 'able to stop fear, remove pain, implant joy and augment pity' (*Encomium of Helen* §8), one might be tempted to conclude that here Aristotle, by sternly and unqualifiedly forbidding the orator to touch the emotions of his audience, also unqualifiedly abjures Gorgianic rhetoric in favour of Platonic philosophy. His enterprise of mediating between Gorgias and Plato would then be doomed from the outset, since the modes of persuasion ostensibly rejected in I 1 are examined in detail later in the *Rhetoric*, and they most certainly do not conform to a programme of exclusively rationalistic persuasion.[9] The temptation should be resisted: one of the crowning virtues of Aristotelian philosophy of mind is precisely that it permits us to drive a wedge between the concept of emotional appeal and that of emotional manipulation. Thought and desire combine in the act of deliberation to constitute the choices which are the precondition for fully rational human behaviour. Philosophical analysis detects intellectual and affective aspects in deliberation, but this analytical distinction is just that: it does not reflect a difference in kind in the soul between reason and passion.

The consequences for rhetorical theory could not be more radical. Whatever version of the Platonic *psychē* one chooses, Platonic emotions are irrational, not in the sense that they are reducible to, say, simple tastes or tactile feelings, but rather because they are, by definition, unmotivated and unmodified by the full-blown, active rationality most evident in philosophical *logos*. In complete contrast, Aristotelian emotions are permeated by reason. When for instance I unhappily perceive a state of affairs as unfortunate and react accordingly, I do indeed perceive it *as* unfortunate: cognitive, evaluative and affective responses are, apart from pathological cases, typically indissoluble. This is not, of course, to pretend that

114

misperception (along any of these dimensions – cognitive, evaluative, affective) does not occur; but it *is* to insist that emotion as such must not and cannot be prised apart from *logos* and then, inevitably, disparaged.

> There are three sorts of credibility [*pistis*] furnished by the *logos*: those residing in the character of the speaker, those residing in the disposition of the hearer, and those residing in the *logos* itself, through its demonstrating or seeming to demonstrate.
>
> (1356A1–4)[10]

Aristotle here acknowledges not only that rhetoric includes aspects irreducible to argument (that is, *ostensible* argument), but also that those aspects enjoy a certain (limited) independence. Explaining the second, emotive, means of persuasion, he says that '[the orator persuades] through his hearers, when they are led into *pathos* by the *logos*; for when pained, or enjoying ourselves, we do not render judgement in the way we do when loving or hating' (1356A14–16).[11] The possibility is thus left open that the *proper* use of rhetorical skill will indeed speak to our emotions, but only when the *pathē* so formed enhance our receptivity to truthful *logos*, rather than setting our feelings at odds with our reasoning. Aristotle's simile likening rhetoric to an 'offshoot' of dialectic and politics (1356A25–7) indicates a refusal either to assimilate or to sunder reasoning and affective motivation: this intricate scheme is intended at once to divide and to unify. Although rhetoric is a 'part and likeness' of dialectic (1356A30–1), in general its arguments, even when valid, do not meet the high (and inappropriate) standards of theoretical investigation: they are *real* arguments for all that.

Perhaps, then, the comment in the first chapter that the arousal of emotion is 'directed at the juryman' without any 'bearing on the issue' might be restricted to abusive emotional manipulation; after all, Aristotle insists a little later that 'one must not *warp* the juryman by leading him into anger or envy or pity; that would be like making the rule one were about to use crooked' (1354A24–6). Were this injunction not limited to *improper* emotional manipulation, then it would, say, permit an orator condemning theft or murder to encourage his listeners to use their practical reason to infer that what he condemns is wrong, but prohibit him from further urging them to react angrily to real wrongdoing: in that case, 'warping' would be caused by any emotional addition whatsoever to reason. But

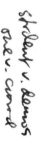

Aristotelian philosophy of mind forces us to realise that the good orator in arguing and in influencing our feelings need not be engaged in two disparate activities. Just as the perception of something as unfortunate is a unitary state, so my persuading you to see it as such is a single, if highly complex, act of rhetoric.

I conclude that what Aristotle rejects is not emotional appeal *per se*, but rather emotional appeals which have no 'bearing on the issue', in that the *pathe* they stimulate lack, or at any rate are not shown to possess, any intrinsic connection with the point at issue – as if an advocate were to try to whip an anti-Semitic audience into a fury because the accused is Jewish; or as if another in drumming up support for a politician were to exploit his listeners' reverential feelings for the politician's ancestors. Harmonising the rational and the emotive features of rhetoric may well prove difficult, but it does not, after all, give good grounds for fearing that Aristotle's attempt to reconcile Gorgias and Plato must founder at the outset. Whether the *Rhetoric*'s later prescriptions for shaping *logos* with *pathos* can be similarly justified, however, remains to be seen.

SPEAKING ON BOTH SIDES

> Further, one must be able to persuade people of opposite cases, just as in syllogisms too, not in order to do both – for one must not persuade people to what is wrong[12] – but so that the state of things should not escape us, and so that if someone else uses *logoi* unjustly we shall ourselves be able to refute them. None of the other arts argues for opposites; dialectic and rhetoric alone do this, because they are both similarly about opposites.
>
> (1355A29–36)

The standard conservative reaction to the sophistical rhetorician was (and is) the claim that he is able to make the worse case appear better.[13] Aristotle does not, unlike the Platonic Gorgias, suggest that it is up to rhetorical expertise itself to ensure that the verbal dexterity it imparts is never used to further evil ends; but he does share the idea that when rhetoric functions as a weapon rather than a tool, it is only for defence.

How is it that the capacity to speak persuasively on both sides enables the rhetorician to recognise 'the state of things'? When philosophers engage in dialectic for the sake of investigation, that is because the truth is not yet known, or at any rate not yet understood and explained according to the high epistemic standards appropriate to philosophy; thus, if they are uncertain about the (im)mortality of the soul, for example, the ability to argue both *pro* and *contra* might very well strengthen comprehension on both sides of the argumentative resources available for resolution of the point at issue. But it is hard to see how an analogous ability might help the upright rhetorician. Surely he should never seek to persuade unless he is certain of the rightness of his cause; and so no need or occasion for rhetoric would ever arise comparable to the need or occasion for investigative dialectic wherever the truth is unknown or not fully clear (in the relaxed sense in which one might be said to have or lack 'knowledge' of such issues as fall within the scope of rhetorical debate).

In asserting that having justice on one's side and knowing it are prerequisites for legitimate rhetorical activity, I do not mean to imply that the competent, honourable rhetorician must approximate to the condition of the *phronimos*, Aristotle's paragon of moral perfection, always reaching and abiding by correct decisions for the right reasons. By Aristotle's lights, one could indeed be an expert in persuasion and never misapply one's skills while nevertheless being something less than a moral exemplar. What I have in mind is rather that if, say, the rhetorician were to elect to pursue someone in the courts on a charge of assault in the belief that that person had attacked the rhetorician's father in the marketplace, both the factual belief that the assault had occurred and the ethical supposition that the attack is an outrage warranting retribution would be as well-founded as such beliefs can be. Again, if acting as a *logographos*, a professional speechwriter, the rhetorician would not produce a discourse for another unless justifiably convinced of his client's *bona fides*.

It might be supposed that the analogy with investigative dialectic would look more promising were we to switch rhetorical genres. Judicial rhetoric concerns only past fact and the application of (let us assume) uncontentious moral principles, so that it affords the ideal Aristotelian orator no grounds for uncertainty. But perhaps deliberative rhetoric, since it concerns future contingencies and the more or less likely outcomes of alternative policies, is a better prospect for comparison with dialectic. Just as philosophers are not sure about the soul, so, one might argue, rhetoricians participating in political debate are not sure about whether, say, the Athenians ought to dispatch a hostile fleet to Sicily. But once more the analogy does not survive inspection. Since Aristotle believes that ethics and politics are fully integrated, his orator should be in no more doubt at the level of principle that imperial expansionism is (let us assume) wrong than he is about the culpability of assault.[14] At the factual level, he should also know as well as such things can be known what the most likely consequence of the expedition might be.[15]

Any linkage between the rhetorical capacity to speak persuasively on both sides, and improved insight into 'the state of things', thus remains obscure. The conclusion which suggests itself is that Aristotle is reacting to a perennial misgiving: since rhetoric is an amoral power, nothing prevents its immoral operation. I have argued that the natural prevalence of truth, its persuasive superiority, is intended to offset mistrust of rhetoric. Perhaps the seemingly fruitless attempt to associate rhetoric's undeniable, and undeniably suspicious, 'two-sidedness' with improvement in knowledge is a further facet of Aristotle's defensive reaction to that misgiving.[16]

SNEAKY QUESTIONS

My procedure up to this point has been to make us doubt that characterisations of investigative dialectic can be transferred to (proper) rhetoric. But the problem becomes considerably more interesting, if not necessarily any more tractable, if we entertain some scepticism about the positive rôle which has been straightforwardly attributed to dialectic hitherto. Only investigative dialectic has been under discussion; but there are other varieties, and any reader of Plato's *Euthydemus* will have learnt that distinguishing between them, and correspondingly between the dialectician/philosopher and eristic/sophist, is not at all straightforward.

Since for Aristotle the classic dialectical encounter involves a respondent attempting to avoid refutation in answering questions on his set topic put to him by the questioner, one of the first issues broached in his disquisition on the theory and practice of dialectic is how such questions are best formulated. In *Topics* VIII 1 he distinguishes between 'necessary' premisses ('necessary', that is, as warranting the questioner's inferences (155B29)), and those which one must get the respondent to concede (155B19). Among this latter class of propositions are those used 'to conceal the conclusion' (155B23): these are 'for the sake of the contest; but since all such business is directed against someone else, it is necessary to employ these too' (155B26–8; cf. 155B10).

118

One might have thought that use of these camouflaging premises would count as a flagrant breach of dialectical propriety; if not an instance of invalidity in the narrow sense, its purpose is still the deliberate confusion of the respondent (cf. 156A7–13).[17] But Aristotle is not dissecting some shady sophistical dodge: 'all such business' refers to dialectic in its entirety, of whatever kind. Nor is this problem limited to premises to be sought from the respondent; 'necessary' ones 'should not be laid out immediately' (155B29–30), again just to make things as difficult as possible. Aristotle sums up:

> to speak generally, one putting questions stealthily must enquire in this way: so that when the *logos* in its entirety has been presented in question-and-answer form, and he has uttered the conclusion, one [presumably the respondent, and everyone but the questioner?] searches for the reason why.
>
> (156A13–15)

According to Aristotle's own theory of demonstration,[18] we understand something when we are in possession of its explanation; and explanation *is* 'the reason why'. So the dialectical questioner succeeds when he bewilders the respondent, when he *deprives* him of the understanding Aristotle himself insists is constitutive of the philosophical enterprise.[19] If this reminds us of anything in Plato, it is Dionysodorus' odious boast that 'everything we ask is similarly inescapable' (*Euthydemus* 276E5).

To reformulate and complicate the puzzle, if all dialectic is 'directed *against* someone else' – is a 'contest' – however can it serve as even a fallible guide to the truth? The point of contests is, after all, winning; if the dialectician invariably competes to win, then will he not fight, and fight dirtily, against an opponent who happens to be defending a true thesis, or attacking a false one? Surely competitive dialectic and rhetoric alike are vivid manifestations of the ruthless, agonistic tenor of Athenian civilisation which tore its fabric so violently that it more than occasionally threatened to dissolve into anarchy.

PHILOSOPHICAL AGGRESSION

Once more help is to be sought by returning to the *Gorgias*. Remember Socrates' insistence that his argumentative challenges and objections are 'not for your sake, but for the *logos*, so that it will advance in the fashion best able to render what is under discussion clear to us' (453C2–4). His model of (investigative) dialectic opens the paradoxical possibility that opponents might, at a deeper level, be partners in the search for truth.[20] The dialectical encounter remains a contest in which questioner and respondent strive to win (within limits, perhaps indeterminate ones). But, on the crucial condition that their motive is philosophical and impersonal, their discussion might track the truth despite its agonistic structure; in fact, it is that very structure which improves dialectic's efficacy as a tool for philosophical research, since its combativeness constantly guards at least against arguments passing muster too easily.

This Socratic precedent certainly enables us to begin to understand how the *Topics* might justifiably offer advice about concealed questioning on the grounds that 'all such business is directed against someone else', without thereby disastrously collapsing the distinction between edifying dialectic and repulsive eristic. But the *Euthydemus* issues a sharp reminder. Only a thoroughly naïve reader of that dialogue would conclude, complacently, that the difference between Socrates and the sophistical brothers is palpably obvious: a large part of the deftness of Plato's denunciation of sophistry lies in the care with which he makes it clear how unclear the gulf separating Socrates from Euthydemus and Dionysodorus might be. Even if huge, it will nevertheless remain invisible to onlookers unaware of the spirit in which they debate. Socrates' dialectical moves may be 'for the *logos*', not for self-aggrandisement at the cost of humiliating others; but that of itself will not help an observer of his dialectical behaviour to discriminate his philosophical aspirations from the brothers' sordid ambitions.[21]

One might protest that the *Topics* does not really attribute such aggressive tactics to the philosopher. Immediately after the manifesto that dialectic 'is directed against someone else', Aristotle seems to say that, in complete contrast to the dialectician, the philosopher does *not* argue combatively:

> it is of no concern to the philosopher and the individual enquirer, if the propositions constituting his argument are true and familiar, and the respondent does not accept them because they are closely linked to the starting-point of his argument, and because he anticipates what will follow. Rather, the philosopher might even be keen for axioms as familiar and close as possible, since scientific arguments are constructed from them.
>
> (155B10–16)

But so far from being complete, the contrast is superficial. First, although Aristotle does intend us to mark the difference between dialectic, which is *essentially* relational, and 'individual enquiry', this means, not that philosophical investigation cannot proceed dialectically, but that it need not. Second, and crucially, the passage does not say that when the philosopher works dialectically, he does not care about winning (for the sake of the truth) without qualification. The implication is instead that if he is thwarted in some particular dialectical match for the reasons stated, he goes away happy because (in this instance) the respondent's refusal to concede the argument (and so *formally* to concede victory to the questioner) is, if anything, a sign that he is on the right philosophical track. One might usefully compare those occasions in Platonic dialogues when Socrates' interlocutors dig their heels in; usually (if not always – consider Protagoras in the *Protagoras*) their refusal to cooperate signifies that Socrates is pursuing a telling line of argument, although his opponent/partner's stalling tactics mean that an explicit *elenchos* cannot happen.

The relevance of all this ambiguity and potential confusion in the sphere of dialectic to the viability of Aristotle's conception of rhetoric should be readily apparent. The natural prevalence of truth dictates that in rhetoric we are prone to be persuaded of the truth (or at the very least are not actually inclined to be taken in by falsehood), while in dialectic we are likely to draw nearer to philosophical understanding of the way things are (and not take each other in with a packet of fallacies). Our point of departure was the *aporia* of how Aristotle's epistemological optimism might be reconciled with his unembarrassed recommendation of what look to be some extremely dodgy argumentative tactics. If a general, 'Socratic' strategy is available for vindicating the presence of agonistic debate within dialectic (that is, if interlocutors can come that much closer to the truth by virtue of impersonally motivated competition), then we might try to transfer that strategy to rhetoric, to vindicate *its* exploitation of some less than scrupulously fair combative techniques. Of course, how successful we would be might vary from case to case; but in large measure it will hinge on one vital issue which has not yet been settled. I have maintained that 'anything goes' is not a rule in dialectic; but I have still to fix even the rough location of the bounds within which dialectical competitors must operate. So, before we can judge the success of something like a 'Socratic' strategy in justifying epistemological optimism in rhetoric, we must first consider just how unscrupulous Aristotle is prepared to imagine the *non*-sophistical disputant in dialectic might be.

RULES OF THE DIALECTICAL GAME

First, Aristotle recommends that the crafty questioner should occasionally resort to self-objection: 'for respondents are not disposed to be suspicious of those who *seem* to be arguing fairly' (156B18–20); if this does not entail that skilful dialectical argument presents the mere semblance of fairness, it also does nothing to exclude it.[22]

Second, note Aristotle's advice with regard to popular beliefs:

> and it is useful to say as well that 'this sort of thing is habitual and widely said'; for if they have no objection, they hesitate to unsettle what is customary. At the same time, because they themselves are making use of such things, they also guard against unsettling them.
>
> (156B20–3)

Now, in his confrontation with Callicles, in the final third of the *Gorgias*, Socrates bitingly dismisses from consideration arguments constructed from premises which may be popularly endorsed, but to which he has not committed himself. The only witness to the truth of interest to him at this point is Callicles, since, by Socrates' own rules, his interlocutor is *committed* to his dialectical assertions (*Gorgias* 471E2–472D4). But since the *endoxa*, the 'reputable opinions', to which the Aristotelian dialectician must attend are beliefs which commend themselves either to everyone, or to the majority, or to the wise (*Topics* 100B21–3), his admirers might contend that the stated goal of paying heed to collections of *endoxa* as comprehensive as possible is a good index of the superiority of Aristotle's method over Socrates': while Socrates gathers dialectical results piecemeal, satisfied with the all too often inconclusive outcomes of his one-on-one encounters, Aristotle's catholicity promises far more substantive results. But throwing in 'this sort of thing is habitual and widely said' in the hope that the respondent cannot find any objection seems expressly designed to cow him, to intimidate, precisely to make him bow to the popular consensus[23] of which Socrates was so scornful. And if the respondent himself also derives his ammunition from *endoxa*, Aristotelian disputants would seem to be in danger of succumbing to a degree of dialectical conformism inimical to genuine philosophical endeavour.[24]

are we investigating or competing?

Aristotle now turns (*Topics* VIII 4) from prescriptions for the questioner to recommendations for the respondent. The remarks he makes about the different species of dialectic go some distance towards countering the unfavourable impression of his method which his readers have perhaps begun to form. This text is of such seminal importance that it deserves quotation *in extenso*:

> people teaching or learning do not have the same targets as people competing, and the latter do not have the same targets as people who spend their time with one another in order to carry out an investigation. This is because the learner must always state what he believes, since no one so much as attempts to teach something false. In contrast, when people are competing, the questioner must at all costs appear to be having an effect, while the respondent must appear not to be affected at all. And in dialectical gatherings, when people propound arguments not to compete, but to test someone and to carry out an investigation, the respondent's goal, and what sort of thing he should grant and what he should not, with a view to the proper or improper defence of his position, have not yet been articulated.
>
> (VIII 5, 159A26–36; cf. *Soph. El.* 10 ff., 171A38–B9)

One might argue that this passage puts paid to my effort to establish that Aristotle's epistemological optimism is fraught with ambiguities, since it so emphatically separates benign varieties of dialectic from malign ones. Take, in particular, my earlier claim that 155B26–8 is to be construed as indicating that cut-throat competition is a generic characteristic of dialectic: the present text suggests to the contrary that only one type of dialectic is brutally agonistic, and that employment of propositions 'to conceal the conclusion' and other such unseemliness go no further than nastily competitive dialectic. Therefore, the complaint runs, my rendering of 155B26–8 and 155B10 as saying that dialectic is 'directed *against* someone else' is a tendentious over-translation: while the Greek could bear such a construction, we can now see that it only means that dialectic is an essentially *relational* activity.[25]

Is this really so? First, that the targets of the different species of dialectic are different need not entail that their procedures are also (entirely) distinct: one moral of the *Euthydemus*, as we have seen, is that sophistry is so readily confused with philosophy because the difference between their respective motivations, while fundamental, might nevertheless remain invisible. All that can be *seen* is aggressive argumentation. Second, perhaps what singles out 'competitive' dialectic as a species is not competition *per se*, but rather the necessity of appearing[26] to strike or avoid a blow '*at all costs*' (159A31). Third, the statement that dialectical gatherings are 'not to compete, but to test someone and to carry out an investigation' should be construed (in the light of all the passages in which a relatively unbridled, global, agonistic tendency in dialectic is made clear) as meaning not that dialectic 'proper' is not a contest, but that its *raison d'être* is not winning, as it is of eristic (*Soph. El.* 171B22 ff.).[27] In a manner reminiscent of the doctrine of double effect, such a stance could be intended[28] as fully consistent with the view that the philosophical disputant sets out to win. In this larger context, therefore, 155B26–8 and 155B10 do speak of genuinely adversarial activity: to translate them as if dialectic were only 'relational' would be weak and misleading. Finally, the quotation ends with Aristotle's explanation that he has rehearsed these purported dialectical *differentiae* because how the respondent in a gymnastic and investigative exercise should best conduct himself has not yet received clarification; in Aristotle's opinion, his predecessors as teachers of dialectic have neglected this issue (159A36–7). So we should inspect what he supposes will fill this gap before reaching any decision on how clean a cut can realistically be made between dialectic and eristic.

FOR APPEARANCES' SAKE

One of the most revealing suggestions of the *Sophistici Elenchi* for coping with fallacies is that sometimes one does better to confront their propounders with 'apparent', rather than 'real', solutions:

> just as we say that one must occasionally elect to argue plausibly rather than truthfully, so too on occasion one should resolve fallacies plausibly rather than in truth. For in general one should fight against eristics not as if they were refuting us, but as if they were appearing to do so; for we deny at any rate that they are arguing, so that one must set things right with a view to not seeming to be refuted.

(175A31–6)

The *Sophistici Elenchi* is supposed to teach us how to avoid sophistical victimisation; and surely it is reasonable to assume that one should not do this by stooping to the eristical level, as Ctesippus does in the *Euthydemus*. But now we are told that even if we are not sophists – but philosophers, presumably? – there are occasions when truth must be sacrificed to appearance. An element of the dialectical situation in ancient Greece whose influence it is almost impossible to exaggerate is its aspect of exhibition, even exhibitionism. Just as athletic competitions – and rhetorical 'displays' – are decided by more or less formally constituted bodies of judges, so dialectical encounters too take place in (semi-)public venues which accommodate an audience, perhaps a partisan one, in whose eyes the debate is lost or won – a situation which the Platonic dialogues bring vividly before our eyes.

Aristotle recommends that when a genuine refutation would seem to the dialectical audience not to hit the mark, one should instead use a counter-argument which, while itself spurious, will nevertheless appear convincing. Thus arguing or refuting 'plausibly' in my translation must be read as '*merely* plausible', in the light of the contrast with arguing or refuting 'in truth'. Furthermore, the Greek original of 'plausibly' is an adverb cognate with '*endoxon*', the key-word of constructive philosophical dialectic; the troubling suggestiveness of this semantic connection must not be pressed too hard, but the realisation that under sophistical assault the Aristotelian philosopher might, at least for the nonce, renounce his allegiance to truth and validity – for appearances' sake – should give us pause. It becomes increasingly difficult to resist the conclusion that in practice, as opposed to the occasional pious injunction, there is no hard-and-fast distinction between 'white' dialectic and 'black' eristic.

But it is not only when facing up to agonistic sophistry that Aristotle advocates what, in my terms, are 'invalid' tactics:

> since such *logoi* take place for the purpose of exercise and of testing someone, not of teaching someone, it is clear that one must argue not only for truths, but also for falsehoods; and not only using truths, but also occasionally using false-hoods. For frequently, when a truth has been posited, the dialectician must eliminate it, with the consequence that he must advance falsehoods. And sometimes, too, when a false-hood has been posited, it must be eliminated by means of falsehoods; for nothing prevents someone believing things which are not the case rather than truths,[29] so that as the *logos*

is formed from what he believes, he will be persuaded rather than benefited.

(161A25–33)

Here Aristotle asserts that the exigencies of the dialectical encounter – that is, the obligation to argue *against* one's opponent/partner – can involve the philosophical dialectician in both asserting falsehoods and propounding false arguments (or at least in deliberately taking advantage of the respondent's falsehoods).

As in the case of the other examples we have canvassed, a purist might protest that this text is of only limited application because it concerns 'gymnastic' and 'peirastic' *logoi*, those for training and testing arguers, not ones developed for the sake of investigation. The authentic philosopher might train himself and his co-workers in this flexible and uncommitted fashion, but would never argue other than validly, for anything but truth, once his serious business was underway. But this objection fails. Admittedly, Aristotle does maintain a loose distinction between 'gymnastic'/'peirastic' and 'investigative' dialectic. At 159A26–36, quoted on p. 123, for example, he slips easily between 'in order to carry out an investigation' and 'to test someone and to carry out an investigation'. However, that is explained by the context (the distinction is between agonistic dialectic and other types – didactic, peirastic, investigative) and clearly at 161A30 ff. arguing falsely is only used by the *echt* dialectician for testing.[30] But, much more importantly, if what we are about really is investigative, then neither of us can know at present where the truth lies; and so we both have no choice but to attack and defend to the best of our ability, impersonally, so that our chances of attaining truth might increase. Or if, as previously mentioned, we know what the truth is, but do not comprehend 'the reasons why', then deliberate exploitation of 'invalidity' might serve to enhance our theoretical understanding.

True, the occasional necessity for combating falsehood with falsehood must be strictly 'peirastic' (for, were it genuinely 'investigative', how would the questioner be certain that the beliefs turned against the respondent were false?); but it is only in such circumstances that one's knowing and deliberate indulgence in 'falsehood' could be neatly circumscribed. Moreover, Aristotle betrays anxiety lest this *ad hominem* approach to correction through dialectic should lead one to refute 'invalidly' *and* eristically, for in the immediate sequel he urges: 'but one converting another properly must convert him dialectically and not eristically, just as a geometrician would do so geometrically, whether the conclusion were false or true' (161A33–6). The comparison is more than a trifle puzzling: if, say, I were to rid you of your false belief that 156 is a prime by reminding you that you believe that no even number is a prime, should that count as mathematical rather than sophistical 'conversion'?[31]

It is time to take stock before returning to the *Rhetoric*. We have hardly exhausted the resources of the dialectical component of the *Organon*, but we have gathered more than enough material for the purpose of comparisons between dialectic and rhetoric. We set out from the conviction that the right way to try to deal with the epistemological optimism enunciated in *Rhetoric* I 1 is not to shrug it off as something special 'for dialecticians', a Platonic *apologia* to be reverently set aside before we begin the grimy, pragmatic business of rhetorical chicanery. That would be a viable option only were dialectic itself always manifestly innocent of playing fast and loose with the truth. But even in the course of our very limited survey of the *Topics* we have discovered quite impressive evidence of dialectic's being a thoroughly agonistic, occasionally coercive activity – in fact, a sort of intellectual spectator sport (a blood sport, at times, too). We have also had repeatedly to take account of texts declaring that there are distinctions to be made between varieties of dialectic; but time and again we have found that such distinctions, if not trifling, do not amount to systematic grounds for the isolation of good dialectical procedure from bad.

RULES OF THE RHETORICAL GAME

Aristotle is undoubtedly committed to a version of what I have called 'the Socratic strategy' to excuse dialectical competitiveness: 'since in business someone who obstructs the common task is a bad partner, it is clear that this also holds for *logos*; because here, too, some common project has been proposed, except in the case of those who compete' (161A37–9; cf. 161A20–1). Opponents *are* partners in the search for truth – in that they argue, precisely because they are opposed. So what are the prospects for a quasi-Socratic vindication of rhetorical combat? I put it so circumspectly because it should be obvious that justifications for ostensibly sharp practice in dialectic and rhetoric must take account of the disanalogy between them in just the respect I have been dwelling on: namely, that whatever implausibility may attach to Aristotle's attempt to show that a good dialectical opponent is at once and thereby a partner, such an attempt cannot even be made for rhetorical opponents (not that Aristotle ever pretends otherwise). There is no rhetorical parallel to peirastic or investigative dialectic, where competitive partnership might flourish; there is only the upright rhetorician fighting witting or unwitting evil, analogous to the philosophical dialectician confronting competitive sophists – whom one must occasionally show up by foul means, as well as fair.[32]

The first item in our catalogue of fishy persuasive techniques comes from *Rhetoric* I 7, where Aristotle is giving instruction in how to concoct arguments in situations where both sides agree on what is advantageous, but differ over how much benefit might accrue from the policy in question (1363B5–6): 'the same things divided into their parts seem greater; for they seem to exceed more' (1365A10–11). Just as with the *Topics*' less scrupulous recommendations, one suspects that the 'seeming' here must be specious appearance, intended to hoodwink the gullible assembly. Is the tactic any better than the merest subterfuge, as if one were to console an infant disappointed with a ten-pence piece by exchanging it for ten pennies?[33] Perhaps there is an answer, but it is at best a partial mitigation. By dividing something into its parts and dwelling over them, my rhetoric might get you to perceive and assess concealed benefits you would otherwise be likely to ignore; this technique thus teaches us to divide up whatever it is we are advocating, not so it might appear greater than it actually is, but rather in order to help the assembly appreciate its real magnitude. (One might even try to forge a further, advantageous link with the problem posed by the triviality of the rhetorician's didactic rôle: if the intention of dividing into parts is benignly informative, then the rhetorician employing this device is doing something to educate ignorance rather than taking advantage of it, albeit in the humble manner appropriate to the proto-intellectualism characteristic of a crowd of ordinary citizens.) The problem with this attempt at justification is that the reference to apparent excess does seem to indicate that the rhetorician should trade on the adult remnant of the childish delusion about the coins, the common cognitive defect which fools us into automatically correlating having more parts with an increase in magnitude.[34]

The next, sure-fire candidate for recognition as an instance of licensed invalid persuasion is this prescription for epideictic oratory:

one should take features [of character] close to the actual ones to be the same with regard to both praise and blame . . . and [when praising] always put the best construction on each of the accompanying qualities . . . and describe those in states of excess as being in states of virtue . . . for it will seem so to the many.

(1367A33–B3)

In the *Symposium* Socrates insists that he will inevitably suffer humiliation on taking his turn to praise *erōs* after what he describes as Agathon's consummately Gorgianic performance (*Symposium* 198C1–5):

on account of my stupidity I had imagined that one must speak the truth about each subject being praised, and once that has been established, make a selection of the fairest of the actual characteristics and arrange them as attractively as possible . . . But, so it seems, it has turned out that this is not the way to go about praising any subject properly: rather, one should heap up the greatest and fairest attributes possible, whether it is so or not; and if this is false, no matter.

(198D3–E2)

Far from being an example of more or less oblique Socratic irony, this is surely an expression of absolutely direct, withering sarcasm. Socrates is not outlawing speech in praise or blame as such; but he is implying that the virtuously philosophical man trying his hand at rhetoric should tolerate no deviation from the truth. The function of legitimate epideictic oratory is indeed to present its subject in as attractive (or unattractive) a light as possible, but for Socrates truth sets unassailable limits on the possibilities, the illumination must be veridical, there must be nothing factitiously cosmetic in it.[35]

Aristotle's advice places him squarely in the company of Agathon *et al*. Suggestively, Cicero records (*Brutus* 46 ff.) that Aristotle is reported to have said of Gorgias that he wrote out commonplaces, like Protagoras, but focused 'on praise and blame of particulars because he thought that the orator's most special characteristic was enhancing by praise or belittling by censure' (Buchheim test. 25). He recommends, say, that we display sensible prudence as icy calculation, substitute 'generous' for 'spendthrift', or represent the excessive timidity of the coward as the moderate caution which belongs only to the brave. 'For it will seem so to the many': the simpletons will fail to notice the distortion, so long as the cunning rhetorician masks his subject's actual features with close, but to them utterly deceptive, *simulacra*. Aristotle says explicitly not only that 'it will seem so to the many', but also that they will 'reason falsely about the motive'. And this is by no means a freakish, if lamentable, exception:

> since praise rests on actions, and exercise of choice is characteristic of the good man, one must attempt to display [the subject of praise] as acting in accordance with choice; useful too is his appearing to have so acted frequently. That is why one must take coincidences and chance events as if they resulted from choice; for if many similar instances are advanced, they will seem to be a sign of virtue and choice.
>
> (1367B22–7)

What has become of the 'natural' prevalence of truth?

TRADING ON AMBIGUITIES

Nor is such disturbing material to be found only in the chapters devoted to epideictic rhetoric. Students of the *Euthydemus* and the *Sophistici Elenchi*[36] require no reminder that perhaps the chief weapon in the sophistical armoury is the deliberate propagation of amphibolies: in whichever of its multiple senses the hapless interlocutor takes some ambiguous term or construction, the merciless eristic will trip him up by then responding as if some other sense had been intended. Aristotle's contemporary Isocrates provides us with some particularly suggestive indications of how extensively – and subtly – a rhetorician might match any dialectical play with ambiguity. In the *Panathenaicus*, having heightened the effect of his fulsome praise of Athens by contrasting her benevolence with Spartan malevolence, he introduces the fiction of a Laconising associate. The intention of this baroque device is presumably to permit Isocrates to raise objections against himself, only to quash them – at least to his own satisfaction. The anonymous Spartan champion suggests that Isocrates' discourse actually has a hidden agenda. Had he merely extolled Athenian virtue at the expense of Spartan vice, his procedure would have been at odds with his previous positive remarks about the Lacedaemonian constitution, an incongruity typical of cheap oratory (*Panathenaicus* 234). Therefore – so the 'associate' says – Isocrates decided to *seem* to speak truly about the cities, *seemingly*

130

condemning the Spartans in the eyes of those ill-disposed towards them, but secretly praising them. How could this be achieved? By means of *logous amphibolous*, viz. those which 'can go both ways and are highly contentious [*epamphoterizein dynamenous kai pollas amphisbēteseis echontas*]' (§240). Exploitation of such *logoi* in contractual disputes for personal gain is shameful but when the topic is 'the nature of men and things' it is 'fair and philosophical' (§241). Now if ever a passage cannot be taken at face-value, this is it.[37] Isocrates has been at pains to distinguish the views of the 'associate' from his own (he explicitly states that he maintained a studied and complete silence on the validity of the diagnosis, §265). After all, he is ascribing to his creature an analysis of his own authorial intentions which, at the very least, robs them of candour – although, paradoxically, this lack of frankness is supposedly an index of 'fair and philosophical' discourse.

The speech-act is so bewilderingly elaborate that we would be well-advised not to agree with Norlin that its claims are 'surely' ironical. Nevertheless, the *Panathenaicus* does contain the idea, however circumscribed, that a deft rhetorician might deliberately turn ambiguity to (benign) advantage. Most interestingly, the condition set on the exploitation of amphiboly is that it occur in a 'philosophical', not a forensic, context. Isocrates' notion of 'philosophy' is apparently rather shallow, negatively and nebulously defined as rhetorical activity distinct from the humdrum legal involvements of the professional *logographoi* whom he affected to despise. Still, perhaps the implication of the *Panathenaicus* is fundamentally Gorgianic: if the context is 'philosophical' (viz. 'rhetorical' and 'epideictic', in Socrates' terminology), then ambiguous *logoi* are to be skilfully deployed for the confusion – that is, delectation – of auditors sophisticated enough to be knowingly, pleasurably taken in.[38] Intelligent, industrious connoisseurs will realise that the *Panathenaicus* teems with 'decorations and falsehoods [*poikilias kai pseudologias*]' (§246) – but wholesome 'falsehood' which 'benefits and pleases [*terpein*]' the listeners. Not that the 'associate' has not spoilt their delight by making all obvious, even to the ignorant (although this artificial, proleptic spoiling move might, within the environment of Isocrates' *tour de force*, be equivalent to his having his cake and eating it).

Thus Isocrates shows us that and how trading on ambiguities might both animate and ornament a rhetorical display. After this tricky elegance, Aristotle's comment on exploitation of amphiboly is disconcertingly blunt, and seems dangerously close to the contractual disputes where abuse of ambiguity is, according to the 'associate', *obviously* unethical. Aristotle's tip for the aspiring rhetorician seems to be to turn legal amphiboly to his advantage, rather than to take measures to avoid it or minimise its influence. If a law is ambiguous, one should 'turn it around and see with which construction either justice or the advantageous will harmonise, and then employ it' (1375B11–13). Admittedly, Aristotle is not urging the orator to interpret an ambiguously formulated law in one sense, when he knows perfectly well that those who proposed and enacted it intended another. Nonetheless, the encouragement to 'turn it around' with an eye to finding and exploiting a partisan interpretation sounds like good advice for a brilliant shyster, not the competent but upright rhetorician delineated in the first chapter of Book I.

A case can be made that Aristotle's recommendations may not be as blatantly opportunistic as the juxtaposition of 'justice' and 'the advantageous' might suggest. *Rhetoric* I 15, while associating 'non-technical proofs', such as laws and other documents, with forensic oratory in particular (1375A23 ff.), does not exclude them from consideration by the deliberative orator as well (cf. 1375A26 ff.), which is just as we would expect. So perhaps the forensic orator looks to what is just, the deliberative orator to what is advantageous, in choosing which interpretation of a disputed document to adopt, rather than one and the same rhetorical professional being prepared to sacrifice justice to expediency when the occasion demands. But, still, there is no suggestion that a single *correct* meaning be teased out and adhered to regardless of whatever motives, noble or base, may have guided the authors of the law, or should guide us in our interpretation of it. The orator's attention is wholly on the purpose to which he wishes to put the document in question, and so on which meaning best suits his purpose.[39]

TRUTH AND TRIVIALITY

Chapter 19 of Book II contains a thesaurus of schemata for arguments about past or future events. Aristotle suggests that it is possible to argue from antecedents to consequents, or *vice versa*, where they are related *naturally*:

> and if what naturally precedes or happens for the sake of a thing has happened [then that thing has also happened]: e.g.

if lightning has struck, then there has also been a thunderclap, and if he tried, he also did it. And if what naturally succeeds a thing, or for the sake of which that thing happens has happened, then the prior event and the event which happens for the sake of the later event have occurred too: e.g. if there has been a thunderclap, then lightning has also struck, and if he did it, he also tried. Of all these cases, some are so of necessity, others for the most part.

(1392B26–32)

Now the most salient feature of the sublunary world in Aristotle's natural philosophy is that by far the greater proportion of the events which occur there are contingent. Nature expresses itself in complex, stable proclivities, but such tendencies can and often do fail to come to fruition, especially when coincidence intervenes. It is only to be expected, therefore, that reasoning about animals, including the human animal, will generally lack demonstrative necessity: 'the enthymeme [rhetorical deduction] and the paradigm [rhetorical induction] must in many cases concern matters which can be otherwise' (1357A13–15; cf. 1396A2–3).

But there is nevertheless something worthy of note in Aristotle's exposition. He illustrates mere natural precedence and consequence with the sequence lightning–thunder, the natural teleological relation with the sequence attempt–action. If, for Aristotle, thunder and lightning are meteorological, rather than celestial, phenomena, and so are not bound by adamantine superlunary necessity, it is still startling to find them grouped together with the example of human intentional action. If we cannot be as sure of the sequence lightning–thunder as that the sun will rise tomorrow, we also cannot entertain any real, even vanishingly small, doubt about the matter. But when we come to the sequence 'he tried, so he did it', our perfectly reasonable doubt is anything but infinitesimal (the reverse inference from action to attempt, if less treacherous, remains outrageously fallible).

One might be mildly inclined to associate the Aristotelian principle that truth naturally prevails with the crude motto 'if it seems so, then chances are it is so', so that, given faulty reasoning about motive and opportunity, it would be safe to argue that if the generals failed to rescue the crews from capsized triremes who were left floating in the water, then they meant to let them drown. But the motto would seem to have less to do with epistemological

133

optimism as I have defined it than with the reasoning from plausibility, what is *eikos*, so characteristic of Greek rhetorical practice (remember that the *Encomium* catalogues causes making Helen's behaviour *eikos*, and so excusable). It is *reasonable* – at any rate, reasonable enough, one hopes, for the purpose of swaying the judges – to assume that if they did so, then they meant to do so. We should therefore acknowledge the possibility that the schema of II 19 for moving from what has really happened to something else which has – as likely as not? – occurred at least skirts the edges of persuasive invalidity.

By the same token, the schema might erode our confidence in how well Aristotle copes with the issue of triviality: if our common appetite for knowledge can be glutted by such idle speculations as this, then the Socrates of the *Gorgias* need not waver in his dismissal of rhetorical persuasion as the befuddlement of the ignorant by the ignorant.[40] Indeed, in what is surely a deliberate reminiscence of the Platonic dialogue, Aristotle *concedes* that 'the uneducated are more persuasive than the educated *among mobs* [*en tois ochlois*]' (1395B27–8).[41]

So does Aristotle disconcertingly give Socrates everything he could want? Not necessarily, and for the most important of reasons. To the Platonically-inspired cognitive élitist, any and every gathering of the common people might very well constitute a 'mob'. But the Aristotelian epistemological optimist might have every reason to protest that only degenerate collections of humanity deserve to be called 'mobs' – the assembly, the lawcourts, are reassuringly often much better than that. On this reading, therefore, the concession of 1395B27–8 to the *Gorgias* is not fatal: one could paraphrase as 'the Platonic Socrates has a point, but it is vastly exaggerated; intellectual standards are not universally so demeaned'. And that finally is why – or so my Aristotelian apologist would claim – the triviality issue need not affect him radically. From a Platonic perspective, the crowds of lovers of sights and sounds flocking to the festivals (*Republic* V) may be no better than an ignorant rabble; but, from the vantage of moderate Aristotelianism, they are more realistically viewed as typical groups of *homo philosophicus*, an animal enamoured of a truth it is equipped to see, but not with any great precision, nor to any great depth.

RAISING PASSIONS

Earlier I tried to lay to rest the fear that Aristotle's warning against emotional manipulation in I 1 cannot mesh with his attitude towards 'the Gorgias/*Gorgias* problematic', but I left hanging how far his later prescriptions for arousing emotion can be justified. *Rhetoric* III 7 establishes a particular connection between effective word-choice and oratorical working on the *pathē* of the auditors:

> appropriate phrasing also enhances the plausibility of the subject-matter; for it is both the case that the soul reasons wrongly as if the truth were being spoken, because people's attitude to things like this is such that they think that things are as the speaker says, even if they are not; and also that the listener always sympathises with [literally, 'shares the *pathos* of'] someone who speaks with *pathos*, even if what he says amounts to nothing.
>
> (1408A19–24)

This is almost undiluted Gorgias, whose rhetorical psychology is nothing but psychopathology, the theory of the dominance of the passive *psychē* by the active *logos*. Its mention of cognitive error induced by emotional distortion confirms that the passage is prescribing full-scale emotional manipulation, not mere appeal to emotions which might *complement* a true *logos*.[42] If his auditors are reasoning faultily,[43] that must be because their supposition that this orator speaks the truth is false; his 'appropriate' phrasing – 'appropriate' for deception – has cozened them. This orator is a sophistical rhetorician pure and simple, a rampant instance of Socrates' worst nightmare (and the persuasive paragon of *The Encomium of Helen*) come to life. And consider Aristotle's last, deflationary, remark: most orators really are 'full of sound and fury, signifying nothing'.

Elsewhere (1418A12–17) Aristotle goes so far as to *proscribe* enthymemes when arousing the feelings, on the grounds that *logos* and *pathos* are like impulses whose simultaneous impact on the soul must either wipe out or, at best, diminish the force they would otherwise have had. This may be a rogue text; nowhere else in the *Rhetoric* does Aristotle give signs of sharing the limiting preconceptions in the philosophy of mind allegiance to which leads both Gorgias and Plato in the *Gorgias* to assume that persuasion either addresses *logos* to the exclusion of *pathos*, or moulds *pathos* by scanting *logos*. Yet even if we are willing to set it aside as a mere freak, we must still conclude that the advice given in Book III on the stimulation and management of emotion carries ominous implications; were they to be generalised, epistemological pessimism, not optimism, would be the order of the day.

The time for final stock-taking has arrived, although we have come no closer than we did in the case of the *Topics* to measuring the full scope for argumentative 'invalidity' left open by the *Rhetoric*. Can rhetorical combat be vindicated, from within the constraints imposed by epistemological optimism? At the beginning I set aside the question of identifying the ultimate metaphysical rationale for such optimism; our puzzle has rather been whether, given such optimism, the range of persuasive techniques which Aristotle apparently tolerates makes good sense. Assessment of this puzzle must be tentative, and calls for nice judgement. It should be clear that, in principle, toleration of almost any mode of persuasion – possibly even the most violent compulsion, not to mention gentle attempts at manipulation – may be purchased at the price of inflating the doctrine that the truth naturally prevails. Were it so strong that people almost could not help believing the truth, no matter how powerful the inducements to endorse falsehood, then anything might as well go in rhetoric, since deceit would 'naturally' prove so massively unpersuasive; the defeat of truth and justice would not only 'deserve censure', it would be an unforgivable disgrace. Needless to say, this would be an all but worthless victory at an exorbitant cost: Aristotle's epistemological optimism is so endlessly provocative a philosophical thesis because it mysteriously contends that, *with effort*, the truth is there to be found – it does not hit one in the face.

So what have we found? Our partial sample has revealed that Aristotle apparently countenances: dividing something into parts so as to make it look bigger; wanton falsification in epideictic oratory; turning ambiguities in legal phraseology to one's advantage; inferences from one member of a contingent natural sequence to the other; and a distressing version of Gorgianic psychopathology. Exploitation of ambiguity and bad inferences could perhaps be artfully reconciled with substantial, serious epistemological optimism, and just possibly misleading subdivision might be so accommodated as well. No reconciliation with either epideictic falsification or emotional manipulation is remotely plausible. How does this compare with our study of 'invalidity' in the *Organon*? There Aristotle seemed to accept: the technique of 'concealing the conclusion'; duplicitous self-objection; conformist intimidation; proffering apparent, rather than real, solutions for sophisms; and deliberate exploitation of false-hood and invalidity in the narrow, logical sense. Concealment, self-objection, and use of falsehood might or might not be open to vindication along the lines suggested by 'the Socratic strategy'; conformism seems to reveal the dark side of Aristotle's method-ological dependence on the *endoxa*, and endoxic refutation shows that Aristotle knows that for spectator sports, even intellectual ones, the appearances are sometimes all-important.

If for no other reason, the pains I have taken to emphasise that our coverage has been anything but comprehensive (although I do maintain that it is representative) should stop us from doing a simple sum and comparing the results – such a decision procedure would be simple-minded, in any event. I originally insisted that we should struggle against the lazy inclination to break the theoretical back of the *Rhetoric* by relegating I 1 to the status of a sop to the Platonists; but reasonable readers might well feel by this point that I have had my opportunity to persuade them that an ambitious conceptual unity informs the work – and failed. Why should the list of impro-prieties I have culled from the *Rhetoric* be taken as evidence for tensions, tolerable or otherwise, in Aristotle's project, rather than as (regrettable, but real) evidence against there being an organic unity combining I 1 with the main structure of the work? The corresponding list of improprieties drawn from the *Topics* is, I hope, a persuasive rejoinder: any scepticism we may experience about Aristotle's awareness of, and responsiveness towards, 'the Gorgias/*Gorgias* problematic' in the *Rhetoric* actually feeds off no more than an unreflective assumption – the assumption that in any comparison between dialectical and rhetorical methodology, rhetoric must inevitably come off worse. The *Topics* material has suggested otherwise.

Does Aristotle pay lip-service to the *Gorgias*, while actually in cahoots with Gorgias? This survey of invalid persuasion in the *Rhetoric* and beyond has yielded no firm answer. My purpose has not been to advance the depressing, reductionistic proposal that if the *Rhetoric* can be dismayingly unethical, at least the *Topics* fares no better. Rather, we should now be clear that the sometimes dubious validity of the persuasive and argumentative techniques Aristotle is willing to condone might well undermine his commitment to epistemological optimism. Since that optimism itself underpins both a major part of his defence of rhetoric against the onslaught of the *Gorgias*, and his reliance on *endoxa* for the development of philosophical theory, the tenability of his neo-Parmenidean conviction that truth prevails in persuasion remains both intensely problematic and profoundly important. But that, of course, is what makes the *Rhetoric* and the *Topics* so intensely interesting – to the dialectically-minded. It comes as no surprise, given that the rhetorician, like the eristic, sets out to win, that truth should go to the wall; nor even that Aristotle expects the truth to prevail none the less: the surprising thing is that his own treatise, time and again, subordinates truth to victory.

6

EPILOGUE
Does philosophy have a gender?

'Will to truth', you who are wisest call that which impels you and
fills you with lust?

(Nietzsche, *Thus Spoke Zarathustra* II 12)

GORGIAS, SOCRATES AND HELEN
ONCE MORE

There is a quick way to conclude that philosophy is, at the very
least, in sympathy with a large set of feminist concerns. Gorgias
could shock with the suggestion that we are all Helens open to
psychic violation only by drawing on deeply entrenched cultural
expectations concerning women in general as symbolised in the story
of the exemplary woman, Helen. Gorgias' threat is that we are like
her; and what she is like is passively vulnerable. Women can be
raped. In Greek society, sexually desirable males, especially youths,
were also liable to physical assault. Rape can also be a form of
humiliation of males, then as now, especially in war: sexual, but
predominantly motivated by the desire to degrade, rather than
to enjoy. It is vital to distinguish the ideology of rape (for example,
all those boys and girls too beautiful – or too chaste – for their own
good) from its practice (where physical beauty is often an
irrelevance). It is the humiliation produced by rape, however vulnerable the victim really is (and so however 'blameless'), which makes
Gorgias so threatening.

As we have seen, what Gorgias implies by erasing distinctions
between seduction and compulsion is that whatever the sex of our
bodies, the gender of our souls in the grip of masterful persuasion
is feminine. The *Encomium of Helen* evokes the daunting vision
of a world populated by crowds of biddable females to be forced

or seduced – it makes no odds – into compliance with the will of the solitary male, the wielder of rhetorical power. Or perhaps what we hear is a challenging invitation to sustain and enhance our own masculinity by becoming dominant speakers ourselves. In any case, although the *Encomium* is not as such about women, it essentially trades on misogynistic assumptions whose various descendants are prime targets for the feminist movement. Thus one might easily think that to the extent that philosophers develop their models of persuasion in contrast and opposition to schemes of rhetorical seduction, they are at least the natural allies of feminists.

But most swift inferences are too swift, and this one is no exception. Philosophy sits easily with feminism on condition that the persuasion it advocates and practises does not incorporate a misogyny akin or alternative to the spectacular version exploited by Gorgias. Again, it is easy enough to feel that if there are difficulties here, they cannot be deeply intractable. Granted, far too much of the philosophical canon constitutes a sorry catalogue of direct and elliptical misogyny, ranging from vicious attack to slighting dismissal. And, of course, the vast majority of philosophers are and have been men whose professional behaviour demonstrably betrays the gender bias writ large in their society. One might nevertheless protest that all this, deplorable as it is, is of at most superficial relevance to 'the Gorgias/*Gorgias* problematic'. Our guiding concern is not so much what philosophy says, as how and why it says it – the distinctive manner of philosophical persuasion, rather than the substantive theses propounded by one or another philosopher. Therefore what matters is not the proliferation of sexist theories in ethics, political philosophy and beyond, but the methodological issue of whether philosophy's characteristic appeals to reason are themselves predicated on objectionable, gendered attitudes. Evidently it will not do to take a hard-and-fast division between substantive and formal aspects for granted. Furthermore, were it demonstrable that the methodological credentials of specifically misogynistic philosophy are impeccable, then this defence immediately evaporates. But such fatal doubts are unwarranted, since the argumentative defects of such work are often all too palpable.[1]

Once more, reassurance is not far to seek. The difficulty of articulating an adequate definition of philosophy is, fortunately, matched by the futility of the attempt: philosophical activity past and present exhibits far too rich a diversity to be captured in any neat formula. Philosophical credos, when paraded as criteria identifying everything worthy of recognition as *authentic* philosophy, are seldom more than unworthy polemical weapons. But it would be quite wrong to infer that anything goes. All philosophers are Parmenides' children. What my credo implies is that we all give our allegiance to the ideal of a distinctive *logos*, one devoted to argumentative, critical, resolutely self-critical exploration. As philosophers we demand and render accounts of what we say, constantly seeking rational justifications which in their turn are subject to scrutiny. The obvious reason that this is nothing like a determinate definition is that what arguments must be, and what they must be like to be good, are themselves central questions philosophers must address, given the necessarily self-reflective nature of their enterprise. Nothing whatsoever precludes the best available answers from being tentative, provisional, or context-bound in one or another fashion: dogmatic absolutism is suspiciously hard to square with critical modesty. But if, these significant qualifications aside, there remains something special to be called 'philosophy', it would seem innocent of misogyny. Philosophers' less remote common ancestor is Socrates. Since the great message we derived from our reading of the *Gorgias* was that real dialectical contests are never vehicles for personal aggrandisement at the cost of victimisation, how could philosophy have a gender? Gender, surely, attaches to the person who propounds or examines the *logos*, not the *logos* itself. And Socrates taught us that we engage in dialectic for the sake, and only for the sake, of the *logos*.

What we shall discover, however, is that some prominent feminist thinkers maintain precisely that the *logos*, philosophical reason itself, no matter how it varies throughout the philosophical tradition, is almost universally harmful just because its misogyny lies concealed beneath a misleading ideology of *false* 'impersonality'. This, finally, is the charge which philosophy cannot afford to shrug off: first just because feminism cannot be ignored, but second because important as the challenge is on its own terms, it can be immediately generalised into a potentially lethal objection to all philosophical claims.[2] We have frequently returned to the political implications of 'the Gorgias/*Gorgias* problematic'. Rhetoric as the royal road to political advantage turned out to be exceedingly difficult to reconcile with conditions congenial to democratic discussion; and the Socratic stance towards the interlocutor seemed to indicate the existence of a semi-secret avenue to intimate and critical engagement with others. But it is a common tenet of sophisticated contemporary feminism that the social structures responsible for the subordination of women intersect with a host of other mechanisms which suppress other social groupings. So if philosophical 'impersonality' cloaks pronounced gender bias, by the same token there is every reason to doubt that it fuels a genuinely egalitarian discourse by abstracting from irrelevant particularities of race or class. The Gorgianic orator makes 'women' of us all; the Socratic philosopher dissembles his attachment to a systematically biased 'rationality', foisted on the naïve in the guise of impartiality. From this perspective, philosophical attacks on rhetoric are just so much rhetoric, and 'the Gorgias/*Gorgias* problematic' is no more than a local dispute between those who scrabble after masculine power.

BEGGING THE QUESTION

The assumption that 'feminine' or 'feminist' philosophy does, or would, pay due regard to relations of personal interdependency and the claims of emotion, as against those of reason, and an aversion to aggressive argumentation, are standard features of much feminist writing occupied with philosophy. Respect for interdependency is viewed as an antidote to exaggerated masculine individualism, and occasionally attributed to a feminine (pre-)disposition to acknowledge the complexities of lived experience, in contrast to the masculine penchant for simplistic abstraction. Whether philosophical thought is typically 'abstract', and, if so, whether it thereby reveals gender bias, are issues to which we shall return; and emotion and aggression are topics with which we have already been much occupied, and will also receive direct attention.

At the outset we should set aside large tendencies within the complex movement of modern feminism which are of only dubious relevance to our questions. It is not difficult to distinguish broadly liberal or egalitarian, neo-Marxist and psychoanalytical feminist traditions. The first will tend not to query the characterisation of philosophical reasoning as impersonal, because it promotes the removal of sexual discrimination where it can perceive no pertinent differences between women and men. Since this feminism fights obstacles to equal opportunity, rather than seeing anything wrong in the opportunities themselves, it is unlikely to view philosophical activity as such as problematic for women, once the unjust barriers excluding them from full participation in it have come down. The second will readily dismiss the claims of rational objectivity as an ideological imposition of the dominant gender and class on those they exploit. The third will propose analyses of philosophical rationality as mere rationalisation. Liberal feminists are inclined to overlook our problem.[3] Neo-Marxist feminists who are true to their principles consign philosophy to the ideological periphery relative to the centre occupied by the forces of female production, biological, domestic and industrial, exploited by men; in their eyes the solution to our problem is all too glaringly obvious. Psychoanalytical feminists reductively refer philosophy to the effects of divergent male and female child-rearing practices; to them there is also no problem, because they fail to recognise that philosophical thought might possess any degree of real independence from gender-specific infantile development.[4]

But even highly pertinent writings often both yield a positive answer to 'does philosophy have a gender?' and take the answer as an unchallengeable point of departure, rather than as a possibility to be verified.[5] An editor of a frequently cited and influential anthology casually airs the opinion that 'it may be that there has only rarely, anywhere, been a *human* act performed or a *human* thought produced, for acts and thoughts have had to occur within the differential opportunities and limits set by the sex/gender system':[6] as if, say, dunking a basketball in a ghetto were to perform a 'black' rather than 'human' act, in light of the 'the differential opportunities and limits set by the race/class system'. Programmatic introductions are often especially revealing:

> Gender is defined by opposition. To be masculine is not to be feminine. Feminine is what is not masculine. What appears on either side of the male–female divide is extremely variable. For instance, whether males tend to be warlike, bookish, competitive, cooperative, individualist or role-oriented is specific to time and place. But where masculinity is associated with any of these, femininity will be associated with the opposite, and, where women are oppressed, taken to be inferior. Philosophy, in so far as it is the articulation of the concepts, dilemmas, explanations and abstractions of a culture, will only be half the story unless both genders contribute equally.[7]

This is intended to establish that there indeed is – or should be – a distinctively feminist 'perspective' in philosophy. The problem

143

is that however generously open-ended definitions of philosophy must be, this one cannot do. It should certainly be conceded that *insofar* as philosophy does a job of articulation or clarification, the neglect or exclusion of any social grouping is a grave defect. But philosophy's primary function is critical and argumentative, and nothing has been said to show that this could, let alone should, be undertaken from a gendered perspective. What one readily concedes is that there are feminine 'stories' of very great importance awaiting philosophical articulation; yet it does not follow that the dialectic which arguers, female or male, apply to such narratives need or could be sexually bipolar.[8]

Another such introduction insists that

> One element in the feminist theoretical programme, then, is to call into question the illusion of the liberal that while others can speak only from their various special perspectives (and so in a partial or partisan way), his own contribution is naturally entitled to hold the centre of the intellectual stage since *he* is a thinker pure and simple, unhampered by any 'perspective' of his own.[9]

There are clearly exaggerated types of liberalism which do assume far too easily that they have achieved neutrality, and that their neutrality goes wider and deeper than they have any right to suppose. But again the language of perspectivalism is anything but clear. No one *is* 'a thinker pure and simple'. Sometimes we strive to think, to the exclusion of all else. Of course we do not thereby think away our intellectual limitations: if anything, intensification of mental effort can help to bring them to light. Thus to the extent that liberals imagine their intellectual condition to be a fair approximation to untrammelled omniscience, they deserve mockery. But does the necessity, assumed here, of speaking from a perspective claim something more? If the idea is that various participants in ethical debate contribute disparate experiences for communal discussion – from a *shared* dialectical perspective – well and good.[10] But this model presupposes that the doing of philosophy, as opposed to what it reflects on, is gender-neutral.[11]

Perhaps the most frequently cited authority for the proposition that philosophy has a gender[12] is Genevieve Lloyd, whose book *The Man of Reason* is devoted to just this question.[13] On the basis of a sequence of historical case-studies about the portrayal of rationality, women, or both in philosophy, she concludes that:

144

Notwithstanding many philosophers' hopes and aspirations to the contrary, our ideals of Reason are in fact male; and if there is a Reason genuinely common to all, it is something to be achieved in the future, not celebrated in the past. Past ideals of Reason, far from transcending sexual difference, have helped to constitute it.[14]

Yet on examination the texts which she assembles show nothing of the sort. She marshals from canonical philosophers prescriptions for what aids rational progress, and proscriptions of what hinders it. There is no doubt whatsoever that the actual and perceived social position of women during any of the historical periods when these thinkers flourished was, to say the least, inimical to whatever philosophical aspirations women might then have entertained. But that can hardly establish that any and all philosophical ideals of rationality are *intrinsically* masculine, as Lloyd illegitimately infers.[15] Misogynists have regularly insisted throughout history that the intellectual endowment of women is markedly inferior to that of men, and not a few philosophers have enthusiastically abetted or even promoted such prejudice. That depressing fact does not entail that characterisations of rationality itself, even in the mouth of the misogynist himself, are themselves misogynistic. (Anti-Semites accuse Jews of miserliness: does this mean that acts of generosity by Jews should oblige the bigot to revise not only his estimation of Jews, but also his conception of generosity?) Historical cataloguing will not settle the issue; and fallacious transitions from the crying need for philosophy about the needs and experiences of women to feminine philosophy must be rejected. So far the vital questions remain unaddressed: What is the effect of the hitherto inevitable, and still continuing, association of women with emotion? What are the implications of philosophy's abstract character and impersonality, if it is correct to emphasise feminine involvement in the concrete and personal? And given that women are the perennial victims of abuse both physical and mental, how wary should they also be of philosophical aggression, disciplined or not?

OTHER PEOPLE

Much recent feminist thinking in ethics and beyond takes its inspiration from reflection on Carol Gilligan's *In a Different Voice*. Gilligan trenchantly criticises the scheme of moral development advocated by Lawrence Kohlberg; this presents a broadly Kantian account, according to which such development marches in step with the capacity to formulate and apply increasingly abstract and more nearly universalisable principles. Tests conducted by Kohlberg allegedly reveal gender difference, with females consistently scoring as less mature. Gilligan undermines this conclusion by emphasising the general inadequacy of Kantian abstractionism as a moral stance. Furthermore, she reinterprets Kohlberg's results (in addition to her own, new data) as revealing a distinctively female 'voice', one which manifests a heightened sensitivity to situational complexities, primarily those involving the rights and interests of others. Gilligan conjectures that this 'voice' is indeed female, but is so as the upshot of (contemporary) child-rearing practices, rather than as a matter of simple biology. In response to this work[16] a widely shared view has emerged that women typically – and rightly – heed particularity in a manner incompatible with a traditionally masculine bias in favour of abstract, impersonal principle.[17]

Does such work demonstrate that for women the cost of admission to philosophy as currently practised is unacceptably high: the sacrifice of personal and emotional involvements which should, on the contrary, be respected by a reformed, feminist philosophy? If we have learnt anything, it is that the issues of the nature of emotion and its relation to rationality are anything but straightforward. In the *Encomium* it suited Gorgias' purpose to represent the soul as an undifferentiated, altogether malleable stuff whose feminine *pathē* are controlled by an external, masculine *logos*. The discussion of the *Gorgias* suggests a strikingly different model, according to which *logos* is internalised and displays a rational independence to be cultivated, although the *pathē* are not (yet) re-habilitated. But in Aristotle we encountered the ideas that emotional response is essential to proper moral habituation, and that at least some feelings are rational insofar as they can be informed and modified by the appeals of reason.

It is quite true that those philosophers who are prone to denigrate emotions as entirely irrational feelings also tend to castigate women as exaggeratedly emotional, either directly, or by way of tying emotion to the body, together with the further premiss that women are mired in their biology. But the variation in the positions we have examined shows that there is nothing inevitable in such associations. To a surprising extent, the very category of 'emotion' is a shifting philosophical (and latterly psychological) construct, although constant factors in its construction have been and remain difference from reason and its passive, merely responsive character. Thus it is indeed inevitable that any philosopher of a rationalistic bent – that is, nearly all of them – will recognise a need for the emotions to be properly schooled by reason: only extremists, however, will insist on their extirpation. And they will all of course also suppose that when we are engaged in philosophy, we might well draw on our emotional experiences, but that reflection on them should be conducted in a rational, relatively disengaged manner. There is nothing here to turn away anyone but the committed irrationalist, who in any case is unlikely to encounter anything more than frustration in philosophical activity.[18]

And what of impersonal abstraction? Here we must tread carefully, making nice distinctions. We initially considered the notion of impersonality when investigating the Socratic insistence that dialectic, as opposed to rhetoric, is for the sake of the *logos*, where this meant at least two things. First, criticism levelled at an interlocutor's statements is not to be taken 'personally', as we say: we shall evaluate this disclaimer shortly. But second, the simple fact that a statement is made by one person rather than another is neither here nor there: all that matters are the argumentative credentials of the *logos*, not its *personal* origins. And this, surely, is a variety of abstract impersonality to which no one could take exception – at any rate no one opposed to authoritarian mystification. If we are intimates, it might be legitimate or even necessary for you to care about the personal fact that *I* have propounded a faulty argument: fallacious reasoning is a defect, sometimes a grave one, and friendship urges you to correct me for my sake. But such concern for me is perfectly consistent with the condition laid on dialectical involvement that when as a philosopher you inspect my arguments, personal feelings have nothing to do with it.

Are there other, potentially objectionable modes of abstraction? We have already commented that there is every reason to anticipate that different participants in dialectic will bring diverse experiences to the discussion. Sometimes it will be a matter of fact that these experiences are unshared; occasionally they will be inaccessible in principle to (some) others.[19] What this entails is that we abstract recklessly at our peril: philosophers cannot afford the luxury of smooth theorising at an altitude above real complexities, when the complexities should not be neglected in their deliberations. Nothing could be more truistic than the rule that one should avoid unjustified abstraction; but, like many such truisms, it is far easier to endorse than to honour. A sensible distaste for the products of unwarranted abstraction should not expand into a condemnation of abstraction *per se*: people try too hard for universal truths just because they are so rare and powerful.[20]

Nevertheless, in yet another sense philosophy not only tolerates, it positively demands a special type of personal involvement. When Callicles refused to play along, Socrates did not lapse into monologue: he was still obliged to carry on a dialogue, albeit with himself. Dialectic *always* engages critically with other intellects. Parmenides' poem recounts how the goddess gave him a truth she advised him to test and which he in turn submits to our critical inspection. Socrates cannot know for himself without putting other people's ideas to the test – or so Plato represents him, addressing his readers in the most complicated of indirect, deliberately baffled dialogues. If the Cartesian *Meditations* develops a self-portrait of an isolated mind reliant only on its internal resources, even its readers are constantly invited to reproduce the journey from doubt to assurance and thus to verify the theory presented. All philosophical thought must reach out to criticise and be criticised, and so can never be reduced to a solitary activity. Philosophers might sit alone writing in their studies, but at the very least they must *imagine* the argumentative reactions of their readers. And that is always to imagine someone who talks back.

AGGRESSION PURIFIED?

In the end we return to the point we have already visited repeatedly, but always inconclusively. And this book will remain inconclusive: 'the Gorgias/*Gorgias* problematic' is something to be continuously thought through, not solved, disposed of once for all. When philosophers assure you that their destruction of your cherished position is a uniformly impersonal and occasionally benevolent exercise, why believe them? If they construct knock-down arguments with such evident satisfaction, if all the philosophy descended from the Greek original retains its deeply agonistic character, why suppose that their professional aggression has been cleansed?[21] Why concede that their attacks belong in a different category from Gorgianic triumphalism? The short answer is that often one should not believe them. Just as philosophy never emerges from the need to redefine its criteria for acceptable argumentation, so too dialectic never casts off the ambiguity which encourages its confusion with eristic, something which the *Euthydemus* and *Topics* show all too well. And sometimes there is no confusion: despite seemly protestations, the argument which knocks us down is a weapon aiming to hurt. But only sometimes. The not so short answer is that even if the argument appears eristical for the excellent reason that it is, lovers of truth of either gender have no other options. Were we already wise, then we could safely forgo argument, with all its attendant perils. Lovers of justice tolerate the obvious evils of an adversarial legal system in the faith that the clash of often self-interested or vindictive advocates will generate as much of the truth as our ignorance can attain. Lovers of philosophical truth put up with traditional accusations of sophistry, and the sophists active in their midst, in the conviction that only their paradoxical competitions have any chance of yielding knowledge. If a philosopher committed to this risky project can be permitted a strictly personal reflection, Socrates was right to insist that correction at the hands of an able dialectician is no unworthy, or even unpleasant, thing. Reader, I await refutation.

12

NOTES

1 MUCH ADO ABOUT NOTHING: GORGIAS' *ON WHAT IS NOT*

1 Buchheim 1989 will serve as my standard source for the original Greek fragments of Gorgias, and Greek and Latin reports about him; this collection not only is the most complete, but also, in general, benefits from judicious textual criticism. The German translation is good, and the explanatory notes often useful.

2 Diels 1884 was the first scholar in the modern period to advance a developmental hypothesis, proposing that Gorgias evolved from 'physicist' to 'eristic' to 'rhetor'; he was challenged by Gomperz, who insisted: 'Der "philosophische Nihilismus" des Gorgias ist aus der Geschichte der Philosophie zu streichen. Seine Scherzrede über die Natur hat ihren Platz in der Geschichte der Rhetorik' (Gomperz 1912, p. 35). Nothing could better illustrate the continuous challenge Gorgias poses to orthodox thinkers – we shall see that *The Encomium of Helen* is also shrugged off as a slight joke. This dismissive comment is fairly typical of more recent judgements:

> even if the treatise *On What Is Not*, or *On Nature* is accepted as showing that Gorgias was a philosopher, it is important to bear in mind that it is an early work, dated to the years 444–1 (Olympiodorus *Commentary on Plato's Gorgias* prooemium 9). There is no evidence that he maintained an interest in philosophy, as distinct from rhetoric, later in his life – unless we think we can find such evidence in his *Encomium of Helen*.
>
> (MacDowell 1982, p. 11)

A late Neoplatonic commentary is not generally the most reliable guide to the chronology of intellectual developments which occurred a millennium earlier. In any case, MacDowell's faith that we can so easily tell what is 'philosophy, as distinct from rhetoric' shows that editing Gorgias is no guarantee that one has learned from him.

3 When Heraclitus says '*philosophoi* must be enquirers into many things' (fr. 35), it is safest to translate in accordance with etymology as 'lovers of wisdom must be enquirers into many things'. Diogenes Laertius

NOTES

famously asserts that 'Pythagoras was the first to call philosophy
"philosophy" and himself a "philosopher"' (1.12). The problem with
exploiting this claim for our purposes is that Pythagoras' *philosophical*
status is far from secure; indeed, one noted authority concludes his
chapter on Pythagoras with the remark that he 'was a philosopher only
to the extent that he was a sage' (Kirk, Raven and Schofield 1983,
p. 238). Cole 1991 lays great emphasis on what he argues is the fourth-
century, specifically philosophical, provenance of the word 'rhetoric'
(e.g. 'the word *rhetoric* itself bears every indication of being a
Platonic invention', p. 2). His thought-provoking argument for the
proposition that rhetoric itself, not just the terminology of 'rhetoric',
is a Platonic and Aristotelian construct, is systematically vitiated by his
neglect of the type of position I have formulated for philosophy and
'philosophy'. And, as we shall see, his thesis fails to do anything like
justice to Gorgias.
4 Coxon 1986 is the most recent, comprehensive and punctiliously
edited collection of fragments of and reports about Parmenides, and
also provides a careful English translation, but his interpretation is a
disappointment. Many of the claims of Owen 1986a have been hotly
contested, but it remains the contemporary classic of Parmenidean
scholarship, and should be consulted before all else. The reader should
be warned that even when Parmenides' text is not uncertain, translation is still contentious, and others may construe the text differently
from me, although I have tried to produce a neutral rendering.
5 *Pace* Coxon 1986, p. 168.
6 Cf. ibid. p. 191.
7 Whether such an admission is or is not compatible with Parmenides'
metaphysical principles is perhaps the most fiercely debated problem in
the interpretation of his philosophy. Mackenzie 1982 is an especially
stimulating, if necessarily speculative, response.
8 Indeed, comparison of rhetoric's meretricious dangers with make-up
eventually became something of a commonplace, for example in
Montaigne's fiercely anti-rhetorical essay 'On the vanity of words':

> those who hide women behind a mask of make-up do less harm,
> since it is not much of a loss not to see them as they are by
> nature, whereas rhetoricians pride themselves on deceiving not
> our eyes but our judgement, bastardising and corrupting things
> in their very essence.
>
> (Montaigne 1991, p. 341)

9 The sense in which Parmenides supposes his false cosmology to be
superior to the competition, not to mention what right he might have
to present it (see n. 7), remain unresolved questions: his deception is
clearly presented as 'better' in the sense of 'better at taking us in', but
is it also 'better' in the sense of deviating as little as possible from the
truth? And if so, is that why it is 'better' in the first sense? Coxon
imagines that Parmenides actually endorses the cosmology which follows
(Coxon 1986, p. 218); for a more subtle analysis, see Long 1963.
10 Descartes' correspondence contains several more or less similar versions

151

of this passage; both their relationship and their dating are disputed. My translation is of the Latin text at Adam and Tannery 1964–76, vol. 4, pp. 174–5.

11 Kahn 1979 is an excellent guide through these complexities.

12 Newiger 1973, *contra* Kerferd (who attempts to assimilate the versions), argues that *MXG* is *real* Gorgias, while Sextus diverges importantly and disastrously from the original. Kerferd's irenic thesis is presented to best advantage in Kerferd 1982, where he concedes that at least in the final section, that on incommunicability, the versions differ significantly, but suggests that they both preserve fragments of true Gorgias:

> I wish to argue that in the third section, at least for the greater part, we have two quite distinct sets of arguments, one set in Sextus and the other in *MXG*, and to conclude that the two sets must be treated as complementary if we are to recover Gorgias' original argument.
>
> (Kerferd 1982, p. 215)

But unfortunately he never comes to grips with the indubitable evidence for heavy reworking by Hellenistic philosophers; his claim, for example, that when reading *MXG* 'we might have expected that Gorgias would have used the Protagorean man-measure principle to argue that one man's sense-perceptions are not going to be the same as another man's sense-perceptions' (p. 220) seems to rely on *M*'s doxographical association of Gorgias with Protagoras – and thus simply begs the question. The general moral is that to aspire 'to recover Gorgias' original argument' is to court disaster.

13 The opinion that in *M* 7 Gorgias is just one more episode in the history of negative dogmatism was the position reached by the Cambridge ancient philosophy group in 1985, and I thank all participants in that seminar for helping me to understand Sextus' procedure.

14 The issue can be pursued with the help of Mansfeld 1988.

15 Sedley persuasively suggests that

> there is every reason to believe that the first section, on those alleged to deny that there is any criterion (*M* 7.49–88), is the work of Aenesidemus himself [the first-century BCE founder of neo-Pyrrhonian sceptical philosophy]. This can be inferred especially from the treatments of Anacharsis and Gorgias, both of which are recast in the rigorously dilemmatic form of argument characteristic of Aenesideman scepticism.
>
> (Sedley 1992, p. 25)

Aenesidemus' authorship of this section would thus help explain the massively disproportionate space allotted to Gorgias (65–87). Sedley endorses the view that *MXG* gets us closer to Gorgias, but makes a very perceptive comment about a highly important formal feature which does recur in *M*, despite all its sceptical refashioning:

> one aspect which remains constant in both versions is the concessive structure of the overall argument: *p*, and even if not

p, *q*, and even if not *q*, *r*. This device is a direct legacy of Gorgias to Aenesideman scepticism, which uses it widely (I know of no serious philosophical use of it between Gorgias and Aenesidemus, other than in Plato's *Charmides*).

(n. 8, pp. 25–6)

But apart from 'serious' philosophy, this type of concessive structure abounds in the rhetorical tradition (e.g. 'I had no desire to kill him; but even if I did, I lacked the means . . .'), and can be found in discussions of *stasis* theory in rhetorical handbooks, for example Quintilian's *Institutiones Rhetoricae* III 6.5, 10. So yet again we find an instance of Gorgias' slipping and sliding between modes of discourse which others strive anxiously to keep apart.

16 Kirk, Raven and Schofield counsel caution: 'the title reported [for Melissus] is probably as usual not the author's' (1983, p. 391), and they issue a specific warning relevant to Gorgias:

> it is sometimes suggested that Gorgias entitled his own work *On Nature, or On What Is Not* in parody of Melissus' title. But the practice of giving titles to prose books seems to have begun only in the sophistic age . . . , so the most we could with any safety conjecture is that Melissus' work was known to Gorgias by the title recorded in 521 and 522.

(n. 1, p. 392; cf. n. 1, p. 102)

Note that while they are properly sceptical about Melissus' having named his own book, they are happy to accept the speculative possibility that Gorgias played off a title imposed on Melissus, which for our purposes is all one could want.

17 For Parmenides, the reader can consult Owen 1986a; Evans 1982 is a modern work whose difficulty is commensurate with its brilliance.

18 In contrast, Kerferd interprets the third section of *On What Is Not* as acknowledging representation, but denying its efficacy:

> Gorgias is introducing a radical gulf between *logos* and the things to which it refers. Once such a gulf is appreciated we can understand quite easily the sense in which every *logos* involves a falsification of the thing to which it has reference – it can never, according to Gorgias, succeed in reproducing as it were *in* itself that reality which is irretrievably *outside* itself. To the extent that it claims faithfully to reproduce reality it is no more than deception or *apatē*.

(Kerferd 1981, p. 81)

Just how this problem of the 'outside' is supposed to work remains obscure to me; but in any event, its textual anchors are to be found in *M*'s version, not *MXG*'s, so that this alternative to a reading which has Gorgias building his case from non-representational *logoi* is doubly unattractive.

19 The text I have translated contains conjectural supplements, but one occurrence of '*psophos*' is certain.

20 Cf.

> si l'on commence par donner des pouvoirs du langage une défi-
> nition hyperbolique, qui lui attribue la capacité de véhiculer les
> choses mêmes qu'il nomme, avec toutes leurs qualités concrètes,
> on se donne la partie belle pour montrer qu'il est incapable d'ac-
> complir les performances que l'on attendait de lui. Mais qui a
> jamais pensé qu'on pouvait se nourrir en lisant le menu?
>   (Brunschwig 1971, p. 81)

21 Passmore 1961, ch. 4 is a superb analysis of the logic of self-refutation.

22 Robinson cannot see anything funny (let alone serious) in Gorgias: 'far
from being profound, they [the arguments of the third part of the work
on nature] are merely embarrassing' (Robinson 1973, p. 58). He also
asserts – without any basis – that 'Plato seems to have viewed Gorgias
neither as a serious thinker nor as having any pretensions to being so
regarded. He viewed him simply as a clever talker' (p. 49). Ch. 3 will
suggest otherwise. Robinson is worth reading as an object-lesson in the
effects of imperturbable conventionalism.

23 Closely analogous uncertainties becloud interpretation of the second
part of Plato's dialogue the *Parmenides* (in fact, thinking about this
dialogue led me to the possibility of reading *On What Is Not* in a
'straight' fashion). The second part of the *Parmenides* consists of a
remorseless sequence of antinomies, propositions suffering from profound logical defects, propounded with apparent seriousness despite the
explicit formal contradictions generated. Just as in the case of *On What
Is Not*, the theme, distorted or not, is of course Parmenidean; and just
as *On What Is Not* has been written off as a bad joke, so too some
baffled scholars have taken the same line with the *Parmenides*. But other
philosophers have suggested, in the spirit of 'straight' reading, that Plato
is here putting on display what he knows full well to be
logically unacceptable – the deep 'mistakes' with which the second part
of the dialogue teems are put there for our benefit (see Owen 1970 for
an elegant exposition and critique of such approaches). Furthermore,
one might just speculate that the anti-Parmenidean propositions
deployed in the *Parmenides* (e.g. 'the one which is not is') are sufficiently reminiscent of the materials exploited by Gorgias in *On What
Is Not* to suggest that the analogies between it and the second part of
the dialogue are not coincidental: perhaps Plato was encouraged to
compose his work by Gorgias' example, read 'straight'.

24 Rosenmeyer writes 'now for the first time it is clearly recognised that
speech is not a reflection of things, not a mere tool or slave of description, but that it is its own master' (Rosenmeyer 1955, p. 231), while
Segal has it that 'Gorgias' denial of the existence of communicability
of true "Being" would not necessarily have hampered his practical activity
. . . nor is he likely to have isolated himself from practical life because
he could demonstrate syllogistically that nothing exists' (Segal 1962,
p. 102). Have these authors forgotten that if they take the treatise at
face-value so as to detach the conclusions of the final section, then they
are in consistency bound to treat the preceding parts in the same fashion?

But, if there is nothing, then there are no things for speech not to reflect; and I suspect that Segal is employing a rather unusual concept of proof, if he thinks that (sincere) demonstration of nihilism would not throw a spanner into the works, practical or not. What is mesmerising about *On What Is Not* is not what Gorgias theoretically demonstrates, but rather his playful refusal to come clean on whether he is demonstrating anything at all. No carefully excerpted selection from our text heralds the autonomy of non-descriptive language; as it pretends to say there is nothing, so it makes as if to say there is nothing to say. Newiger, too, disappoints by attempting to portray Gorgias as a mildly interesting empiricist philosopher of a relativistic bent. Even Brunschwig's otherwise incisive study falls into this trap of 'theoretical' reduction: 'Gorgias, qui fut . . . par son *Traité du non-être*, l'un des premiers théoriciens de l'impossibilité de communiquer' (p. 79). He concludes on a note very close to Rosenmeyer's: 'Gorgias, penseur de la rhétorique, débarrasse ainsi le langage de sa fonction d'information pour mieux dégager sa fonction d' influence' (p. 83).

2 IN PRAISE OF FALLEN WOMEN: GORGIAS' *ENCOMIUM OF HELEN*

1 Stephanie West, the most recent commentator on *Odyssey* IV, remarks of line 279, which describes the mimicry, that 'it is not actually recorded that Aristarchus athetized this line, but the scholia emphasise its absurdity in terms which imply that he must have done . . . The line is awkward in expression and implausible in content' (Heubeck, West and Hainsworth 1988, p. 211). She does not explain what should be faulted in the expression, which is impeccable; and her later reference to 'this strange trick' (ibid.) suggests that she imposes inappropriately realistic criteria on Homer. But her admission that 'there may be more to this curious detail than meets the eye' (ibid., p. 212) betrays some uneasiness; perhaps she half-realises that this striking and significant description of Helen's powers hardly deserves to be expunged from the text.

2 Although he does not mention him by name, MacDowell is an enthusiastic, if superficial, Isocratean: 'what he does is not in fact to praise Helen, but to defend her conduct against criticism; *Defence of Helen* would really have been a more appropriate title' (MacDowell 1982, p. 12).

3 Loraux 1981 is primarily responsible for recognition of the manifold significance of one extremely important type of epideictic speech, the funeral oration (although she registers caveats against assimilation of *epitaphioi* to the *Aristotelian* model of epideictic discourse (pp. 227–9)).

4 Some are unwilling to accord it much value even within these tightly circumscribed terms: for example, 'his text contains . . . a largely irrelevant introduction and a bravura digression on the various forms persuasive speech may take' (Cole 1991, p. 76); but Cole's contention that full-blown rhetoric only emerged as a child of fourth-century philosophy systematically warps his readings of Gorgias, who must be

denied the self-reflective sophistication demonstrating that Cole's evolutionary thesis is false.

5 Goldhill 1990 argues most convincingly for this conclusion.

6 MacDowell translates 'of an action virtue' and comments: 'one might have supposed that *aretē* just meant 'merit', virtually equivalent to *kosmos*. But it is in accordance with the archaic use of the word to regard it as applicable primarily to action' (MacDowell 1982, p. 33). This cannot be right. Although it is true that *'pragma'* could mean 'action', there is no evidence for a limitation of *generalised 'aretē'* to action. Instead, there are abundant passages demonstrating that *'aretē'* can function as the equivalent of *'andreia'*, that is, 'courage' (see Dover 1974, pp. 164–7), and one might indeed translate accordingly. My alternative rendering takes *pragma* as equivalent to 'thing' in the widest possible sense, so that in this phrase Gorgias refers broadly to anything from a superb hunting-hound to a well-constructed and -tuned lyre.

7 As in 'the martial array [*kosmos*] of bronze and iron' (§16), where *'kosmos'* refers to phalanxes in fighting-order.

8 MacDowell glosses *kosmos* as follows: '"goodness", "merit", the thing which brings renown, the proper condition in virtue of which a city is a good city, a body is a good body, etc. (Not "ornament" here, because it is the good order of the thing itself, not an extraneous addition . . .)' (MacDowell 1982, p. 33). This unqualified exclusion of 'ornament' is thoroughly misguided. Although the reassuring formula implied by §1's strictures, 'praise (only) the praiseworthy, blame (only) the blameworthy', certainly does disqualify deceitful *kosmos* for the nonce, Gorgias' careful tactic is surely to arouse our suspicions, then – temporarily – to still them, and finally to confirm them emphatically. Therefore the last thing readers should do in reacting to §1 is to suppress their initial responses to *all* the connotations of *kosmos*.

9 MacDowell reads *elechthē* instead of *ēlenchthē*, translating 'the other was reputed to be because he said he was', and comments on *elechthē*: 'the reading of late manuscripts, perhaps merely a medieval conjecture, but it must be preferred to the oldest manuscripts' *ēlenchthē*, which does not make sense' (MacDowell 1982, p. 34). Why not? Elsewhere he explains:

> *ēlenchthē* is translated by Diels–Kranz 'die Fama trog', but it cannot mean this. If right, it would have to mean something like 'he was proved not to be because he claimed he was'; but *dia* would then be absurd.
>
> (MacDowell 1961, p. 121)

There is no absurdity once one recognises that this surprising expression is a cardinal example of *paradoxologia*: the divinity of Helen's beauty is so obvious that Tyndareus' claim virtually refutes itself. Buchheim rightly rejects MacDowell's arguments and translates 'der andere, da er vorgab, es zu sein, bloßgestellt wurde' (Buchheim 1989, p. 5). Isocrates' description of Theseus' parentage ('said to be the son of Aegeus, but born of Poseidon' (*Helen* 18)) is a pedestrian simplification of his master's conceit.

10 We have no way of knowing whether the *Encomium* was in the first instance a script for public recital or a text for private reading (although the contrast is not as marked in the ancient context as it is today: there are reasons to believe that 'private' reading might still, as a rule, have been aloud, and in company). But no feature of my interpretation depends on a resolution of the performance/reading issue.

11 The classic study remains 'Agamemnon's Apology' (Dodds 1951, pp. 1–27). Many features of his discussion have been challenged, but without affecting the possibility that Gorgias' theological assumptions might well have been contentious. In the *Odyssey* Helen confesses that she 'repented the reckless folly [*atē*] which Aphrodite gave, when she led me thither from my dear fatherland' (IV 261–2). The connection here with overdetermined explanations of human action is evident; and West comments appositely on *atē*: 'mental aberration supernaturally imposed, folly, infatuation . . . Helen is not disclaiming responsibility for her actions; she means that she acted under the influence of overwhelming passion, not rationally or from calculation' (Heubeck, West and Hainsworth 1988, p. 210). I am not nearly so confident as she is that Helen determinately 'means' one thing rather than the other; but the passage certainly does suggest a theology at variance with Gorgias' convenient assumptions.

12 Verdenius perceptively notes a most disturbing implication of the juxtaposition:

> there is a kind of '*Verfremdung*' in the fact that Gorgias in his *Encomium on Helen* included a theoretical section in which he recommends deception as a form of persuasion and in fact identifies the two. This may suggest to the reader that the defence of Helen, too, is deceptive, which contradicts the announcement at the beginning of the speech, that it will 'show the truth' (§2).
>
> (Verdenius 1981, p. 125)

Of course, he illicitly exaggerates: while Gorgias hints at an assimilation of persuasion and deception, he does not explicitly identify them, and nowhere does he 'recommend' deception in so many words. But Verdenius is right to draw our attention to the *implied* threat.

13 Cole's reading of fr. 23 is consistent with his systematic misinterpretation:

> if epic narrative under the patronage of the Muse makes the poet into an eyewitness of what he cannot in fact have seen or heard, drama works the same transformation, but on the audience rather than the author . . . The dramatist was thereby pledged to do his best to deceive the audience into thinking – for the duration of the performance – that they were seeing and hearing what they could never have seen or heard; and the audience was similarly pledged not to resist this effort at deception. This is evidently the line of reasoning behind Gorgias' famous assertion.
>
> (Cole 1991, p. 38)

Cole here supposes himself to be describing the *pre*-rhetorical environment of 'oral poetry and oral eloquence'; but the description is incoherent, and in any case inapplicable to Gorgias' assertion. The incoherence springs from a bizarre consequence of the claimed analogy between poet and dramatist, namely that the Muse-inspired poet would *himself* have to be deceived, if he is to be correlated with the dramatist's *audience*. Rather, as one would anticipate, the Muse conveys to him the power both to enlighten and deceive *his* audience (surely the implication of Hesiod, *Theogony* 27). And Cole cites the fragment as an example of the archaic attitude towards the function of poetry, an attitude supposed to antedate the rhetorical revolution. He can do so only by ignoring the quite novel tension which Gorgias has generated between *alētheia* on the one hand, pleasure (in deception?) on the other.

14 Adkins remarks most acutely:

> etymologically speaking, a *dynastēs* is simply 'one who can'; and what Gorgias says *logos* can (*dynatai*) do is uncontroversial and based on empirical observation. But since the 'for' clause is an explanation of *dynastēs*, and follows it, the incautious reader may suppose that Gorgias has justified his use of *dynastēs* in the full sense of 'potentate'; as the reader will certainly have interpreted it, since *dynastēs* never occurs in its etymological sense.
>
> (Adkins 1983, pp. 109–10)

15 Cole insists that 'there is nothing, however, to suggest that, as some critics have maintained, Gorgias intended this analysis of the power of *logos* to be an indirect glorification of his own profession' (Cole 1991, p. 146), but refuses to accord such passages as §8 the attention they deserve.

16 In a passage regularly cited as a parallel to the *Encomium* (and perhaps one which betrays the influence of Gorgias on him), Euripides describes not *logos*, but rather persuasion as a *tyrannos* (*Hecuba* 816 ff.).

17 Strictly speaking, my claim fits just post-Cleisthenic Athens, and is perhaps uncontentious only for the period after Ephialtes' reduction of the powers of the Areopagus in 462 ensured that the Council and Assembly enjoyed untrammelled control of public affairs (what his reforms actually entailed remains puzzling).

18 E.g. Plato, *Apology* 17B, or Isocrates' contention that his enemy condemned the 'power' (*dynamis*) of his *logoi* (*Antidosis* 4).

19 See the section 'Evils of rhetorical education: sophists and sycophants' in Ober 1990, pp. 170–4.

20 Although Ober concedes that 'probably most Athenian citizens – even those who attended the Assembly regularly – never exercised their right to speak there' (Ober 1990, p. 79), he still argues that

> *isēgoria* changed the nature of mass experience of the Assembly from one of passive approval (or rejection) of measures presented, to one of actively listening to and judging the merits of complex, competing arguments. Skill in public speech became an increasingly important leadership skill, since all major matters

were decided on the basis of speeches delivered in the Assembly. The political life of the citizen became much more intense and personally meaningful, as he was forced to think about and choose among the various policy options presented to him.

(ibid.)

Maybe so; Ober has certainly sketched a very inspiring portrait of radical participatory democracy, but only at the cost of neglecting some of his own evidence (see n. 19). No description could better summarise what is threatened by Gorgias' evocation of '*logos* the great *dynastēs*'. Ober contends that the Assemblymen were no longer 'passive': Gorgias suggests that the persuader alone functions actively. Ober maintains that the auditors did not merely listen, they also judged 'arguments': later sections of the *Encomium* will implicitly deny that the *psychē* possesses any faculty of active rationality for such assessment (the next chapter shows that although Plato most emphatically disputes this psychology, he too denies that this faculty can be employed in democratic debate). Ober's phrase '*forced* to think about and *choose*' is itself a nice instance of *paradoxologia*: one might have thought that the element of compulsion in the democratic situation as he describes it sits uneasily with the exercise of unconstrained choice.

21 Adkins complains that '*logoi* are the agency of persuasion; but they appear merely in a prepositional phrase. To perceive the *logos* is essential; but there is no word for perception' (Adkins 1983, p. 110). This seems excessively harsh; he is straining to uncover the 'inconsistency and invalid argument' of his title. The prepositional phrase is quite adequate to signal agency.

22 Cf. 'these [poetical elements] did not form a mere embellishment of speech, but served the very practical purpose of making the audience more easily inclined to accept the persuasive tricks by heightening the pleasure of listening' (Verdenius 1981, p. 119); and

> thus the *metron*, the formal aspect of the *logos*, seems to play a significant part in causing the emotive reactions upon which persuasion rests; and it is, therefore, natural that conscious formalism is so important in the carefully balanced antitheses, rhyming cola, calculated sound-effects, and metrical patterns in Gorgias' own style.
>
> (Segal 1962, p. 127)

23 Segal asserts that

> §7 ... presents a purely physical *pathos*, an objective act, which arouses pity; in §9, however, the *psychē* and its emotions are discussed, and the application of the same term, *pathos*, to the *psychē* in a different context there helps to give to this subjective emotion an objective, physical reality.
>
> (Segal 1962, p. 105)

Adkins objects that 'the language is vivid; but I cannot agree that the combination of emotional adjectives with nouns of physical

NOTES

description, or *vice versa*, commits Gorgias to any particular philo-sophical or psychological theory' (Adkins 1983, p. 110). In the light of my strictures at the end of Ch. 1 against viewing Gorgias as a theo-rist, philosophical or otherwise, I am in broad agreement with Adkins' conclusion, but dissent from his grounds for it. He regards Gorgias as a skilful 'sophist' in the traditional, pejorative sense, that is, as rather less than a theoretician, while I contend that Gorgias is provocatively *anti-* rather than *sub-*theoretical. My complaint against Segal arises from the conviction that it is quite wrong to saddle Gorgias with (in any case untenable) hard-and-fast distinctions between subjective and objec-tive, psychical or emotional and physical, as Segal does most implausibly in the statement that 'the *psychē* is thus not yet the completely spiritualised or dematerialised entity which it is to become for Plato, though, on the other hand, Gorgias probably did not think in terms of such a consistent materialism as Democritus' (Segal 1962, p. 106).

24 De Romilly suggests that this section is intimately linked to its prede-cessor:

> now is it not a likely inference that these devices [antithesis, punning, wordplay and rhyme], which were meant to subdue the audience and produce on the listeners' souls such and such a feeling, were derived from the wonderful power that they had in magic song and that some poets had already imitated with a thrilling and impressive effect?
>
> (de Romilly 1975, pp. 18–19)

MacDowell counters that 'magic, like poetry, produces emotional effects. But that does not mean that poetry is a kind of magic, or *vice versa*; the connection between them is somewhat overstated by J. de Romilly *Magic and Rhetoric* ch. 1' (MacDowell 1982, p. 37). But it is MacDowell who overstates his case: what is or should be at issue is not whether Gorgias marks a distinction, but rather what he takes it to be. Buchheim usefully remarks that Gorgias' language might well characterise *logoi* as themselves instrumental, rather than mere conduits for the communication of *dynamis* originating elsewhere: 'zu erwägen ist, ob damit nicht nur, wie die Grammatik des Ausdrucks vorschreibt, gemeint ist, daß die Beschwörungen aus Reden bestehen oder durch Reden gegeben werden, sondern daß sie gerade durch ihre sprachliche Form einen göttlich wirkenden Charakter erhalten' (Buchheim 1989, p. 166).

25 MacDowell comments that '*psychēs hamartēmata* and *doxēs apatēmata* make a rhyming pair of the kind which Gorgias likes, and that, for him, is a good enough reason to put both phrases in' (MacDowell 1982, pp. 37–8). This is remarkably fatuous. MacDowell neglects two far from trivial points. First, '*hamartēmata*' recalls '*hamartia*' in §1. There the error was that of praising the blameworthy or blaming the praise-worthy; but now we learn that (some) *logoi* have the effect of encouraging error by means of emotional manipulation, in this instance magical, but not necessarily so, given what we have already been told about poetry. This reinforces the (pleasant) trouble we ought to be

160

having over Gorgias' self-reference. Second, the errors and deceptions in question are *technai*: inasmuch as *logoi* are tools, various arts can put the inherent *dynamis* of *logos* to work (this is another issue which the *Gorgias* will dispute).

26 I owe this interpretation to Adkins:

> he now uses the fact that *logos* is masculine, *psychē* feminine. He writes *ho men oun peisas*, 'the one who persuaded', which might refer either to Paris or to the *logos*, while *hē peistheisa*, 'the one who was persuaded', might refer either to Helen or to her *psychē*. Since it is not Helen's *psychē*, but Helen, that is being blamed, the hearer is likely to interpret the second participle as referring to Helen, the first to Paris, with the result that it is suggested that Helen was compelled by Paris using *logos* as an instrument: a proposition *prima facie* even less easy to accept than that her *psychē* was compelled by *logos*. There is verbal dexterity also in *peithesthai* [translated 'obey']. Since it is the passive of *peithein*, if A *peithei* B, B *peithetai*; but the range of usage of *peithesthai* with the dative spans 'be persuaded, obey, trust in': the word may suggest that *logos* compelled Helen not merely to be persuaded but to trust in and obey what was said.
>
> (Adkins 1983, p. 113)

27 Dover's summation is just: 'the element common to all that was said of women by the Greeks is the woman's inability to resist fear, desire, or impulse' (Dover 1974); not only is the female an unresisting object, she also characteristically yields emotionally, as a reader of the *Encomium* would expect.

28 While the homosexual lover had no need to conceal his desire, and it was possible for him to boast to his friends of its attainment (Plato, *Phaedrus* 232A), the boy whom he pursued was expected to resist seduction and had to bear reproaches if it was known that his resistance was overcome. It seems to have been felt that the boy who yielded had assimilated himself to a *hetaira* [concubine] (Aeschines I.111, 131, 167, 185), detracting from his future rôle as a citizen-warrior, and that he had been worsted in a contest with his seducer.

> (Dover 1974, p. 215)

Dover 1978, although some of its contentions have been severely criticised, remains magisterial. Its comments on the potential assimilation of the passive partner in a homosexual relationship to women and other inferiors ('Dominant and subordinate roles', pp. 100–109) are full of interest for the student of Gorgias, especially the remarks on '*hybris*', 'assault', an Attic legal term which takes in specifically sexual attack:

> it is not only by assimilating himself to a woman in the sexual act that the submissive male rejects his role as a male citizen, but also by deliberately choosing to be the victim of what would be, if the victim were unwilling, *hybris*. The point of the fierce

161

sanctions imposed by Attic law on *hybris* was that the perpetrator 'dishonoured' (*atimazein*) his victim, depriving him of his standing as a citizen under the law, and standing could be recovered only by indictment which in effect called upon the community to reverse the situation and put down the perpetrator. To choose to be treated as an object at the disposal of another citizen was to resign one's own standing as a citizen.

(Dover 1978, pp. 103–4)

29 '*Peithō* is not at this date a name of Aphrodite ... but an independent goddess with erotic among other functions' (M. L. West 1978, p. 161). The erotic associations of persuasion are, of course, grist to Gorgias' mill:

> Sappho called *Peithō* a daughter of Aphrodite (90.7 f. = 200, cf. 96.26–9, and 1.18); Paris *peith' erō* [persuaded by *erōs*] Helen's heart (Alc. 283.9); the prostitutes of Corinth are *amphipoloi Peithous* [handmaidens of Persuasion] (Pind. fr. 122.1–2); and so on ... Hence a lovely person can be thought of as formed by *Peithō* as well as by the Charites: Ibycus 288 ... cf. Th. 349 n. *Peithō* is coupled with the Charites also in Pind. fr. 123.14, and becomes one of them in Hermesianax 11.

(ibid., p. 162)

30 '*Meteōrologoi*' could encompass theoreticians we would call 'meteorologists', 'astronomers' and 'astrologers'.

31 'The force of the *logoi* thus works directly upon the *psychē*; they have an immediate, almost physical impact upon it' (Segal 1962, p. 105).

32 It is plausible to assume that Gorgias intends his expression to be recognised as a polemical re-working of the famous dictum, '*opsis tōn adēlōn ta phainomena* [appearances are a vision of the unapparent]': for an interpretation of the conflict between Anaxagoras and Democritus over its proper interpretation, see Wardy 1988.

33 Cole is anxious to minimise the significance of this passage: 'the reference is to one very specific, not especially popular form that artful eloquence can take [viz. either prepared judicial speeches or epideictic ones]' (Cole 1991, p. 148). Given that the contests are 'necessary', a reference to epideictic oratory is not possible; and how could Cole know, *pace* Gorgias, that these *logoi* were 'not especially popular'?

34 Discussion of the implications of the use of the word '*ochlos*' will be reserved until Ch. 3, since Plato deliberately re-employs the vocabulary of 'crowds' in Socrates' onslaught on Gorgias.

35 MacDowell favours the translation (a) 'under compulsion' over (b) 'compelling, persuasive', on the grounds that

> the objection to (b) is that Gorgias maintains that the discourses of scientists and philosophers are also persuasive, so that *anagkaious*, if interpreted in this way, fails to distinguish lawcourt speeches from the kinds of speech mentioned in the other parts of the sentence.

(MacDowell 1982, pp. 39–40)

But there is no reason to assume that Gorgias is looking for an absolutely exclusive characterisation; and while (a) achieves a good ironic effect in the *compelled* pleader who *persuades*, (b) delivers the thematic fusion of compulsion, persuasion and pleasure.

36 Cf. how Palamedes assures the Achaean princes that hackneyed flummery is serviceable only when pleading 'in a crowd [*ochlos*]', and that in addressing them he avails himself of nothing but the facts, 'teaching the truth and not deceiving', unlike the rogue Odysseus (Gorgias, *Defence of Palamedes* 33).

37 The issue of how such dialectic might receive justification is taken up in Chs 3 and 5.

38 In §19 it means something like the turbulent 'contention of love' which Helen's eye, struck by Paris' looks, transmits to her *psychē*.

39 Cf. 'once again, Gorgias is trying to equate *peithein* with a causal sequence, for the effect of a drug does not depend on the patient's choice: cure or death follows irrespective of the patient's wish' (Adkins 1983, p. 114).

40 Segal concludes that

> the processes of the *psychē* are thus treated as having a quasi-physical reality and, perhaps more significant, as being susceptible to the same kind of control and manipulation by a rational agent as the body by the drugs of the doctor.
>
> (Segal 1962, p. 104)

The problem with this reading is that it fails to take account of the fact that *magic* is in question: is a witch or wizard 'a rational agent'? De Romilly is aware of the difficulty, but seeks to circumvent it:

> certes, il s'agit toujours de drogues (*pharmakōn, epharmakesan*) et même de discours qui ensorcellent (*exegoēteusan*), mais le souci d'expulser les humeurs est digne d'Hippocrate ... Et il est manifeste que Gorgias entend mettre en parallèle deux sciences comparables, dont l'une est relative au corps et l'autre à l'âme, et qui sont la médecine et la rhétorique. Il entend faire une science de la magie du verbe.
>
> (de Romilly 1973, p. 162)

She elaborates on this interpretation in a later study:

> he classifies drugs methodically in order to evolve a clear notion of the various possibilities with which one could reckon. This leads us from the level of magic and incantation to the level of empirical medicine. But it also separates two notions that had long been joined; for, although Gorgias started from inspired poetry and real magic, for his rhetoric he did not count on anything like inspiration.
>
> (de Romilly 1975, p. 21)

Her arguments do not withstand inspection. Hippocratic doctors were extremely eager to distance themselves from traditional healers and magicians (as Lloyd conclusively demonstrates in his chapter 'The criticism

of magic and the inquiry concerning nature' (G. E. R. Lloyd 1979, pp.
37–49 in particular)) – but Gorgias mixes magic with medicine. So the
idea that he effected a transition from magic to science is untenable,
since there is no 'separation' of the 'two notions'. On the contrary, as
Adkins argues, the notions are deliberately confused:

> *pharmaka* in §14, closely associated with 'humours' (*chymoi*), a
> scientific term, predominantly suggests scientific medicine; but
> *pharmakeuein*, which has the same range as *pharmaka*, when
> brought into association with both *goēteuein* and the earlier use
> of *pharmaka* readily calls to mind the full range of usage, and
> binds together the argument of §14 with that of §10, where,
> Gorgias hopes, a causal sequence has already been conceded.
>
> (Adkins 1983, p. 114)

If anything, Gorgias' drugs are reminiscent of Helen's mood-altering
pharmaka, 'many noble, many baneful', which also fall within the expertise of a 'doctor' – surely not a practitioner of 'empirical medicine'
(*Odyssey* IV 220–32).

41 Some slight evidence for the rationalising tendency sought by de Romilly
(see n. 40) is to be discovered here, if anywhere.

42 Reading '*ameleia*' with MacDowell, rather than '*alētheia*' with
Buchheim, whose textual judgement for the latter, vexed portions of
the *Encomium* tends to falter.

43 '*Eisoikizein*' for psychic infiltration is a significant metaphorical
precedent for Plato's magnificent descriptions of the citadel of the soul
yielding to hostile colonisation or siege, e.g. '*hē paranomia . . . eisoik-
isamenē* [lawlessness . . . made itself at home]', *Republic* 424D.

44 Perhaps this is the original for Plato's psychic model in *Philebus* 39A–B.
But if so, it is the complications which Plato introduces which are of
greatest interest. His modification of Gorgias is not merely a matter
of positing both a scribe and a painter in the soul; rather, the decisive
break with Gorgias' psychology comes from Plato's insistence on a
plurality of active and passive processes, perception, memory, imagination and, most important, *judgement*.

45 Baxandall 1971 testifies to the severe limitations of the rhetorical legacy
of antiquity as a contribution to the emergence of Humanist art
criticism.

46 MacDowell denies the connection: 'was Euripides answering Gorgias or
Gorgias answering Euripides? Probably neither. There is no resemblance
in details, and no strong reason to link Gorgias' discussion of Helen
with anyone else's' (MacDowell 1982, p. 12). The quotation from
Barlow in n. 47 is sufficient answer.

47 Another irony – Menelaus is succumbing to Helen's beauty as
Helen once had to Paris'. The power of *opsis*, appearance, which
Gorgias so stresses in his *Encomium on Helen* (16–19), operates
here too, and the gap between a reasoned mental conviction and
the ability to act on it, yawns so widely that it casts the whole
scene into irony. The outcome has rendered the debate futile for

Hecuba. By showing that persuasive words can persuade, but fail to lead to consistent action, Euripides may have in mind Gorgias' gross overestimation of them in his *Encomium* (10–14) and be demonstrating a different view.

(Barlow 1986, pp. 207–8)

On the *Troades* I am particularly indebted to Simon Goldhill's contribution to our joint Cambridge rhetoric course.

48 'One may imagine the twinkle in Gorgias' eye as he reveals in the very last word that he regards the whole paradoxical composition as a game' (MacDowell 1982, p. 43). Indeed, one may.

3 IN DEFENCE OF REASON: PLATO'S *GORGIAS*

1 Obviously my approach to Plato condemns out of hand any conception of (early) dialogues as more or less factual reportage of actual Socratic conversation; my Socrates is a fictional character, not a representation of a historical personage. However, this approach has no difficulty in accommodating the presumption that many of the preoccupations or even particular arguments attributed to his character Socrates by Plato were, as a matter of historical fact, manifested or enunciated by the real Socrates, even if its advocates see little potential gain and much actual loss in the traditional scholarly practice of mining Plato as a seam of historical information about Socrates.

2 Because he overlooks this possibility of indirect philosophical communication, Dodds' treatment of the dialogue, despite many fine points, is fundamentally flawed: 'for the modern reader the main interest of the *Gorgias* does not lie in its formal "dialectical" arguments, whose logic is seldom entirely convincing and sometimes transparently fallacious' (Dodds 1959, p. 30).

3 Williams has an undefended and unfair opinion of the relation between the dialogues, but gives powerful expression to at least one of the aspects of the *Gorgias* which have ensured its enduring fascination for philosophers:

once at least in the history of philosophy the amoralist has been concretely represented as an alarming figure, in the character of Callicles who appears in Plato's dialogue the *Gorgias*. Callicles, indeed, under the conventions of Platonic dialogue, engages in rational conversation and stays to be humbled by Socrates' argument (an argument so unconvincing, in fact, that Plato later had to write the *Republic* to improve on it). What is unnerving about him, however, is something that Plato displays and that is also the subject of the dialogue: he has a glistening contempt for philosophy itself, and it is only by condescension or to amuse himself that he stays to listen to its arguments at all.

(Williams 1985, p. 22)

165

NOTES

4 Irwin provides a useful schematic representation of the dialogue's structure:

> since each of the first two interlocutors is found to need the support of his more extreme successor, the refutation of Callicles implies the refutation of his predecessors too (508A–C). More briefly, the structure is this (using initial letters for the positions of the three interlocutors):
> (1) If G, then P.
> (2) If P, then C.
> (3) But not C.
> (4) Therefore not P.
> (5) Therefore not G.
>
> (Irwin 1979, p. 9)

The existence of such inferential relations demonstrates that any interpretation which seeks to isolate the Gorgias section from its successors is bound to misconstrue the true status of many of its arguments by ignoring whatever relevant modifications emerge in the Polus and Callicles sections. My hope is to avoid this pitfall while according the first section the attention it deserves yet tends not to receive. For example, after denying that Gorgias is either a 'sophist' properly so called or 'an original philosophical thinker', Dodds declares that the extant examples of Gorgias' writing 'make the impression of a dazzling insincerity, an insincerity so innocently open as to be (except in the funeral oration) entirely void of offence' (Dodds 1959, p. 8). This condescending attitude towards the real Gorgias unfortunately ensures that his handling of the Platonic Gorgias is seriously inadequate.

5 Dodds glosses *dynamis* as '"point" or "function" (Lat. *vis*)' (Dodds 1959, p. 190); fine as far as it goes, but his patronising insensitivity to Gorgias' achievement (see n. 4) keeps him from picking up the resonance of the word Plato carefully puts in his Socrates' mouth.

6 Irwin's consistent rendering of *legein* as 'speak' rather than 'mean', e.g. 'how are you speaking?', 'don't you understand how I'm speaking?', merely confuses the Greekless reader.

7 The fussy strictures of the ancient commentator Olympiodorus on the conversational proprieties (Olympiodorus 2,10) are wide of the mark, but his hunch is valuable. That is, he appreciates and emphasises that Socrates encourages Chaerephon to understand what is to be asked (2,8), while Polus, as his teacher's product, is all too anxious to launch into his *own* display.

8 Cole comments:

> it is in philosophical texts that we first hear of this discipline; and the word *rhetoric* itself bears every indication of being a Platonic invention. There is no trace of it in Greek before the point in the *Gorgias* (449A5) where the famous Sophist – after hesitation and (possibly) a certain amount of prompting from Socrates (448D9) – decides to call the art he teaches the 'rhetorly' – that is, *rhētōr's* or 'speaker's' – 'art' (*rhētorikē technē*).
>
> (Cole 1991, p. 2)

NOTES

This claim, which underpins Cole's major thesis, that 'rhetoric' properly understood is a fourth-century invention, collapses immediately. So far from its being the case that the word 'rhetoric' is flagged here as a Platonic invention, the description of it as 'so-called' – a description Cole overlooks or ignores – strongly implies that the word 'rhetoric' was current outside, and predated, the Platonic writings (conversation with Malcolm Schofield has brought this home to me). For Cole, Plato and Aristotle are 'the true founders of rhetoric as well as of philosophy' (p. 29). His stated adherence to a 'revolutionary' rather than 'evolutionary' model of the genesis of rhetoric (p. 28) is nothing more than subscription to a reductive schema submerging all else beneath supposed Platonic and Aristotelian influence. Thus, on the one hand, in philosophy he entirely fails to recognise Parmenides' centrality, as explained in Ch. 1 (revealingly, Parmenides receives only a single paragraph from Cole (p. 59)); on the other, in rhetoric he cannot, consistently with his dominant theme, appreciate Gorgias' provocation of philosophers – and everyone else who might dispute the mastery of persuasive power.

9 Vickers 1989 might be retitled *In Defence of Rhetoric against Plato*:

> I have long felt that the account of rhetoric, and politics, in the *Gorgias* was a violent travesty of both disciplines, but not until I sat down to write the studies that form chapters 2 and 3 (in part) of this book did I realise just how systematically Plato distorted both evidence and argument to build up his case.
>
> (p. vii)

In the event Vickers' 'defence' turns on his association of (rhetorical) free speech with the emergence and maintenance of democratic institutions. He cites *Gorgias* 452D–E and comments:

> to Plato, of course, it was deplorable that the rhetorician, not the philosopher, should have such power, but to the majority of students of rhetoric down to the Renaissance its great attraction was just this promise of success in civic life, and its upholding of liberty.
>
> (p. 7)

Thus from the outset, by blandly overlooking the *coupling* of freedom for the rhetorician with control over his fellow-citizens, Vickers shows himself to be disappointingly purblind, at best, to what the issues are. Later he does attempt to grapple with the political repercussions: Plato

> has crudified the argument, for the power traditionally ascribed to rhetoric was not the unscrupulous power of the tyrant, autocrat and voluptuary at once, but the power to influence decisions in open meetings. What is actually a mark of democracy – which Plato abhorred – is turned by him into an attribute of tyranny.
>
> (p. 99)

So much for *logos* the great *dynastēs*. Despite (or because of?) his obsessive fury at the *Gorgias*, Vickers manifests no awareness whatsoever of

167

the real Gorgias' historical and theoretical significance, or of the way
the *Gorgias* reacts to Gorgias (e.g. Gorgias is a 'dialectician's dummy',
p. 95). Nor has he any interest in what dialectic might be (pp. 125 ff.
betray almost total misunderstanding of the logic of *elenchos*), or *how*
it competes with rhetoric; nor any understanding of the virtual
coincidence of rhetoric and politics in Athens (e.g. consideration of 'the
rival claims of politics and philosophy to represent the good life'
(p. 103) is a 'switch' from the topic of rhetoric *per se*). He naïvely
identifies the sophists as political theorists espousing an ideal of liberal
democratic consensus, anathema to the Popperian, authoritarian
monster who is Plato. Such examples of analytical and scholarly
shoddiness could be multiplied almost indefinitely.

10 Dodds comments *ad loc.*:

> with this vague and pompous phrase compare the claim of
> Gorgias' pupil Isocrates that the art of discourse is *pantōn tōn
> enontōn en tē tōn anthrōpōn physei pleistōn agathōn aition* ['of all
> things in human nature the cause of most goods'] (*Nicocles* 5, *cf.*
> also *Pang.* 3–4).
>
> (Dodds 1959, p. 208; he fails to acknowledge that his
> gloss is identical to Olympiodorus 5,1 in every detail)

But whatever its tone, the expression is hardly 'vague', if one pays due
regard to the pragmatics of idiomatic speech; rather, Socrates, the 'infantile' philosopher, *refuses* to understand what Gorgias says.

11   The rôle that *logos* may play in this process entitles it to be called
a 'wielder of power' (*dynastēs*: *Helen* 8), but not necessarily a tech-
nician (*dēmiourgos* [Socrates' word, not Gorgias', at *Gorgias*
453A2]). Later writers can speak of rhetoric as a form of power
(*dynamis*), or as possessing a *dynamis* of its own, but art and
dynamis are distinct enough that at times (*cf.* Arist., *Rhet.* I 2
1356A32–4; I 4 1359B12–14; Quintilian 2 15 2) *dynamis* is
explicitly contrasted with the exact knowledge (*epistēmē, scientia*)
that regularly accompanies art.

> (Cole 1991, p. 148)

True, Socrates' interest in expertise is emphatic and, obviously enough,
a distinctive Platonic conception of what counts, or rather *should* count,
as *technē* is in play in the *Gorgias*. Nevertheless, this provides no reason
not to believe that Gorgias offered tuition, or that such tuition must
primarily have been intended to convey persuasive power to his pupils.

12   Readers may well feel very restive with this uncritical sketch of philosophical procedure – and so they should. The compelling (if often
intractable) issues involved in criticism and attempted vindication of the
impersonal model of philosophical activity are broached in the epilogue.

13   At *Phdr.* 261CD Socrates speaks more accurately: forensic rhetoric
is concerned with the just and the unjust, but *dēmēgoria* (the
deliberative branch) with the good and the bad, a wider field
which includes questions of expediency as well as of rightness;

NOTES

he also recognises (261AB) that rhetoric can be exercised *en idiois* ['in private'], and on trivial matters (the epideictic branch).

(Dodds 1959, p. 205)

It is Dodds, not Socrates, who implies not only that there is nugatory praise and blame, but also that all epideictic is trifling. And the difference between the *Gorgias* and the *Phaedrus* here is not a matter of 'accuracy': Gorgias expresses himself as he does because for him there are no significant distinctions between the public venues wherein rhetoric holds sway, while the Socrates of the *Phaedrus* is concerned to keep a tamed and purified persuasion within its proper place(s).

14 The sense of *ochlos* is strongly negative: e.g. *ochlos mallon ē stratos*, 'a mob rather than an army', Herodianus 6.71, *hoi toioutoi ochloi*, Thucydides 4.126 (and in opposition to *dēmos*, 7.8). In Xenophon, Charmides, expatiating on the difference between private dialectic and competition 'before the masses' (*en plēthei*), maintains that innate shame and fear are more to the fore 'in crowds' (*en tois ochlois*) than in private gatherings (*Memorabilia* 3.4–5). For the range of terms used to designate the Athenian citizen body, see Ober 1990, p. 11. Cf. 'it [rhetoric] is a means invented for manipulating and stirring up the mob and a community fallen into lawlessness' (Montaigne 1991, p. 342, from 'On the vanity of words': 'mob' translates 'une tourbe'). Dodds provides a useful Platonic reference:

both in Plato and elsewhere the word commonly conveys a tinge of contempt; it would scarcely be employed in this connection by a good democrat. This is not, however, a point on which Socrates and Gorgias would disagree: at *Euthyd.* 290A3 Socrates is made to use similar language – *dikastōn te kai ekklēsiastōn kai tōn allōn ochlōn kēlēsis* ['the bewitchment of juries and assemblies and other crowds'].

(Dodds 1959, p. 205)

However, he misses the possibility that the passages are much more intimately related, unlike Cole, who on the basis of the magical metaphor suggests that *Euthydemus* 289E4–290A4 is 'almost certainly' a reminiscence of the *Encomium*; although he typically spoils the insight by adding the caveat that 'this is probably yet another instance of later "rhetoricisation" of traditional material' (Cole 1991, p. 148).

15 For discussion of the 'digression' in the *Theaetetus* (171D–177C), where Socrates contrasts philosophical leisure with the hurried constraint of the lawcourts, see Burnyeat 1990, pp. 31–9.

16 One might note in passing that an Athenian tragedian was conceived of as 'teaching' the entire assembled city, and that his production was evaluated by a jury selected on egalitarian principles; the denial in the *Gorgias* that instructing a multitude is even possible thus effectively robs of all legitimacy an Athenian institution we regard as one of radical democracy's signal triumphs. Indeed, much later in the dialogue Socrates makes this absolutely explicit. Taking advantage of the definition in the

169

Encomium of poetry as '*logos* with metre', he extracts Callicles' agreement that tragedy aims its *logoi* at a great *ochlos*; so tragedians are just rhetoricians, and thereby flatterers of the motley crowd (502B1–D9). This dismissal is exceedingly hard to reconcile with what seems to us the provocative character of much extant Greek tragedy; Dodds' defence cannot command assent:

> although Euripides could on occasion enforce unpalatable truths (as in the *Troades*), there are passages in some of his plays where we cannot but suspect him of 'playing to the gallery'; and if a poet of his rank could at times yield to the temptation, it is likely that lesser men offended more often and more grossly.
>
> (Dodds 1959, p. 321)

17 See Ch. 4, 'Protagoras and Isocrates: the genius of evasion'.
18 This is Olympiodorus' interpretation (7,1).

19   It is doubtful that this naïveté extended, as Plato would have us believe, to a complacent exaltation of his own uninformed presentation of a theme over the informed one of an expert (*Gorgias* 452E1–8, 456C2–6, 459C3–5), for Gorgian discourse operates perforce in situations where expertise as Plato understands it is not available.

> (Cole 1991, p. 152)

This is all premised on Gorgias' so-called 'announced scepticism' (p. 150), evinced primarily by *On What Is Not* read as straightforward assertion of 'sceptical' epistemology, a scepticism promptly disregarded by its author, e.g.

> to accept the isolated testimony of Plato at this point is to read the presuppositions and methods of later rhetoric into a characteristically fifth-century phenomenon. Gorgias' scepticism, like Protagoras' relativism, obviously shared the rhetorician's recognition of the problematic character of human communication. But having recognised the problem, both men chose, by and large, to circumvent it rather than seek a solution along rhetorical lines.
>
> (p. 152)

The real Gorgias would certainly not have adopted the position which Plato ascribes to his character, but not for the reasons Cole adduces. He imagines that the operation of 'Gorgian discourse' is limited to pockets of uncertainty; in fact, the *logos* as extolled by Gorgias knows no limits and exerts a uniform compulsive force.

20 The 'blame students, not teachers' defence swiftly became a *topos* in the rhetorical tradition, appearing, for example (in unacknowledged debt to the *Gorgias*?), in Isocrates, *Antidosis* 251–3.
21 It would seem that representatives of the American gun lobby who protest that there is nothing menacing about responsible weapons enthusiasts might find venerable support in the *Gorgias* as well as the Constitution.

22 After Irwin 1979, p. 25. Liddell, Scott and Jones' 'refute' must be avoided; Socrates may hesitate because he foresees that the *elenchos* will issue in a refutation, but he does not say that what he is engaged in is just refutation, pure and simple. However, neither Dodds nor Irwin copes adequately with the translation of '*pros to pragma*', and so neither of them perceives the subtlety of Socrates' position.

23   *Philonikounta* [E4] should not be deleted, as Headlam suggested: for Socrates can hardly deny that he *legei pros Gorgian*: what he denies is that he *legei philonikōn pros Gorgian*. There is no real inconsistency with D4, where with *philonikountas* we naturally understand *pros allēlous*.

(Dodds 1959, p. 214)

This is fine, with the addition that Socrates affirms that he *legei philonikōn tou kataphanes genesthai* ('speaks in a competition to clarify the issue'). Socrates contends against obscurity in the *logos*; if that inevitably entails speaking *pros Gorgian* ('against Gorgias'), the necessity nevertheless remains extrinsic to Socrates' stated intentions, which concern discovery of the truth to the exclusion of all else. These matters are further explored in Ch. 5's discussion of Aristotle on dialectic, and in the Epilogue.

24 Irwin pertinently comments:

Gorgias has argued that the rhetor will be more persuasive than the expert among the non-expert and ignorant. Socrates now suggests that the rhetor makes himself appear to know more than the expert, which Gorgias has not so far conceded. Socrates must assume that the rhetor can persuade his audience only by appearing to know more than the expert. But this assumption is dubious. Why could a rhetor not appear to know the *relevant* facts, even though in general the expert knows more about the subject? Or why could the rhetor not be more persuasive because he appeals vividly and powerfully to people's feelings? . . . On the other hand, the confinement of rhetorical success to the inexpert is a good ground for suspicion. If the rhetor could claim to have the objectively better case, why should it not persuade the experts in the subject as well?

(Irwin 1979, pp. 123–4)

25 In his chapter 'The Socratic elenchus: method is all', Gregory Vlastos wrestles with the profound problem of how Socrates can legitimately regard dialectic as an instrument for the discovery of truth – as he does – when, to all appearances, his procedure could in logic do no more than establish inconsistency among his interlocutor's beliefs. Consistency can be achieved without truth. Vlastos speculates that the answer is to be found in what he calls 'the tremendous assumption': 'whoever has a false moral belief will always have at the same time true beliefs entailing the negation of that false belief' (Vlastos 1994, p. 25). Consideration of Vlastos' problem as such lies beyond the scope of this book, although we have touched on, and shall

return to, closely related matters. Here it must suffice to point out that our possession of such hypothetical omnipresent true moral beliefs would constitute no objection to my use of the idea of Socratic moral idiocy, since such 'idiocy' has been defined in terms, not of true belief, but of an absence of knowledge (which Vlastos would not dispute).

26 The sufficiency thesis is a paradox which Plato himself would come to reject as his psychology developed, and would accordingly modify, in the *Phaedrus*, his vehement rejection of rhetoric as the indefensible manipulation of ignorant emotion.

27 This is why Irwin's complaint is beside the point:

> Gorgias does not promise to 'teach virtue' in the sense of making people virtuous ... He only promises to tell his pupils the sorts of things that are just and unjust. Learning this and acting justly or being just are, for Gorgias and for most people, two very different things.
>
> (Irwin 1979, p. 126)

The text contains no such distinction between 'making' and 'telling' and, were it there, Gorgias would lose greatly in trying to take advantage of it.

28 Olympiodorus says 'he calls apodeictic conviction "necessity"' (19,9); Dodds glosses *ou ... anankazeis* 'by logical arguments' (Dodds 1959, p. 245). Cf. 475A5, 475B2, 475B8.

29 'Not "I do not talk to the vulgar" – for Socrates interrogated all sorts of people (*Apol.* 22A–D) – but "with people *en masse* I do not even attempt discussion"' (Dodds 1959, p. 248).

30 Olympiodorus (20,2) sees this vividly (*allos allēn echei doxan* ('each man has a different opinion')), although he is thinking, non-Socratically, of the many 'listening to a demonstration'.

31 When Callicles himself is eventually bested by Socrates, he accuses him of being dialectically 'violent' (*biaios*) (505D4–5: undertranslated by Irwin as 'you're so insistent, Socrates' (Irwin 1979, p. 83); Dodds' paraphrase ('what a tyrant you are!' (Dodds 1959, p. 332)) is much better).

32 Not that the interpretation of Socratic midwifery is unproblematic: Burnyeat 1990 should be consulted.

33 Cf.

> those who complain that they cannot resist him, or cannot see where they stand after having discussed with him, are merely bewildered by the power of thorough analysis ... Whereas the magic of the sophists aimed at producing illusion, Socrates' magic rests on the obstinate destruction of all illusions. It is the magic of implacable truth ...

and

> Gorgias represented the deceiving power of style, or of the choice and arrangement of arguments, which could create at will any

NOTES

kind of emotion. Socrates represents the stimulating power of reasoning and discussion, when devoted to the search of truth. But in both cases this power was bewildering, amazing, magical.
(de Romilly 1975, pp. 36–7, 37)

34 In fact the identification of Socrates with *erōs* in Alcibiades' speech is much more complete and emphatic than I have indicated, since further features of his description are obvious reminiscences of what other speakers had said: for example, the anecdote about Socrates' toughness during the Potidaean campaign recalls elements of Socrates' report of Diotima's erotic lesson.

35 We have not only a subjective contradiction between Callicles' personal values and the levelling tendency of his hedonistic doctrine, paralleling the conflict between his élitist convictions and his political rôle as friend and flatterer of the Athenian *dēmos*; in the *kinaidos* case there is also an objective incompatibility between this form of pleasure and the pursuit of a political career in Athens.
(Kahn 1983, p. 107)

36 To add yet another suggestive text:

Agathon: Socrates, I am not able to speak against you; let things be as you say they are.
Socrates: It is the truth, beloved Agathon, that you are not able to speak against, since there is no difficulty in speaking against Socrates, at any rate.
(*Symposium* 201C6–9)

37 Kahn misses this fundamental point: 'it is the central thesis of this study that all three arguments are in a deep sense *ad hominem*: directed against the man and not only against his statements' (Kahn 1983, pp. 75–6). He thinks that the 'amoral conception of rhetoric can be consistently stated', which is true enough; but he believes that only the threat of 'public hostility and grave personal risk keeps Gorgias from stating it (p. 84). There is no textual evidence to support this judgement; why does Kahn so lightly accuse Gorgias of hypocrisy? As he admits, the *deliberate* fallacies he detects in the refutation of Polus can hardly underpin Socrates' positive theses, the Socratic Paradoxes espoused in the *Gorgias* (pp. 110–11). *Mutatis mutandis* this criticism applies to Kahn's analysis of the refutations of Gorgias and Callicles, to the extent that there he also claims to detect the *ad hominem fallacy*. Were Kahn correct, the *Gorgias* would ironically be the ultimate *vindication* of Gorgias (as Cicero imagines it to be: see Ch. 4, 'Cicero: the ideal orator'). On his reconstruction, the grand confrontation of dialectic and display is just a deceptive superstructure, concealing the fundamental working of persuasion on Platonic readers susceptible to the emotional impact of the image of Socrates' life, rather than the rational force of his arguments.

38 I have already mentioned Vlastos' (n. 25) insistence that Socrates refuses to be satisfied with coherence, and (sometimes) claims to achieve truth,

173

and the 'tremendous assumption' which is supposed to solve the quandary: all interlocutors possess true moral beliefs for Socrates to call upon if required for purposes of refutation. Vlastos' solution is appealingly provocative and powerfully argued, but I find myself inclined to reject it, albeit with considerable misgivings. Vlastos concedes that evidence in favour of his interpretation is exiguous; he accounts for this by appealing to Socrates' 'epistemological innocence', an innocence beginning to break in the *Gorgias* itself, which manifests a new methodological awareness and enunciates the claims to certainty which so impress Vlastos. On balance I find this line implausible because vindication of the 'tremendous assumption' would create at least as many and as intractable problems as it would eliminate – an objection Vlastos never properly confronts. Therefore I prefer to suppose that Socrates' 'epistemological innocence' remains unsullied: the aporetic dialogues are entirely open to a sceptical construal by those so inclined, and the dogmatic flashes of the *Gorgias* are unjustified without the transcendental psychology of the *Meno* (which Vlastos in any case invokes as the immediate successor to the unstable epistemology of the *Gorgias*).

Perhaps a more important source of disagreement is over what is, and what is not, taken for granted. Vlastos is entirely occupied with the problem of how to make the transition from coherence to truth. But that (1) there is such a thing as objective truth; that (2) there is a well-founded distinction between cooperative dialectic and competitive eristic; and that (3) interlocutors can and do regularly express sincere dialectical commitments are taken absolutely for granted in Vlastos' exegesis. His reader is given no clue that the *Gorgias* is about *rhetoric* in particular: all one learns from Vlastos is that the dialogue contains *elenchoi* concerning cardinal ethical issues, and that these *elenchoi* are fitted out with highly charged methodological prescriptions. Thus he conceives of the puzzle as an epistemological quandary *internal* to philosophy, to be met using his meta-elenctic principles. My overall reading is radically different. So far from his taking (1)–(3) for granted, on my interpretation Plato's dominating concern in the *Gorgias* is to explore their viability in light of the threat posed by the writings of the real Gorgias. For Vlastos, *logos obviously* means '(deductive) argument'. For me, dialectical *logos* is indeed argumentative; and the fact that its persuasive force derives from rationality of itself constitutes a move against Gorgias. Thus Vlastos' reading is at once too stringent, in that it formulates the issue with unwarranted logical specificity, and far too complacent, in that it takes for granted the very conditions for the possibility of philosophy which are under debate. His *Gorgias* is essentially a set of provisional epistemological pronouncements on *how* philosophy can be done so as to track truth; my *Gorgias* is essentially a pitched battle with rhetoric over *whether* philosophy can be done. The *Gorgias* targets hostile alternatives *to* philosophical discourse, rather than articulating choices between alternative models *of* philosophical discourse. It will not have eluded the reader's attention that however deep my disagreement with Vlastos, only an interpretation which stimulated me greatly could have called forth so protracted a reply.

NOTES

39 Dodds cannot take the device of dialogic monologue too seriously: 'inge-
nious and successful though it is, it reveals the underlying tension
between Plato the Socratic "dramatist" and Plato the philosopher' (Dodds
1959, p. 331). He seems to miss the *philosophical* (rather than 'dramatic')
significance of question-and-answer as an investigative technique.
40 Dodds misconstrues Callicles' remark as meaning he 'finds Socrates'
arguments more logical than convincing' (Dodds 1959, p. 352). Irwin
catches the mistake and plumps (without argument) for the third option
I have enumerated:

> though Callicles is still not entirely convinced, Socrates does not
> suggest (contrary to Dodds) that he is unreachable by rational
> argument. Though Socrates has previously suggested that
> Callicles' desires are disordered (505C), and mentions here the
> misguided 'love' (*erōs*; see 481D) that prevents him from being
> convinced, he still insists that rational persuasion can make
> Callicles re-direct his desires.
>
> (Irwin 1979, p. 233)

41 Olympiodorus says that 'continual use of good *logoi* subdues the *pathē*
by enchantment and perhaps cuts them out' (39,8), as if Gorgianic incantation rather than Socratic dialectic were in question. In fact, he thinks
that the point of *our* reading the dialogue is 'to cut out the *pathē*' (40,4).
This excision is supposed to be the result of the dialogue's *logoi*, although
Olympiodorus confesses that Socrates' arguments are sometimes
enthymematic (*anakephalaiōdōs*), sometimes 'diffuse' (*apotadēn*).

42 Socrates' version of these incidents conceals the serious questions
of policy sometimes at stake and the solid grounds for measures
taken against these politicians. His story is a perversion of the
historical conditions, as far as we know them.

(Irwin 1979, p. 235)

43 As I stated at the outset, my intention is neither to produce another
complete commentary on the dialogue, nor even to chase down every
plausible connection between Gorgias and the *Gorgias*: so sensitive,
fecund and elaborate is Plato's response that even the apparently more
limited exercise would swiftly expand into full-scale commentary. The
reader familiar with the dialogue should now be prepared to develop a
novel appreciation of well-studied texts: for example, the concluding
eschatology, in which the *psychē* is stripped of the body, stripped of all
cosmetic *kosmos*, describes a mythical situation in which deception is
absolutely impossible, in which judgement is invariably correct. In other
words, a situation in which Gorgias is impossible.

4 AFTERLIVES

1 See Too 1995 for an innovative and controversial reassessment of
Isocrates' true originality as a rhetorical self-construction.
2 See Loraux's shrewd comments on the fifth-century Athenian 'rupture
entre un passé panhellénique et un présent hégémonique' (Loraux 1981,

175

p. 71); in the fourth century international events oblige Athenian ideology to return to a version of that past.

3 Nor, it would seem, the same as those employed in philosophical debate, at least in 'eristic', the unfavourable aspect under which Isocrates routinely sees and contemptuously dismisses 'philosophy' (as we, not he, would understand the term): he warns Alexander off 'eristic' as unseemly for monarchs, who should brook no contradiction (*pros hautous antilegein*) from their fellow-citizens (*To Alexander* 3). Isocrates apparently perceives no awkwardness in continuing to refer to persons now forbidden any opportunity of dissent as 'fellow-citizens'.

4 Vickers suggests that Isocrates reaffirmed 'a fundamental distinction that Plato tried to erode', viz. that between persuasion and compulsion (Vickers 1989, pp. 155–6). Thus he fails to understand that Gorgias himself introduced the essential, provocative collapse of the dichotomy, and that, in some instances, Plato is reacting to Gorgias' challenge, rather than 'trying to erode' it. But, second, Vickers' entire discussion of the *Gorgias* betrays that he fatally overlooks the crucial possibility that logical compulsion need not be an act of violation.

5 It is not as if Isocrates simply *ignores* the danger that in these novel circumstances all rhetoric, including his own, is a ridiculous irrelevance. Before broaching the topic of 'calumny' (probably Demosthenes') against Philip, he insists that he should 'express himself with his *customary* frankness' (*emoi te prosēkein meta parrēsias hōsper eithismai poieisthai tous logous*, *To Philip* 72). Again, he represents his intimates, shocked at his intention of presuming to advise Philip, as protesting that he will consider Isocrates 'grossly deluded about the *dynamis* of both his *logoi* and his own thought' (21–2). But – so we are blandly assured – they were swept off their feet by the unparalleled brilliance and profundity of what Isocrates read to them, and humbly withdrew their previous objections.

6 Unless otherwise indicated, translations are from Hubbard and Karnofsky 1982.

7 '*Kekēlēmenoi*': cf. '*kekēlēmenos*' ('mesmerised', Hubbard and Karnofsky) for the effect of the great *logos* on Socrates (328D4–5). But, as usual, Socrates' complaint that he was at a loss for words is dripping with irony, as the immediate sequel discloses: 'but when I realised that he really had finished, I recovered, with some difficulty, my presence of mind . . .'. A good *logos* restores and vivifies one's critical faculties, rather than dissipating them. Socrates is hinting that if Protagoras' talk has a profound effect, that is not by virtue of its rational power – thus the recurrence of the imagery of enchantment.

8 See Ch. 1, 'Who was Gorgias?', p. 7. Whether Isocrates adapted this particular *topos* of sophistical vilification from Plato, or it was already available for general exploitation in the fourth century, cannot be settled.

9 See Ch. 3, 'Rhetorical feasting, philosophical plain fare?', pp. 52–8.

10 Here I depart from Hubbard and Karnofsky, who mistranslate: 'if, therefore, you can give us a clearer *demonstration* that excellence can be taught, please don't stint us, but give a *demonstration*' (emphasis added). The geometrical/logical overtones of 'demonstration' should at all costs be avoided. Hubbard and Karnofsky do, however, correctly render the

NOTES

occurrence of *'endeixasthai'* in 317C7 as 'show off'. Not that in 320B8–C1 Socrates is saying anything as crass as 'show off, please'; but Plato's choice of vocabulary again serves to keep very much alive the issue of how to speak. And, of course, the dialogue famously sets Socrates' favoured method of 'short speech' (dialectical question-and-answer) against Protagoras' 'long speech' (exemplified most obviously by the 'great *logos*' itself).

11 This translation diverges from that of Hubbard and Karnofsky. Scholarly debate has raged inconclusively over the authenticity of the 'great *logos*' as Protagorean doctrine, opinions ranging from the assurance that it is a light adaptation of an original text written by Protagoras himself to the position that it is a Platonic composition designed purely with the requirements of the dialogue in mind. Thus it might even be possible to contend that what I shall describe as Isocrates' modification of Plato's text is actually an instance of his fidelity to the *real* 'great *logos*' of Protagoras, which has disappeared. Although I am not attracted by this sort of inconclusive speculation, my interpretation of Isocrates remains unaffected by it, since all my points can be reformulated in terms of a reaction to Gorgias, the *Gorgias* and the historical, rather than the Platonic, Protagoras.

12 This translation diverges from that of Hubbard and Karnofsky.

13 This translation diverges from that of Hubbard and Karnofsky.

14 Translation after Norlin.

15 Translation after Norlin, but retaining *logos* transliterated in place of his disastrous, if understandable, disambiguation, 'speech'.

16 That such a reference is intended is further supported by Crassus' later response to Scaevola, when he states that when in Athens he remained unshaken by the philosophers' attack from all sides on rhetorical pretensions to government and to *scientia*, even that by Plato, the initiator of the dispute, whose *Gorgias* he read diligently; only to conclude with the rhetorical flourish which furnishes this chapter with one of its epigraphs: that Plato 'was most an orator when heaping scorn on them' (I 45–7).

17 See Ch. 1, 'Who was Gorgias?', p. 6.

18 Again, supporting evidence is to be found in Crassus' riposte to the philosophers. After expatiating on the formidable learning which even the enemies of rhetoric must concede is necessary for 'copious' speech in court or Senate, taking in knowledge of public affairs, mores, the law and human nature, he concludes with this rhetorical question addressed to hostile philosophers:

> but if the power of the orator is nothing other than the power of speaking in a well-organised way, elegantly and at length [*composite, ornate, copiose loqui*], I ask, how could he achieve that very thing without that knowledge which you do not concede to him? For the capacity [*virtus*] of speaking cannot arise, unless the things said have been perceived by the man who says them.
>
> (I.11.48)

19 Shortly, Scaevola will take issue with just this Isocratean exaltation of the power of the word:

177

who will concede to you that in the beginning the human race, scattered in mountains and forests, enclosed itself in walled towns not because it had been forced to this by the advice of the prudent, but because it had been enticed by the speech of the eloquent? Or indeed that the remaining expedients for either the establishment or conservation of communities were set up not by wise and strong men, but rather by the eloquent and those who speak elegantly?

(I 36–7)

The following catalogue of culture heroes confirms the impression that, to a degree, in Scaevola Cicero is doing little more than representing the clichéd attitude of bluff Roman resistance to effeminate Greek ingenuity. If originally times were hard, they were put right under the compulsion of strong wisdom, not by yielding to cajolement. But matters are more complicated than they appear on the surface. First, Cicero ironically has Scaevola couch his rejection of Crassus' vision of the supremacy of persuasion in terms of the categories of *Greek* culture, wisdom/compulsion vs. eloquence/enticement. Second, he must also borrow from Greek philosophy the tactic of associating rhetoric narrowly with flattery. Third, his traditionalist scepticism is expressed very eloquently and ornately.

20 In effect Crassus is espousing a Romanised version of the scheme of rhetoric supervised by philosophy described in Plato's *Phaedrus*. The *Phaedrus* does not come within the scope of this book, but it is enough for the reader to know that its delineation of a 'science' of the emotions presents a historically important opportunity for reconciling a rhetoric, newly purged, with philosophy, a solution which can, as here, be combined with the evasive manœuvres inherited from Isocrates.

21 Translations will be from Behr's Loeb edition, occasionally with modifications.

22 Loraux 1981 is excellent on how Aristides' *Panathenaicus* is a discourse superficially comparable with the Panathenaic orations of the classical era, but from which all civic significance has evaporated (pp. 260–5).

23 Elsewhere (200 ff.), he contends that if rhetoric is indeed, as Plato would have it, 'the craftsman of persuasion', then *ipso facto* it cannot involve yielding to the preconceptions of the audience, since to persuade, he claims, is *by definition* to overcome an opposing opinion – as if all attacks were frontal.

24 I am at a loss to understand how Vickers, whose enthusiasm for Aristides is presumably considerable, since he reused Aristides' title (*In Defence of Rhetoric*) and castigates the *Gorgias* at comparable length and with comparable vehemence, can conclude that 'like Isocrates, Aristides restores force and persuasion to their rightful positions as mutually exclusive opposites' (Vickers 1989, p. 173).

NOTES

5 ARISTOTLE'S *RHETORIC*:
MIGHTY IS THE TRUTH AND IT SHALL PREVAIL?

1 I am not questioning the universal scholarly presumption that the *Rhetoric* takes serious note of the *Phaedrus*; to mention only what is perhaps the most obvious and generally recognised influence, Aristotle's various schemata for organising emotional proclivities within a typology of character surely take their original impetus from the notion of 'scientific' psychology advanced in that dialogue. My concern is not to exclude the *Phaedrus* from consideration, but rather to ensure that the vital contribution of the *Gorgias* to the formulation of Aristotle's views receives the attention it deserves.

2 The correct translation of this passage is a matter of debate; for defence of my construal, see Grimaldi 1980, p. 27. The alternative (defended by e.g. Cope 1877, pp. 22–3) is to translate 'necessarily they [viz. the losing parties] are defeated through their own fault'. But since it is only Aristotle's claim that truth and justice enjoy a natural superiority which has a bearing on my argument, I can accept either rendering of the latter part of the sentence.

3 Tyler Burge argues on behalf of what he calls 'the Acceptance Principle': 'a person is entitled to accept as true something that is presented as true and that is intelligible to him, unless there are stronger reasons not to do so' (Burge 1993, p. 467). But many contemporary philosophers would find such a principle strikingly contentious, and Burge himself limits it in such a fashion as to bring out the contrast with Aristotle very distinctly:

> in areas like politics, where cooperation is not the rule and truth is of little consequence, or philosophy, where questioning is as much at issue as belief, we engage in complex reasoning about whether to accept what we hear or read. Reasonable doubt becomes a norm. But these situations are not paradigmatic. They are parasitic on more ordinary situations where acceptance is a norm.
>
> (p. 484)

4 Cole puts the matter very neatly:

> rhetoric is that part of any self-consciously calculated piece of communication which fails to meet a philosopher's standards of accuracy, coherence, and consistency, but is still necessary if the communication is to be fully successful. Rhetorical discourse is not the opposite of philosophical discourse but rather, in most situations, its complementary contrary, and only capable of being identified and studied by reference to the appropriate philosophical counterpart.
>
> (Cole 1991, p. 13)

5 Recent Aristotelian scholarship abounds with alternative explanations of what sort of argument might sustain his confidence in the (eventual) accessibility of truth to human enquirers; Jonathan Lear's idealistic

179

and Terence Irwin's Kantian interpretations (Lear 1988, Irwin 1988) have proved particularly fertile. My own explanation, which attributes Aristotle's faith in the utility of his dialectical method as an instrument for discovering absolute truth to his philosophical biology, is to be found in 'Aristotle and his predecessors on mixture' (in Wardy 1990).

6 The *locus classicus* for discussion of Aristotle's dialectical method remains '*Tithenai ta phainomena*' (Owen 1986b); the most important subsequent modifications to Owen's reading mostly involve enlarging the range of data coming within the scope of the method (see e.g. 'Saving Aristotle's appearances' in Nussbaum 1986). The scholarship is voluminous, but Denyer is noteworthy for putting together material from the *Rhetoric* with the standard 'philosophical' passages which constantly recur in the literature (see 'Our natural flair for the truth' (Denyer 1991), pp. 183–5).

7 It might be objected that since the first chapter of the first book is so manifestly at odds with the remainder of the *Rhetoric*, my issue is merely a pseudo-problem; there is no consistency, but none should be sought, since the lack of theoretical cohesion is the consequence of imperfect textual integration:

> what is now regarded as the first chapter of Book 1 was apparently originally addressed to students who had completed a study of dialectic (such as is found in the *Topics*) and who had little knowledge of rhetoric, though they may have been aware of the existence of handbooks on the subject. For them Aristotle explains the similarities between dialectic as they know it and rhetoric as he understands it but does not comment on the differences. The chapter as a whole is very Platonic and contains echoes of several of Plato's dialogues.
>
> (Kennedy 1991, p. 26)

Of course I agree that the Platonic cast of *Rhetoric* I 1 is very marked; but I attribute this to Aristotle's earnest engagement with 'the Gorgias/*Gorgias* problematic', rather than to its origin or purpose. Kennedy is right that 'chapter 1 creates acute problems for the unity of the treatise' (p. 27); but his conclusion that

> despite other possible interpretations, it is probably better to acknowledge frankly that chapter 1 is inconsistent with what follows, that it is far more austere in tone than Aristotle's general view of rhetoric, and that the difference results from addressing different audiences and from the attempt to link the study of dialectic with that of rhetoric
>
> (p. 28)

is far too hasty. If I am right that 'the Gorgias/*Gorgias* problematic' is at the heart of the matter, then 'the attempt to link the study of dialectic with that of rhetoric' must be much more than a passing fancy: in which case the degree of incoherence into which Aristotle (supposedly) lapses might well be an index of the pressure to which he submits

NOTES

in order to maintain his distinctive position with regard to that problematic.

8 Indeed, in the *Sophistici Elenchi*, Aristotle lists this very limitation, among other weaknesses, as useful for refuting someone: lengthy argument is a good thing 'since it is hard to see many things at once' (174A17–18).

9 But the Stoa did endorse something like such a programme, advocating, for the most part, an extreme, Socratic renunciation of anything but a rigorously 'informative' variety of rhetoric: see Atherton 1988.

10 A connection with a common later tripartition of aspects of persuasion is more than plausible:

> and because, as I have already said on numerous occasions, we lead people to our opinion in three ways, either by teaching or by winning them over or by moving them, one of these three we must openly display, so that it might seem that all we want to do is teach; whereas the remaining two should be interfused throughout the whole of our speeches like the blood in our bodies.
>
> (Cicero, *De Oratore* II 310)

However, the speaker, Antonius, emerges here as an unabashed follower of Gorgias. His orator is a dissembling sophist who lulls us with the pretext of instruction only the better to lower our resistance to his emotional trickery; work on the *pathē*, so far from cooperating with anything like philosophical *logos*, lies concealed in ambush within the Trojan horse of rational appeal.

11 Cf. Cicero's 'those who speak either concisely or calmly can teach the judge, but cannot move him' (*De Oratore* II 215). Aristotle would not demur, although he might well have taken exception to the capping phrase, 'on which everything depends'.

12 Kennedy comments: 'this principle, important as a response to the criticisms of Plato, appears only in a parenthetical remark and is not repeated in the prescriptive parts of the treatise' (Kennedy 1991, p. 34). This is not quite right. Although his translation follows modern editions of the text in placing the Greek original of the words 'for one must not persuade people to what is wrong' within parentheses, the paratactic construction of that original does not make it some sort of minor aside. Furthermore, its not being repeated is of no significance unless one supposes that *Rhetoric* I 1 is *not* 'prescriptive'.

13 The best-known exposition of this conservatism is the contest between the Just and Unjust *Logoi* in Aristophanes' *Clouds*.

14 This claim might seem much less plausible in its application to state policy than to interpersonal ethics; but the *Politics* betrays no more doubt about the validity of Aristotle's political science than does the *Nicomachean Ethics* about the correctness of his moral theory. His delineation of the ideal *polis* would seem to ensure that in his view the rhetorician in politics *must* eschew imperialism.

15 Of course, his knowing as much as can be known about the 'probabilities' (to be understood in an unsophisticated, pre-statistical manner,

181

NOTES

to avoid anachronism) is fully compatible with their being so distributed that even the best-placed predictor is radically uncertain about what will really happen. But such uncertainty does nothing to support the contention that an ability to promote conflicting policies in a persuasive way aids us in seeing 'how things are' (or 'how they might be').

16 Grimaldi supposes that the statement 'it is characteristic of one and the same art to see both what is plausible and what is apparently plausible, just as it is up to dialectic to see both the syllogism and the apparent syllogism' (1355B15–17) is yet another Aristotelian response to worry about the ethical status of rhetoric:

> Aristotle's reference to dialectic and the apparent syllogism is clearly to the *Sophistici Elenchi* . . . And so our passage asserts: the art of rhetoric enables one to see that which persuades to the truth as well as that which persuades to what is not true, although its object is the truth as far as that is possible.
>
> (Grimaldi 1980, p. 33)

But his own reference to the *Sophistici Elenchi* shows that his interpretation is unsound: if an 'apparent syllogism' is a piece of reasoning which is only speciously valid, then the apparently plausible must be a piece of discourse which appears to be persuasive, but is not, not one which persuades us, but of the wrong thing. This specious plausibility must of course gull the inexpert speaker, not his potential audience, since if *they* found it plausible, and so were persuaded, it really would be plausible. Now given Aristotle's epistemological optimism, from his perspective it might indeed happen, even frequently, that a falling away from the truth is responsible for some rhetoric's merely apparent plausibility; but that does not alter the fact that what Aristotle is here talking about is what persuades or what seems to persuade *tout court*, not 'that which persuades to the truth' or to its opposite.

17 And cf. *Soph. El.* 12: people say they are 'just asking questions because they want to learn' – and so avoid setting out explicitly what they want to (seem to) prove/refute (172B21–4).

18 It makes no odds to my argument whether one conceives of this theory as recommending that explanations be cast in the terms of the *Posterior Analytics'* apodeictic syllogisms, or simply that one acquire accounts of 'the reason why' expressed non-syllogistically.

19 There is another passage which might initially take us aback at *Soph. El.* 33: 'the strong *logos* is the one which has us most at a loss' (182B32 ff.); but a distinction is made here between genuine syllogisms which leave unclear which reputable opinion is to be rejected, and eristical ones, which just have us asking 'how shall I answer that?' and 'how did I get into *this* mess?' (cf. also 171B10 ff.).

20 But the typical Socratic personal *elenchos* is reduced at *Soph. El.* 172B35 ff. to getting someone to contradict his own *superficial*, socially approved, beliefs and desires.

21 I am not arguing that there is nothing to choose between the sophists' fallacies and (some of) Socrates' arguments in the *Euthydemus*, only that there is not everything, and that it would not just be such

182

dimwits as Isocrates, if he is to be identified with the anonymous carping critic at the end of the dialogue, who might be prone to confuse dialectic and eristic. The constant refrain of the *Euthydemus* is that the sophists' victims are 'thunderstruck' by their fallacies (e.g. 276D3); but the famous image of the *Meno* ascribes a numbing effect to Socrates' dialectic just as easy, and as understandable, for his victims to resent.

22 There is a partial parallel at *Rhetoric* III 7: one reprimands oneself for exaggerated language – because then people *think* one is in earnest (1408B2 ff.). Aristotle similarly advocates resorting to the artifice of 'natural' language at III 2 (1404B18 ff.), and says that we must not 'overact' (III 7, 1408B4 ff.).

23 This consensus cannot always be complete, since otherwise the *aporiai* generated by the appearance or reality of conflict between *endoxa* to which the Aristotelian philosopher reacts would never arise; but the threat remains that his consensual method may be open to conformist abuse.

24 Implicit, perhaps, in *Topics* I 2, 101A30–4; cf. *Rhetoric* III 7, 1408A34–6. Finally, there is an explicit comparison between rhetorical and elenctic procedures at *Soph. El.* 174B19 ff.

25 Cf. *Soph. El.* 170A12 ff. for a purely relational '*pros tina*': the sophistical refutation is *only* a relational refutation, if at all.

26 The emphasis at 156B18–20 on producing an appearance of argumentative fairness was said to do nothing to dispel the worry that this appearance is merely specious. If competitiveness 'at all costs' is the defining characteristic of agonistic dialectic, then it may be that samples of the other species of dialectic cannot indulge in *completely* untrammelled unfairness beneath a gloss of fairness; but that is not a very reassuring concession. (The label 'agonistic' does not imply that the other species of dialectic are *not* agonistic, on the common understanding that a genus and one of its subordinate species might share a designation, justified in this instance by the hypothesis that specifically 'agonistic' dialectic is so to the exclusion of all else.)

27 Note that Aristotle is careful to make preserving one's reputation a third, but definitely *non*-philosophical, motive for engaging in sophistry (175A12–16).

28 I hedge my claim with this qualification because, just as the doctrine of double effect is notoriously problematic, so we might decide that the boundaries between species of dialectic are considerably more porous than Aristotle is always prepared to admit (although at other times he is ready to concede quite casually that real dialectical situations are very fluid; for example, 'those practising are incapable of abstaining from agonistic dialectic' (164B13–15)).

29 At first blush, this denial might seem flatly incompatible with epistemological optimism. But, on reflection, it emerges that Aristotle must mean that this or that *individual* bucks the optimistic trend. And this solution finds support in the context, which is describing explicitly peirastic argument, that is, the sort of argument conducted with immature, ignorant individuals.

30 And note the careful distinctions at *Soph. El.* 171B3 ff., 172A21 ff.

31 The parallel makes (some) sense in the light of Aristotle's careful comparison between eristic arguments and cases of faulty scientific reasoning at *Soph. El.* 171B3 ff. The geometer arguing *qua* geometer does so 'in accordance with his subject-matter', even if he gets it wrong; that is, he stays inside his expertise. The dialectician does so too, although he has no special subject-matter. In consequence, the faulty scientific reasoner is comparable, in some ways, to the eristic – although not in all. Aristotle still has grave problems because he has to make the dialectician's field 'the common things', and that is too vague a specification to establish in the case of dialectic a firm distinction between being 'in accordance with his subject-matter' and not being – which puts the rhetorician in the same boat.

32 Note the comparison with rhetoric at *Soph. El.* 174B19 ff. – there is no cooperation.

33 There is a counterpart in special offers, guarantees, etc.: a guarantee is for twelve months (all those months), not one (measly) year. But you can get slim and fit in twenty-eight days (not a whole month).

34 The quotation from Meleager immediately after this passage might suggest that Aristotle is thinking of qualitative rather than quantitative division – Meleager specifies what *sort* of evils there are in the sack of a city, not how many. It thus appears that Aristotle has not sufficiently distinguished between quantitative and qualitative components; none the less, his abstract description of the case is resolutely quantitative.

35 Furthermore, the potentially explosive implications of Aristotle's 'cosmetic' recommendations are not restricted to the epideictic genre, damaging as that in itself might be, for he says that victory in general goes to the man who *seems* wise, virtuous and benign (1378A6 ff.) – so the speaker is always constructing his own encomium, as it were.

36 Aristotle refers us to the *Topics* for how to deal with ambiguities (1419A20 ff.).

37 Norlin, the Loeb editor, comments with confident brevity on the last quotation: 'surely this is ironical' (vol. II, p. 520).

38 Not that Isocrates fails to pull out all the moralising stops at the end, declaring his approbation of auditors who prefer educational to epideictic *logoi*, *logoi* which aim at truth to those which seek to disturb opinions, *logoi* which upbraid and censure to those which are for the sake of pleasure and delight (§271).

39 In later rhetorical treatments of ambiguity as a cause of legal dispute, the two approaches, by appeal to honourable or dishonourable motives and by appeal to ordinary linguistic usage, tend to be combined: see e.g. *Ad Herennium* II 16, Cicero, *De Inventione* II 116–18.

40 Cf. III 14 on the sorts of things people tend to pay attention to (1415B1 ff.) – with not a word about truth.

41 But note Aristotle's *reasons*: he quotes Euripides ('they speak in a more cultured way') approvingly because the mob speaks of what it knows, of what is close to home, whereas the educated waffle on about generalities and principles. *That* determines what sort of 'reputable opinions' – including ones that are only 'true as a rule' – are to be

NOTES

used. Note too that deliberative oratory is less 'ill-willed' than forensic, precisely because it deals with such generalities (1354B ff.).

42 The idea of 'sympathy' raises yet a further problem, best illustrated by Antonius' claim in Cicero's *De Oratore* that since

> it is impossible for the listener to be pained, to hate, to feel ill-will, to be terrified of anything, or to be reduced to tears of pity, unless all those emotions [*motus*] which the orator wishes to produce in the judge, are seen to be stamped or rather branded on the orator himself,

(II 189)

and counterfeit emotion will not do, then: 'no mind is so ready to embrace the power of the orator as to be inflammable, unless the orator in his approach to it is himself alight and burning' (II 190). Since effective eloquence demands feeling, and feeling cannot (the story goes) be convincingly faked, the successful orator will himself often be in the throes of passion. From the Aristotelian perspective, this chain of reasoning might seem to open up the quite appalling prospect that the orator will not only gull his audience intellectually, he will also on occasion suffer distorting *pathē* in order to be able to manipulate them emotionally. But there is a way out. For the Aristotelian, the *pathē* are deplorable not intrinsically, but only if cognitively erroneous or affectively inappropriate. However, since the envisaged situation is one of deception, anything like the Ciceronian condition of sincerity laid on eloquence would bizarrely demand that the orator deceive himself; and while self-deception is an acceptable concept, deliberate, knowing self-deception is not (barring irrelevant subtleties). Therefore the Ciceronian condition is, it would seem, an option only when deceptive oratory has been eliminated from consideration, with whatever plausibility (Antonius' autobiographical protestations of sincerity (II 189-90) are revealing in this connection). But that finally leaves us with the materials for constructing a dilemma of 'sympathy'. If the speaker is always upright, then since his sincere emotions might nevertheless cloud his judgement, he will communicate erroneous *pathē* to his auditors and innocently mislead them. But alternatively, if counterfeit emotion can, *pace* Antonius, win conviction, then the orator is an unmoved, just as he is an unconfused, manipulator, and Socrates' darkest suspicions are realised. Of course, epistemological optimism combined with the condition of sincerity would dissolve the dilemma, but only by compounding implausibilities.

43 At 1404A1 ff. Aristotle blames the need to use a highly-wrought delivery on the wickedness of the audience; at 1415B4 ff., a highly-wrought proemium is 'irrelevant to the argument' and 'directed at a vulgar listener'. So, is the rhetorician's excuse the moral degeneracy and stupidity of his audience? One must also take account of Aristotle's advice that the narrative in a speech for the defence should be very selective about mentioning past events – only such as, if they had *not* occurred, they would stimulate 'pity or indignation' in the auditors (1417A8 ff.). Again, at 1419B24 ff., part of the purpose of the epilogue

NOTES

is to whip up feeling; this task is separate from, and subsequent to, the
relation of what the facts were and how important they were, as if intellect and emotion were separate – or separable by the devious orator
(1377B31 ff. is also open to this disturbing interpretation).

EPILOGUE:
DOES PHILOSOPHY HAVE A GENDER?

1 For example, it is far from clear that Aristotle's notorious pronouncements on slaves and women are consistent with either the foundations
  of his natural philosophy or the basic principles of his dialectical method.
  Lear 1988 (pp. 197–208) and G. E. R. Lloyd 1983 (pp. 94–105) ably
  expound this topic, and Lear in particular argues convincingly that
  Aristotle is guilty of incoherence.
2 This thought is related to Michèle Le Dœuff's explanation of why her
  superb book's title must end, or perhaps not end, with 'etc.'
3 Thus more or less all that Janet Radcliffe Richards finds it necessary to
  say about women and logic is this:

> being illogical is not having strong feelings, or mixed feelings,
> or changing your mind, or being unable to express things and
> prove things, or anything of the sort. It is maintaining that incom-
> patible propositions are both true, and in doing so maintaining
> *nothing*, since to make an illogical statement is to make no state-
> ment at all. But since this is so, and since the purpose of language
> is to convey information, to use language at all is to rely on logic.
> (Radcliffe Richards 1982, pp. 37–8)

So far as it goes, this is a reasonable version of some traditional
Aristotelian lore, although its assumption that language is (primarily?)
for the transmission of information is at best simplistic, if convenient.
The difficulty is that it does not go anywhere near far enough. Properly
sceptical feminists might well concede the *bona fides* of the Principle
of Contradiction, while nevertheless finding the logical canons which
are acceptable to the philosophical community, and which incorporate
rather more than the avoidance of flat inconsistency, intensely problematic. This is not to dispute the views which Radcliffe Richards
expresses on feelings etc.: rather, it is to complain that her excessively
narrow idea of logic and illogicality blinds her to very real difficulties
besetting philosophical feminism.
4 Not that the latter two tendencies need remain apart. This is a
  characteristic expression of psychoanalytical reductionism on the part
  of a neo-Marxist:

> because the problem for the boy is to distinguish himself from
> the mother and to protect himself against the real threat she poses
> for his identity, his conflictual and oppositional efforts lead to
> the formation of rigid ego-boundaries ... Thus, the boy's
> construction of self in opposition to unity with the mother, his

186

construction of identity as differentiation from the other, sets a
hostile and combative dualism at the heart of both the community men construct and the masculinist world view by means of
which they understand their lives.

(Hartsock 1983, p. 296)

As one anticipates,

the female construction of self in relation to others leads in
an opposite direction – toward opposition to dualisms of any
sort, valuation of concrete, everyday life, sense of a variety of
connectednesses and continuities both with other persons and
with the natural world.

(ibid., p. 298)

Exponents of this approach routinely assert that their project is
not reductionistic, but no more persuasively than their non-feminist
analytical colleagues.

5 Lorraine Code epitomises the dogmatic approach:

because engagement in the project [viz. 'of remapping the
epistemic terrain'] is specifically prompted by a conviction that
gender must be put in place as a primary analytic category, I start
by assuming that it is impossible to sustain the presumption of
gender-neutrality that is central to standard epistemologies: the
presumption that gender has nothing to do with knowledge, that
the mind has no sex, that reason is alike in all men, and man
'embraces' woman.

(Code 1993, p. 20)

6 Harding 1983, p. 312.
7 Griffiths and Whitford 1988, p. 6.
8 Subsequently Griffiths and Whitford urge that

since the feminist perspective is necessarily critical, feminist
philosophy is not a way of articulating women's experience
in parallel with men's: it is not a form of relativism. This is a
particularly important point. That which a feminist perspective
enables us to perceive is valid for everyone.

(Griffiths and Whitford 1988, pp. 7–8)

I find this very hard to understand, because the universally valid is
ipso facto not intrinsically perspectival, even if one might well have to
get into a certain position to perceive it. Surely their point is important – female experience provides rich and neglected materials for
philosophical exploration – but counts against their contention that
such work constitutes philosophy *from* a feminist perspective, rather
than philosophy feminists would like to see done.

9 Frazer, Hornsby and Lovibond 1992, p. 11.
10 Consider Le Dœuff's 'heuristic principle':

what we ask of a culture is precisely that it should teach us to
analyse what is said and notably to interpret the way in which

people retransmit another's thought or thought which is not theirs. For the way something is said is largely formed of retransmissions (every book contains a library), which we also need to be able to read.

(Le Dœuff 1991, p. 66)

11 I cannot be sure whether Frazer, Hornsby and Lovibond would resist this conclusion. Their volume, unlike Griffiths and Whitford, is devoted to ethics in particular. There are, for example, well-recognised difficulties besetting the type of neo-contractarian liberalism exemplified by Rawls which lend much additional substance to scepticism about the possibility of non-perspectival ethical and political deliberation. Thus it might be that their reference to liberal 'illusion' is confined to specifically ethical objectivist pretension, in which case their limited perspectivalism is unobjectionable; but they leave the scope of their remarks ambiguous.

12 For example, when Lorraine Code writes that

the ideals of rationality and objectivity that have guided and inspired theorists of knowledge throughout the history of western philosophy have been constructed through processes of excluding the attributes and experiences commonly associated with femaleness and underclass social status: emotion, connection, practicality, sensitivity, and idiosyncrasy

(Code 1993, p. 21)

she attaches a note explaining that Lloyd's book provides the documentation supporting this claim.

13 Although Lloyd too is keen to distance herself from relativism: 'the claim that Reason is male need not at all involve sexual relativism about truth, or any suggestion that principles of logical thought valid for men do not hold also for female reasoners' (G. Lloyd 1984, p. 109). Code evinces an exceptional attitude. The conviction that 'differing social positions generate variable constructions of reality and afford different perspectives on the world' (Code 1993, p. 39) is avowedly relativistic, but the relativism is supposed to be 'mitigated':

the position I am advocating is one for which knowledge is always *relative to* (i.e., a perspective *on*, a standpoint *in*) specifiable circumstances. Hence it is constrained by a realist, empiricist commitment according to which getting these circumstances right is vital to effective action. It may appear to be a question-begging position, for it does assume that the circumstances can be known, and it relies heavily upon pragmatic criteria to make good that assumption.

(ibid., p. 40)

That is putting it mildly. In truth, her position does not just beg questions: it is either incoherent or viciously relativist. If the sense in which the thesis that 'circumstances can be known' is substantial enough to do the work required, it self-defeatingly transcends the perspectivalism it is meant to support. But if its sense is consistently determined

NOTES

only from a particular point of view, no matter how perverted, then so
are all the available pragmatic judgements of 'effective action'. Code's
commitments to empiricism and realism – those she has a right to –
are anything but robust.

14 G. Lloyd 1984, pp. 107–8.
15 She is concerned not to paint at least some of her philosophers as
villains:

> the exclusion of the feminine has not resulted from a conspiracy
> by male philosophers. We have seen that in some cases it happened
> despite the conscious intent of the authors. Where it does appear
> explicitly in the texts, it is usually incidental to their main
> purposes; and often it emerges only in the conjunction of the
> text with surrounding social structures – a configuration which
> often is visible only in retrospect.
>
> (G. Lloyd 1984, pp. 108–9)

In every case the conclusion follows if one combines text with social
structure. In no case did it follow when the text was taken on its own
– at least when the text was written by a major philosopher such as
Plato, Aristotle or Descartes. (Sartre is another matter – but I
would contend that his status as a philosopher, let alone a major one,
is open to doubt.) This book is not the place to trace out and
evaluate the details of Lloyd's exegeses. Since her thesis is premissed on
the detailed conclusions of the case-studies, my reader must go through
The Man of Reason to reach an informed judgement: I can merely record
my own verdict that when it mattered, the exclusion of the feminine
emerged *only* in conjunction with surrounding social structures not
often, but always.

16 Not that Gilligan's approach has been endorsed uncritically: her
failure fully to recognise the sociopolitical particularity of the child-
rearing practices on which she builds her theory has been severely
attacked, and also the feminist psychology she employs in their
interpretation.
17 Code is a good example: 'extrapolating from what Gilligan has done,
it is possible to make sense of how it is that actual, historically
situated, gendered epistemological and moral subjects know and respond
to actual, complex experiences' (Code 1988, p. 198).
18 Even the consistent expression of irrationalism is a tricky matter, as Le
Dœuff's anecdote tellingly illustrates. She says that she discovered that
in philosophically sceptical feminist circles the political demands of
feminism were regularly disabled by indefinitely reiterated challenges
to their philosophical legitimacy. But

> in other women's groups I have heard it said, a little too often for
> my liking, that rationality is a masculine thing, so that women
> trying to disengage themselves from the colonialist grip of the
> patriarchy should, urgently and once and for all, throw rational-
> ity into the bin. I made a few attempts to tell them how lucky
> they were to find the question so simple: there are so many

189

different forms of rationality, depending on which fields one
considers, that it is sometimes hard to make out a common core.
If we cannot determine exactly where rationality begins, the notion
suddenly seems boundless, which is no small subject for reflection.
And then to maintain that rationality must be rejected by women
because it is a masculine thing is an idea which is always advanced
like a reasoned argument and is indeed trying to rationalise
something, even if its premisses are open to dispute. In reply I was
told that I was once more proving that I was colonised to the mar-
row.

(Le Dœuff 1991, p. 23)

19   Leaving open the question as to whether there are essentially 'feminine' and 'masculine' ways of knowing, it is none the less reasonable to maintain that there is a range of experiences which could
not be known in ways similar enough from knower to knower to
produce 'common' knowledge in differently gendered subjects.
Experiences which depend upon natural biological differences, in
areas of sexuality, parenthood, and some aspects of physical and
emotional being, must be different for women and for men to the
extent that it would be impossible for them to know them in anything like 'the same' way.

(Code 1988, p. 198)

Doubtless there are experiences which cannot be experienced by the
other sex (John Updike's fantasising depiction of a woman urinating in
The Witches of Eastwick conveys much more about Mr Updike's mind
(and gullibility?) than what it is like (so I am assured) for a woman to
piss). But Code is playing fast and loose with language. If there is
something I cannot experience, then we might say I cannot know it;
but that is not tantamount to my inability to know *about* it, perhaps
in a manner and to a degree sufficient for my reflecting philosophically
on this strictly inaccessible experience. In fairness, I should point out
that she makes the statement quoted precisely to *deny* that experiences
which are the exclusive preserve of one sex or gender or the other might
successfully serve as the basis on which to construct an alternative ethics,
or ethical theory. (The Marxist proposition that certain uniquely
privileged insights are only available from the perspective of the
oppressed, by virtue of their proximity to the reality of production, is
given feminist expression in Hartsock 1983.)

20   I have made a particular plea in favour of taking seriously a
certain kind of story – first-person accounts of experiences . . . I
have suggested that reflection upon epistemological and moral
matters which is responsibly attuned to such narratives might be
able to retain a kind of contact with human lives that is often
lost in formalistic and abstract-theoretical structures.

(Code 1988, p. 200)

I agree wholeheartedly. But all the pleas Code enters on behalf of the
validity of experience seem readily translatable into strictures against

NOTES

simplistic over-generalisation of a sort very much at home within what she calls 'malestream' philosophy.

21 Janice Moulton approaches our central preoccupation only to veer away from the heart of the matter:

> the philosophic enterprise is seen as an unimpassioned debate between *adversaries* who try to defend their own views against counterexamples and produce counterexamples to opposing views. The reasoning used to discover the claims, and the way the claims relate to other beliefs and systems of ideas are not considered relevant to philosophic reasoning if they are not deductive. I will call this the Adversary Paradigm.
>
> > (Moulton 1983, p. 153: it emerges later that eccentrically she identifies 'deductive' and 'rational' (p. 157))

She explains that her objection to this method rests on its status as a paradigm, quite apart from the opinion that 'conditions of hostility are not likely to elicit the best reasoning' (p. 153). I am encouraging healthy scepticism about the tenability of the claim that philosophical aggression has been *purified*; Moulton fails to see that it at least pretends not to be a refined form of bullying. Bizarrely, her Socrates is not a threatening, adversarial figure:

> one victim of the Adversary Paradigm is usually thought to be a model of adversarial reasoning: the Socratic Method . . . *Elenchus* is usually translated as 'refutation', but this is misleading because its success depends on convincing the other person, not on showing their views to be wrong to others.
>
> > (p. 156)

True, one argues directly with the interlocutor; but refutation to one's face is refutation for all that, Socrates' opponents tend to emerge convinced, at most, that they do not know what they thought they knew, and the aggressive character of refutation is none the less problematic for all Socrates' soothing remarks – in which Moulton perceives no irony.

191

12

BIBLIOGRAPHY

Adam, C. and Tannery, P., *Œuvres de Descartes* (12 vols), Paris, 1964–76.
Adkins, A. W. H., 'Form and content in Gorgias' *Helen* and *Palamedes*.
Rhetoric, philosophy, inconsistency and invalid argument in some Greek
thinkers', in *Essays in Ancient Greek Philosophy*, vol. 2, eds J. P. Anton
and A. Preus, Albany, 1983.
Aristides (ed. C. A. Behr), *Works* (vol. I), London, 1973.
Aristotle (ed. W. D. Ross), *Ars Rhetorica*, Oxford, 1975.
——*Topica et Sophistici Elenchi*, Oxford, 1979.
Atherton, C., 'Hand over fist: the failure of Stoic rhetoric', *Classical Quarterly*
38 (1988), 392–427.
Barlow, S., *Euripides* Trojan Women, *with Translation and Commentary*,
Warminster, 1986.
Baxandall, M., *Giotto and the Orators: Humanist Observers of Painting in
Italy and the Discovery of Pictorial Composition 1350–1450*, Oxford,
1971.
Brunschwig, J., 'Gorgias et l'incommunicabilité', *La Communication*, Actes
du XVe Congrès des Sociétés philosophiques de langue français, vol. I
(1971), Montreal, 79–84.
Buchheim, T., *Gorgias von Leontini, Reden, Fragmente und Testimonien,
herausgegeben mit Übersetzung und Kommentar*, Hamburg, 1989.
Burge, T., 'Content preservation', *The Philosophical Review* 102 (1993),
457–88.
Burnyeat, M., *The* Theaetetus *of Plato*, with a translation by M. J. Levett,
Indianapolis, 1990.
Cicero (eds E. W. Sutton and H. Rackham), *De Oratore*, Books I and II,
London, 1988.
Code, L., 'Experience, knowledge and responsibility', in *Feminist Perspectives
in Philosophy*, eds M. Griffiths and M. Whitford, London, 1988.
—— 'Taking subjectivity into account', in *Feminist Epistemologies*, eds L.
Alcoff and E. Potter, London, 1993.
Cole, T., *The Origins of Rhetoric in Ancient Greece*, London, 1991.
Cope, E. M. (ed. J. E. Sandys), *The Rhetoric of Aristotle with a Commentary*,
Cambridge, 1877.
Coxon, A. H., *The Fragments of Parmenides, a Critical Text with Introduction,
the Ancient Testimonia and a Commentary*, Assen/Maastricht, 1986.

• Denyer, N., *Language, Thought and Falsehood in Ancient Greek Philosophy*, London, 1991.

Diels, H., 'Gorgias und Empedokles', *Sitzungsberichte der Königlichen Preuß. Akademie der Wissenschaften*, Berlin, 1884, 343–68.

Dodds, E. R., *The Greeks and the Irrational*, Berkeley, 1951.

• —— *Plato* Gorgias, *a Revised Text with Introduction and Commentary*, Oxford, 1959.

Dover, K. J., *Greek Popular Morality in the Time of Plato and Aristotle*, Oxford, 1974.

—— *Greek Homosexuality*, London, 1978.

Evans, G., *The Varieties of Reference*, Oxford, 1982.

Frazer, E., Hornsby, J. and Lovibond, S., *Ethics: A Feminist Reader*, Oxford, 1992.

Gilligan, C., *In a Different Voice: Psychological Theory and Women's Development*, Cambridge, Mass., 1982.

Goldhill, S., 'The Great Dionysia and civic ideology', in *Nothing to Do with Dionysos? Athenian Drama in its Social Context*, eds J. Winkler and F. Zeitlin, Princeton, 1990.

Gomperz, H., *Sophistik und Rhetorik. Das Bildungsideal des eu legein in seinem Verhältnis zur Philosophie des V. Jahrhunderts*, Berlin, 1912.

Griffiths, M., and Whitford, M. (eds), *Feminist Perspectives in Philosophy*, London, 1988.

◄ Grimaldi, W. M. A., *Aristotle*, Rhetoric I, *A Commentary*, New York, 1980.

Harding, S., 'Why has the sex/gender system become visible only now?', in *Discovering Reality, Feminist Perspectives on Epistemology, Metaphysics, Methodology, and Philosophy of Science*, eds S. Harding and M. Hintikka, Dordrecht, 1983.

Hartsock, N., 'The feminist standpoint: developing the ground for a specifically feminist historical materialism', in *Discovering Reality, Feminist Perspectives on Epistemology, Metaphysics, Methodology, and Philosophy of Science*, eds S. Harding and M. Hintikka, Dordrecht, 1983.

Heubeck, A., West, S. and Hainsworth, J. B., *A Commentary on Homer's Odyssey*, vol. 1, Oxford, 1988.

• Hubbard, B. A. F. and Karnofsky, E. S., *Plato's Protagoras: A Socratic Commentary*, London, 1982.

✦ Irwin, T. H., *Plato* Gorgias, *translated with notes*, Oxford, 1979.

—— *Aristotle's First Principles*, Oxford, 1988.

Isocrates (ed. G. Norlin), *Works* (vols I and II), London, 1980, 1982.

Kahn, C. H., *The Art and Thought of Heraclitus*, Cambridge, 1979.

. —— 'Drama and dialectic in Plato's Gorgias', *Oxford Studies in Ancient Philosophy* I (1983), 75–121.

Kennedy, G. A., *Aristotle, A Theory of Civic Discourse*, Oxford, 1991.

Kerferd, G. B., *The Sophistic Movement*, Cambridge, 1981.

—— 'Meaning and reference. Gorgias and the relation between language and reality', in *The Sophistic Movement*, ed. K. Voudouris, Athens, 1982.

✦ Kirk, G. S., Raven, J. E. and Schofield, M., *The Presocratic Philosophers* (second edition), Cambridge, 1983.

Le Dœuff, M., (trans. T. Selous), *Hipparchia's Choice: An Essay Concerning Women, Philosophy, etc.*, Oxford, 1991.

• Lear, J., *Aristotle, the Desire to Understand,* Cambridge, 1988.
Lloyd, G., *The Man of Reason: 'Male' and 'Female' in Western Philosophy,* London, 1984.
Lloyd, G. E. R., *Magic, Reason and Experience, Studies in the Origins and Development of Greek Science,* Cambridge, 1979.
—— *Science, Folklore and Ideology, Studies in the Life Sciences in Ancient Greece,* Cambridge, 1983.
Long, A. A. 'The principles of Parmenides' cosmogony', *Phronesis* 8 (1963), 90–107.
Loraux, N., *L'invention d'Athènes, Histoire de l'oraison funèbre dans la 'cité classique',* Paris, 1981.
MacDowell, D. M., 'Gorgias, Alkidamas and the Cripps and Palatine manuscripts', *Classical Quarterly* n.s. 11 (1961), 113–24.
—— *Gorgias* Encomium of Helen, Bristol, 1982.
Mackenzie, M. M., 'Parmenides' dilemma', *Phronesis* 27 (1982), 1–12.
Mansfeld, J., ' "*De Melisso Xenophane Gorgia*": Pyrrhonising Aristotelianism', *Rheinisches Museum* 121 (1988), 239–76.
Montaigne, M. de (trans. M. A. Screech), *The Essays of Michel de Montaigne,* London, 1991.
Moulton, J., 'A paradigm of philosophy: the adversary method', in *Discovering Reality, Feminist Perspectives on Epistemology, Metaphysics, Methodology, and Philosophy of Science,* eds S. Harding and M. Hintikka, Dordrecht, 1983.
Newiger, H.-J., *Untersuchungen zu Gorgias' Schrift Über das Nicht-seiende,* Berlin, 1973.
Nussbaum, M. C., *The Fragility of Goodness, Luck and Ethics in Greek Tragedy and Philosophy,* Cambridge, 1986.
Ober, J., *Mass and Elite in Democratic Athens. Rhetoric, Ideology, and the Power of the People,* Princeton, 1990.
Olympiodorus (ed. L. G. Westerink), *In Platonis Gorgiam,* Leipzig, 1970.
Owen, G. E. L., 'Notes on Ryle's Plato', in *Ryle, A Collection of Critical Essays,* eds O. Wood and G. Pitcher, London, 1970.
—— 'Eleatic questions', in his *Logic, Science and Dialectic, Collected Papers in Greek Philosophy,* ed. M. Nussbaum, London, 1986a.
—— '*Tithenai ta phainomena*', in *Logic, Science and Dialectic, Collected Papers in Greek Philosophy,* 1986b.
Passmore, J., *Philosophical Reasoning,* London, 1961.
Pliny (ed. W. H. S. Jones), *Natural History* (vol. 8), London, 1968.
Quintilian (ed. H. E. Butler), *The Institutio Oratoria,* Books I–III, London, 1980.
Radcliffe Richards, J., *The Sceptical Feminist, A Philosophical Enquiry,* Harmondsworth, 1982.
Robinson, J. M., 'On Gorgias', in *Exegesis and Argument, Studies in Greek Philosophy presented to Gregory Vlastos,* eds E. N. Lee, A. P. D. Mourelatos and R. M. Rorty, *Phronesis* suppl. 1, Assen, 1973.
Romilly, J. de, 'Gorgias et le pouvoir de la poésie', *Journal of Hellenic Studies* 93 (1973), 155–62.
—— *Magic and Rhetoric in Ancient Greece,* London, 1975.

Rosenmeyer, T. G., 'Gorgias, Aeschylus and *Apate*', *American Journal of Philology* 76 (1955), 225–60.

Sedley, D. N., 'Sextus Empiricus and the atomist criterion of truth', *Elenchos* 13 (1992), 21–56.

◢ Segal, C., 'Gorgias and the psychology of the *logos*', *Harvard Studies in Classical Philology* (1962), 99–155.

Too, Y. L., *The Rhetoric of Identity in Isocrates*, Cambridge, 1995.

Verdenius, W. J., 'Gorgias' doctrine of deception', in *The Sophists and their Legacy*, ed. G. B. Kerferd, *Hermes* Einzelschriften 44, 1981.

✷ Vickers, B., *In Defence of Rhetoric*, Oxford, 1989.

✦ Vlastos, G., *Socratic Studies*, Cambridge, 1994.

Wardy, R., 'Lucretius on what atoms are not', *Classical Philology* 83 (1988), 112–28.

—— *The Chain of Change: A Study of Aristotle's* Physics VII, Cambridge, 1990.

—— 'Rhetoric', in *Le Savoir grec*, eds J. Brunschwig and G. E. R. Lloyd, Paris, 1996a.

—— 'Mighty is the truth and it shall prevail?', in *Essays on Aristotle's* Rhetoric, ed. A. Rorty, Berkeley, 1996b.

West, M. L., *Hesiod* Works and Days, *edited with Prolegomena and Commentary*, Oxford, 1978.

Williams, B., *Ethics and the Limits of Philosophy*, London, 1985.

INDEX